THE INNER WORKINGS OF AMERICAN FOREIGN POLICY

Today as never before, the conduct of American foreign policy affects every aspect of our lives. In a very real sense, it makes the difference between peace and nuclear disaster.

There have been many discussions of American foreign policy from the point of view of reporters and scholars. Now, here is a fascinating report from the inside—how American foreign policy is made and how it works in all its manifold ways—by a professional foreign-service officer.

TEMPLE WANAMAKER

is a graduate of Stanford University and has served in various posts for the State Department—in Spain, the Dominican Republic, Israel, and the Bahamas. He is now principal officer in Cordoba, Argentina. From January 1960 to September 1962 he was Director of the Office of Public Services.

BANTAM MATRIX EDITIONS

american foreign policy today

•

by Temple Wanamaker

•

with a preface by Dean Rusk

BANTAM BOOKS
NEW YORK/TORONTO/LONDON

AMERICAN FOREIGN POLICY TODAY
Bantam Matrix Edition published November 1964
2nd printing

Library of Congress Catalog Card Number: 64-25023

Bantam Books are published by Bantam Books, Inc. Its trade-mark, consisting of the words "Bantam Books" and the portrayal of a bantam, is registered in the United States Patent Office and in other countries. Marca Registrada. Printed in the United States of America. Bantam Books, Inc., 271 Madison Ave., New York 16, N. Y.

CONTENTS

PREFACE

The author of this useful book is seasoned with the experience of more than twenty years as a Foreign Service officer. After graduating from Stanford University, Temple Wanamaker entered the Foreign Service in 1941. His succession of posts, broken by wartime service in the Navy, took him to Spain, the Dominican Republic, the Philippines, Israel, and the Bahamas. In 1960 he became Director of the Office of Public Services in the Department of State.

This office plays a key role in the Department's efforts to acquaint American citizens with the realities of our foreign policy. These efforts include issuing pamphlets, arranging conferences with private organization and community leaders, sending officers to speak throughout the country, and answering letters from the public, which in times of crisis have exceeded fourteen thousand a week.

While engaged in this work, Mr. Wanamaker was in a unique position to recognize the growing public interest in foreign policy. He became convinced of the need for a small book which could explain to the American citizen the main elements of our foreign policy. This book, which he took leave of absence without pay in order to write, is his response to that conviction. I believe he has succeeded in describing the realities of our foreign policy and in providing a background against which current news on foreign affairs can be seen as parts of a whole rather than as unrelated segments.

DEAN RUSK

AUTHOR'S NOTE

Perhaps one can best appreciate one's country when seeing it from a distance. The military and economic strength of the United States, and its way of thinking, have given it a pre-eminent position in world affairs—so much so that people on all continents follow with intense interest American political conventions, campaigns, and elections. They realize that the outcome may well have an effect upon them. Yet many people in the United States are not fully aware of their country's role and the effect that its decisions may have on other nations.

As an officer in the Foreign Service of the United States since 1941, I have served in a number of posts abroad, and observed how other countries look at America. When I returned in 1958 for duty in the Department of State in Washington, I was assigned to the Bureau of Public Affairs and eventually became Director of its Office of Public Services. This office supplied information on foreign affairs to the American public through pamphlets and publications, by answering communications sent to the White House and to the State Department, acting as liaison with nongovernmental organizations, and holding conferences. I became increasingly impressed with the desire of American citizens to be informed on what their country was doing abroad and why. I also became increasingly aware that many lacked understanding of the government's objectives and actions and the machinery through which it carried on its foreign policy. Although there was an abundance of material on practically every area of the world and every topic, I felt that there was a need for a small book, simply written, that would give the interested citizen, in broad outline, the framework of our foreign policy and a basis for interpreting intelligently the foreign news in his daily newspaper.

During the preparation of the manuscript, many changes occurred in international affairs. Change is, of course, a basic principle of history. The enemies of World War II have become the allies of today. And it is impossible to predict our relations twenty years hence with the antagonists of today. In my chapter on the Congo, for example, I close with the successful operation of the United Nations in Katanga in early 1963, which eliminated the threat to the integrity of the Congo posed by an independent Katanga under Tshombe. Yet today Tshombe has returned from exile to become the prime minister of the central government of the Congo. The lessons one must learn are that change is continual and that nothing is beyond the realm of the possible.

The broad framework of foreign affairs, however, changes much more slowly. The purpose of this book is not to chronicle current events, but to use them as examples of the fundamentals of policy within the broad framework.

In writing this book I have drawn on the knowledge and experience of my colleagues in the Department of State, the Foreign Service, the Agency for International Development, and the United States Information Agency. I am deeply grateful for the assistance they have given me. In particular, I am indebted to:

Roger W. Tubby, Assistant Secretary of State for Public Affairs in 1961 and 1962, and Robert J. Manning, his successor in that position, for their sympathetic understanding of my purpose in writing this book and their support which made it possible;

Benjamin Bock, a fellow Foreign Service officer, who read the entire manuscript chapter by chapter as it was written and, from a fund of knowledge and common sense, made many suggestions for improvement;

Dimitri Dejanikus, Chief of the General Publications Division, Office of Media Services, Department of State, for his warm encouragement since the beginning of this project and his always helpful advice;

Mrs. Ruth Hale Ayers and Mrs. Helen Eaton McKinlay for their competent and cheerful secretarial services.

TEMPLE WANAMAKER

I. THE FRAMEWORK

Several years ago the Secretary of State received this telegram from a man in South Carolina:

> VERY MUCH OPPOSED TO YOUR MEDDLING IN FOREIGN AFFAIRS. WHY DON'T WE MIND OUR OWN BUSINESS?

This telegram, which undoubtedly would strike a responsive chord in many a citizen, confused and frustrated by the news in his daily paper, poses two other questions—"What is foreign affairs?" and "What is our own business?"

Foreign affairs has been defined as the activities of a nation arising from its dealings with other nations. A nation can't avoid being involved in foreign affairs unless it is able to seal itself off from the rest of the world, as did Japan before 1853. Because of its insular position in the Western Pacific and a determination to have as little as possible to do with foreigners, Japan was able to follow a policy of isolation for over two hundred years until the arrival of Commodore Perry's fleet in 1853.

I believe we would agree with the drafters of the Constitution that among our proper concerns are "to form a more perfect Union, establish Justice, insure domestic Tranquility, provide for the common defense, promote the general Welfare, and secure the Blessings of Liberty to ourselves and our Posterity." Meeting these concerns would seem to be *our* business. The world is now so inter-related that events anywhere can have an effect upon our domestic tranquility, defense, welfare, and liberty. Minding our business, therefore, means being very much concerned with what is happening abroad and, where advisable and possible, taking action.

From the beginnings of its existence as a nation, the United States attempted to avoid becoming involved in European problems. The Atlantic Ocean, controlled by a friendly British fleet, served as a barrier to European expansion. The United States was thus able during the nineteenth century to remain aloof from world issues, except where its interests were concerned, and to develop a continent with a minimum of European interference.

Prior to World War I the United States had been, with few exceptions, a spectator rather than a participant in the mainstreams of international politics. With our entry into that war, President Wilson's enunciation of the Fourteen Points setting forth his plans for a better postwar world, and his participation in the peace conference, the United States found itself looked to as a leader. The refusal of the Senate to give its consent to the Treaty of Versailles, including the Covenant of the League of Nations, marked our return to the role of spectator. World War II and the attack on Pearl Harbor rudely jolted us out of it.

On February 5, 1945, at the second plenary meeting of the conference at Yalta, Churchill, Roosevelt, and Stalin discussed the maintenance of peace and order in Germany at the end of the war. In response to Churchill's question concerning the role of the United States, Roosevelt "replied that he did not believe that American troops would stay in Europe much more than two years. He went on to say that he felt that he could obtain support in Congress and throughout the country for any reasonable measures designed to safeguard the future peace, but he did not believe that this would extend to the maintenance of an appreciable American force in Europe." [1] Yet the United States did not withdraw from Europe. Today it has close to four hundred thousand men in uniform stationed in Europe.

This one fact illustrates how greatly the nature of our country's role in foreign affairs has changed within one generation.

The United States emerged from World War II a far stronger country—the only major nation to have done so. For a few years we held a position of overpowering strength in relation to the rest of the world, but it was not in the cards to expect to hold this position indefinitely. The United Kingdom and the countries of Western Europe made a spectacular recovery, and the Soviet Union learned the secret of the bomb. In place of one superpower there were

[1] *Foreign Relations of the United States—The Conferences at Malta and Yalta, 1945* (Washington, D. C.: Historical Division, Department of State, U. S. Government Printing Office, 1955), p. 617.

now two. Even this situation will probably not last too long. If the trend toward unification in Europe should continue, in spite of temporary setbacks, there may well be three superpowers. Eventually there will be others. This is all part of the process of change.

Factors Shaping Foreign Policy

Upon our adaptability to change and our leadership of it will depend our ability to influence events to move in the direction we would like them to go. That ability is the measure of the success of our foreign policy, which is the sum of the courses of action we take to carry out our objectives in relation to the rest of the world. A number of factors shape a nation's foreign policy. Chief among them are (1) its judgment of its relationship to the changes brought about by the fundamental forces shaping the world, (2) its aspirations and beliefs, and (3) its goal and subsidiary objectives leading to that goal.

THE FUNDAMENTAL FORCES

Our position in the world has changed radically; the world likewise has not remained static. Changes have been taking place at such a fast pace that it would not be inappropriate to speak of some of them as revolutions, for they have contributed to the breakdown of the old order just as surely as armed revolt. Let us examine some of the fundamental forces causing these changes.

EQUALITY AND NATIONAL IDENTITY. A twofold struggle is going on around the world for equal rights and opportunity—for the individual and for the nation. The desire of the individual for equality—one man, one vote—goes hand in hand with the desire of the colony to become an independent nation with full right and opportunity to run its own affairs. A nation has been defined as a body of people associated with a particular territory who are sufficiently conscious of their unity to seek or to possess a government peculiarly their own. The nation, like the individual, seeks recognition of its identity and of its equality with other nations.

The quest for nationhood has reached flood proportions.

At its founding in 1945 the United Nations had 51 members. As of June 1963, there were 111. Forty-five of them, of which 29 are in Africa, gained independence since World War II.

The question no longer arises as to whether a certain colony will become free, but when. The colonial power's objective should be to make the transition as smooth as possible. If the thrust toward equality and national identity is resisted, it will break into violence. This happened in the American colonies in 1776, and it would be foolish not to expect the same to happen elsewhere.

This fierce pride a new country has in its existence was well illustrated by a debate which occurred in the parliament of the Republic of the Congo on December 7, 1962. One of the deputies, Joseph Maboti, introduced a resolution to suspend the plan sponsored by the Secretary General of the United Nations. This is what Mr. Maboti said: [2]

> The Thant plan may be good or bad, but it cannot be applied without approval by the sovereign Parliament of an independent land.
>
> We cannot allow a new neo-colonialism in our land now that we are independent, even if that neo-colonialism is coming under the auspices of the United Nations. The decisions about the future of Katanga must be made here, not in the United Nations chambers in New York.

One of the most backward areas of the world is likewise not immune. This story with a Cairo dateline appeared in *The New York Times* of October 1, 1962, on Yemen:

> Hohsen el-Ainy, Foreign Minister of the new republic of Yemen, asserted here today that his government was "firmly established." He appealed for international recognition and material help.
>
> "Of course if there is aggression against us, we will defend ourselves with all our means. Of course, we could be wiped out, for we are small and weak.
>
> "But worry about that will not stop us now. We could not ask permission of outsiders to do this. We have done what we believe in, what we believe we must do to earn respect and freedom.
>
> "We are not the first to revolt for such a purpose. I believe Americans were the first. Perhaps we are the last. We have been so backward in everything."

[2] *The New York Times,* 8 December 1962.

The drive toward equality and national identity springs from the deep-seated desire of people to be free. While using the slogans of the revolution of freedom, communism seeks to divert this force into channels that lead to suppression of individual rights and extinction of a nation's capacity to act independently. Although constantly proclaiming that its triumph is inevitable, communism in reality is running against the tide. Coercion has not stifled the spirit of self-determination even behind the Iron Curtain. The uprisings in East Germany in 1953 and in Poland and Hungary in 1956, the freedom of action which the satellite states have demanded and have gained in the past few years, and the fierce debate over ideology now raging between the Soviet Union and Communist China are evidence that not even people and states in the Communist bloc want to be run from Moscow.

Every newly independent nation has been anxious to secure membership as soon as possible in the United Nations. Admittance is a recognition of its separate and equal station. Once a nation is confident that its existence is not subject to challenge, it is usually willing to enter into cooperative arrangements with other nations. The industrialized democracies of Western Europe have, in the European Economic Community (the Common Market), surrendered certain traits of sovereignty to a common authority.

RISING EXPECTATIONS. The second fundamental force is the concept that proper utilization of modern technology can provide a better life, not at some future time, but right now, not just for the few, but for everybody. Modern technology provided the means, and the American genius for organization showed how to use it. A large population in an area without internal tariff barriers made feasible mass production based on standardization and interchangeability of parts. Paying the workers sufficient wages to enable them to buy the products of the factories made possible a mass market and a steady rise in the standard of living.

The Indian farmer and the Bolivian miner are now aware of the possibility of a better life, and they want it. They are no longer content to exist at a subsistence level just because their fathers and grandfathers before them did so without hope of anything better. If they cannot see progress under the existing government and social structure, they will, most likely, turn to radical solutions. Communism is there with what purports to be the answer.

The drive for a better life has been well termed "the revolution of rising expectations." U Thant, the Secretary General of the United Nations, has called it "the revolutionary concept of a meaningful future."[3] Recognition of this force underlies our aid programs and the Alliance for Progress.

SCIENCE. In the fields of science and technology, we have made very rapid advances without perhaps realizing how they are affecting our lives. In the realm of flight, we have gone in two decades from breaking the sound barrier to constructing planes capable of flying several times the speed of sound to planning to put a man on the moon. The electronic computer, automation, and progress in the fields of chemistry and atomic science are bringing about change faster than any previous generation ever experienced. Nowhere has there been more progress than in the development of new weapons of destruction.

One of the most important advances of all has been in agriculture. In the United States today it takes only 15 man-hours of labor to produce 100 bushels of corn; half a century ago it took 135 man-hours. This new knowledge is having its effect abroad. France is now facing the problem of food surpluses, and Japan has finally been able to meet its own requirements in rice. Although the Communist bloc is familiar with the methods, it has not yet been able to achieve this breakthrough in food production.

POPULATION EXPLOSION. World population, held in check by what the pessimistic British economist Malthus called the iron law of war, famine, and pestilence, did not reach 1 billion until 1830, but it climbed to 2 billion in 1930, and to 3 billion in 1961. By the year 2000 the world can expect to have some 6.2 billion people. The nearly 2 million babies born each week provide the statistic that the world's population is increasing at an average of 2 per cent a year. This increase, however, it not uniform throughout the world. The developed countries have a lower rate of increase; 1.7 per cent a year is the rate in the United States.

The rate of population increase in the less developed countries tends to be higher and in some of them exceeds 3

[3] Speech on 2 December 1962 at Johns Hopkins University, Baltimore, quoted in *The New York Times*, 3 December 1962.

per cent a year. To a large extent Western science and organization are responsible. Introduction of modern sanitary measures, inoculations against endemic diseases, campaigns against malaria, and shipment of foodstuffs in time of famine have greatly reduced the death rate and prolonged the average life expectancy. It is estimated that, if present rates of growth were to continue, between now and the year 2000 the population of North America would grow from 200 to 300 million, while the population of South and Middle America would grow from some 200 to 600 million.

In some of the poorer areas, the population increase is outpacing the increase in gross national product (a country's total annual output of goods and services). After consumption needs are met in a country in these circumstances, few resources remain to build the roads, dams, and factories which could increase the country's productive output and thus make possible a higher standard of living.

The United Nations is now beginning to give serious attention to the question of population growth, for it presents a serious obstacle to a less developed country's economic growth, even with the help of foreign aid. The problem is well illustrated by the $1 billion Aswan High Dam in Egypt, scheduled for completion in 1972. It will increase Egypt's arable land by one-third; yet during the years of its construction Egypt's population will have grown by one-third.

RESULTS OF THE FUNDAMENTAL FORCES. The less developed countries in Africa, Asia, and Latin America have begun to feel the full effect of these forces only in recent years, and the results have not necessarily been constructive. The drive toward equality and national identity has brought new nations into existence before some of them had sufficient trained men to run them. Inability to fulfill rising expectations has caused frustration, discontent, and occasional outbreaks of violence. Science, while it may provide jet airline service to the capitals, has only begun to increase the crop yields of the farmers. The upsurge in population threatens to outstrip production. Yet mankind is capable of harnessing these forces to produce a much more abundant life. North America, Western Europe, Japan, Australia, and New Zealand have reached a stage of development which has within its power the providing of a decent standard of living for all their citizens.

Yet the per capita gross national product in the rich

nations, the "haves," has been increasing faster than in the poor nations, the "have-nots." Americans now have a per capita gross national product of about $3,000 a year whereas the bulk of the world's population has less than one-tenth as much. The gap between the rich nations, mostly in the northern hemisphere, and the poor nations, mostly in the southern hemisphere, is growing.

OUR ASPIRATIONS AND BELIEFS

A foreign policy which ignores the drive towards equality and national identity, the rising expectations of mankind, the impact of science and technology, and the rapid increase in population will not over the long run be successful. The winds of change blow too strongly. Foreign policy in a democracy must also reflect the beliefs and aspirations of the people in whose name it is executed.

The Declaration of Independence and the Constitution set forth the fundamentals for which we stand:

1. Belief in God. Our country believes in moral values, and its conscience has been shaped by the Bible. It would be against our nature to lie about our intentions or to enter into treaties with no intention of honoring them.

2. "A decent respect to the opinions of mankind." We were concerned about what others thought of our revolt against the British Crown, and we are concerned today with world opinion. We want to appear to do right in the eyes of others.

3. Our conviction that "all men are created equal, that they are endowed by their Creator with certain inalienable rights, that among them are Life, Liberty, and the pursuit of Happiness." We have consistently maintained that people everywhere are entitled to these rights, and have used our influence as a government to that end, although here at home we have not yet fully conceded these rights to those of our citizens whose skin may be a different color from that of our own.

4. Governments derive "their just powers from the consent of the governed." Although we have dealt with dictatorships, we have never been happy in that relationship. Although we have held dependent territories, we have done so only as a temporary measure until the inhabitants could decide their future for themselves. We acquired Cuba, Puerto Rico, and the Philippines from Spain as a result of the Spanish-Ameri-

can War. Cuba became a republic in 1902, and Puerto Rico through free elections opted for its present status as a self-governing commonwealth associated with the United States. In the Philippines we laid the groundwork for eventual self-government through a nation-wide public school system and through staffing the civil service as rapidly as possible with Filipinos. In 1934 Congress passed legislation providing for the islands' independence. On July 4, 1946, the Philippines became an independent nation.

5. "That whenever any Form of Government becomes destructive of these ends, it is the Right of the People to alter or to abolish it." This was and still is a revolutionary doctrine which has inspired many a people in their drive to independence. It is a doctrine which sometimes we have forgotten.

6. The right of the people to have "Representation in the Legislature, a right inestimable to them and formidable to tyrants only."

7. The independence of the judiciary.

8. The pre-eminence of civil power over the military.

OUR GOAL

These aspirations and beliefs have set the pattern for our way of life. Its maintenance and improvement depend, however, not only on what we do at home but also on what others do abroad. Therefore, of vital interest to us is a world environment that permits and encourages our development as a people and as a nation. That world environment is the goal of our foreign policy.

On April 2, 1917, President Wilson, in asking Congress to declare war against Germany, stated, "The world must be made safe for democracy." Since then these words have often been attacked as being hopelessly idealistic; yet in essence they were realistic. They meant that we thought a German victory would not result in the kind of world that would best promote our own national interests.

In his address to the Senate two months earlier, President Wilson had set forth his ideas on the conditions necessary for the future maintenance of the peace. He said:[4]

[4] Address to the Senate, 22 January 1917, "The Conditions of Permanent Peace," as quoted in *Readings in American Foreign Policy*, edited by Robert A. Goldwin (New York: Oxford University Press, 1959).

> I am proposing . . . that no nation should seek to extend its polity over any other nation or people, but that every people should be left free to determine its own polity, its own way of development, unhindered, unthreatened, unafraid, the little along with the great.

The basic goal of our foreign policy has not changed. In his State of the Union message on January 11, 1962, the late President Kennedy put it this way: [5]

> Yet our basic goal remains the same: a peaceful world community of free and independent states—free to choose their own future and their own system so long as it does not threaten the freedom of others.
>
> Some may choose forms and ways we would not choose for ourselves, but it is not for us that they are choosing. We can welcome diversity—the Communists cannot. For we offer a world of choice—they offer the world of coercion. . . .

The ancient Egyptians constructed pyramids out of thousands and thousands of blocks of stone. The final block was at the very top, the apex. It might be helpful to think of foreign policy as a five-sided pyramid, each policy action as one of the building blocks, each side as one of the main elements or courses of action, and the apex as the goal. If the blocks are laid in coherent fashion and each side is constructed in relationship to the others, they should eventually produce a pyramid—provided, of course, that unforeseen calamities do not change the nature of the ground on which the structure is being built and provided the plans of the architect are substantially correct. The goal will not be reached until the last block has been put in place.

As set forth by Dean Rusk, the Secretary of State, the five major elements of our foreign policy are: [6]

> 1. To deter or defeat aggression at any level, whether of nuclear attack or limited war or subversion and guerrilla tactics.
> 2. To bring about a closer association of the more industrialized democracies of Western Europe, North America, and Asia (specifically Japan) in promoting the prosperity and security of the entire free world.

[5] *The Department of State Bulletin* (Washington, D. C.: U. S. Government Printing Office, 29 January 1962), p. 159.

[6] Television program, "Five Goals of Foreign Policy," 24 September 1962. From *The Department of State Bulletin* (Washington, D. C.: U. S. Government Printing Office, 15 October 1962).

3. To help the less developed areas of the world carry through their revolution of modernization without sacrificing their independence or their pursuit of democracy.
4. To assist in the gradual emergence of a genuine world community, based on cooperation and law, through the establishment and development of such organs as the United Nations, the World Court, the World Bank and Monetary Fund, and other global and regional institutions.
5. To strive tirelessly to end the arms race and reduce the risk of war, to narrow the areas of conflict with the Communist bloc, and to continue to spin the infinity of threads that bind peace together.

Chapters IV through VIII examine in detail each of these elements or courses of action.

Factors Affecting the Execution of Foreign Policy

Once a course of action has been decided upon, then it must be carried out. Let us assume, as an example, that, in pursuit of the objective of ending the arms race and reducing the risk of war, we have agreed to meet with the Russians to discuss the reduction of armaments. The United States has a strong domestic base in these negotiations, for its capacity to inflict nuclear damage is as great, if not greater, than that of the Soviet Union. This fact is certainly an incentive to the Russians to reach an agreement. Both sides in the negotiations know the maximum objectives which they would like to reach and the minimum objectives which they must reach if they are to sign a treaty. In between there exists a certain latitude, an opportunity for freedom of action. Within this area the competence and skill of the negotiators are important. Even if, following full consultation with our allies, agreement should be reached and a treaty signed, it cannot come into effect without the concurrence of the Senate. The attitude of the Senate will depend to a large extent upon the attitude of our citizens.

Thus, looking at the carrying out of any foreign policy, we can see two main factors over which we have some control which will influence the outcome. These are our domestic base and the attitude of our citizens.

THE DOMESTIC BASE

Military might is only one of the elements of the domestic base. A strong economy is another, and is necessary to backstop our military commitments abroad and to finance programs of economic assistance. A third element is our performance in relation to our professed ideals. Our influence with the newly independent states of Africa is weakened by incidents, of which they are very much aware, of racial discrimination in the United States.

The United States is considered to be the most powerful nation in the world, but it contains only 6 per cent of the world's population. While it cannot dictate to others, it can have a tremendous influence in shaping events. The stronger the domestic base, the greater the influence. Yet over 5 per cent of our labor force is unemployed; the industrial plant is producing at less than full capacity; school and health facilities are not adequate; cities have their slums; and equality for all men is not yet a fact. We are making progress in correcting these weaknesses. The speed with which we do so will determine how soon we can mobilize our full force in support of our national objectives.

THE CITIZEN

We may agree on our objectives but have many different points of view as to the best ways of reaching them. Do we best promote our interests by encouraging the admittance of Communist China to the United Nations or by keeping it out?—by extending or by denying economic assistance to Indonesia?—by supporting or by withholding our support from the United Nations' action in the Congo? These alternate courses of action are subjects of ceaseless debate in a democratic society and should be.

Our form of government depends for its vitality upon citizen participation in the political process. The President, Vice President, and Members of Congress reach office through the votes of their fellow citizens. Their election, and even more their re-election, depends upon whether the policies they advocate reflect the wishes of the majority of the electorate. For that reason, no foreign policy, no matter how brilliantly conceived, can be successful unless it has the support or, as a minimum, not the active opposition of the majority. It can't have support unless it is understood. If John Doe is not clear as to his country's objectives, then he certainly can't be expected to endorse with any enthusiasm specific policies designed to achieve those objectives. It would be foolish to expect him to support the United Nations if he were unconvinced of the value of the United Nations to the United States. It would be equally unrealistic to expect him to support foreign aid if he could see no benefit to his or to his country's interests.

Our form of government thus places a heavy responsibility upon the executive branch to explain its policies and upon the citizen to learn enough about them so that he can make an informed judgment. The citizen, however, plays a much more direct role in foreign affairs than he usually realizes.

He can be effective in making his views heard if he joins with others who share his point of view. Nongovernmental organizations such as the Chamber of Commerce, the League of Women Voters, and the National Council of Churches, speaking for thousands and in some cases for millions, can have great influence on policy by molding public opinion and presenting their viewpoints to the legislative and executive branches. Labor unions have sometimes taken policy into their own hands, as did the International Longshoremen's Union by boycotting vessels of countries known to be trading with Cuba.

Foreign diplomats, students, and visitors obtain their strongest impressions of the United States not from contacts with the government but from the people they meet. Dozens of official receptions have far less effect on the attitude of an African diplomat toward the United States than failure to secure adequate housing for his family in Washington or to be served in a restaurant. Many of the young men and women from the developing countries who study in the United States return to important positions in their own countries. Their feelings toward the United States stem not so much from what they learned at school as from their relationships with Americans.

II. THE MAKING OF FOREIGN POLICY—THE APPARATUS

An administration sets forth its goal and the component courses of action it proposes to follow to attain that goal—based on its awareness of the forces shaping the world, its judgment of the country's capabilities, and its estimate of what the Congress and the American people want and will support. Each step in the process of moving toward that goal becomes part of our foreign policy.

Let us use an example. Our goal is "a peaceful world community of free and independent states." One of the components is "a closer association of the more industrialized democracies." There are many ways of working toward that closer association. One of them is through closer economic ties. One way of bringing about closer economic ties is to increase the volume of trade. An effective way to increase the volume of trade is to lower tariffs. For that reason, John F. Kennedy proposed to Congress legislation which would give him the authority to reduce U.S. tariffs so that he could bargain with other countries, the Common Market in particular, for reciprocal reduction of tariffs. After passage of the Trade Expansion Act of 1962, the administration was then able to open discussions with the Common Market. At every step in this process—the preparation of draft legislation, the passage of the bill through Congress, and the negotiations with the Common Market—decisions had to be made as to what to insist upon and what compromises to accept. The administration hardly ever gets exactly what it wants. If it insisted upon a whole loaf, it would probably get none. Carrying out a foreign policy, like politics, is the art of achieving the possible.

In our government a number of people have a say in the making and carrying out of foreign policy. This chapter examines what they do, how they do it, and how they tie in with one another.

THE PRESIDENT

The President is the key figure, for only he can make the ultimate decision. The President wears a number of hats. He is the head of state and the symbol of his country to people abroad. He is the Commander-in-Chief of the armed forces. He is the chief of the entire executive branch of the government, appoints its top men, and uses the government machinery to execute his policies. He is the leader of his political party and accordingly responsible for giving life to his party's platform and for carrying his party to victory in the next elections.

The President's authority, although great, is under our check-and-balance system limited by the Congress and by the courts. The Constitution gives the President the power, with the advice and consent of the Senate, to make treaties, provided two-thirds of the Senators present concur, and to appoint ambassadors and other officials. Although the President is the Commander-in-Chief of the armed forces, only Congress can declare war. The President can act only within the scope of existing law. If he requires additional authority, he must ask Congress for it. Congress may or may not pass the enabling legislation and, if it does, it may do so in a form far different from what the President requested. As an example, although Congress, by passage of the Trade Expansion Act, substantially met the President's request for authority to reduce tariffs, it added an amendment, much against the administration's wishes, which had the effect of depriving Poland and Yugoslavia of most favored nation treatment under our tariff laws, thus leaving the President without the discretionary authority he needed to conduct relations with those countries.

If the President feels strongly enough about a proposal and is willing to risk a head-on collision with Congress, he can sometimes achieve his own way by leaving Congress no alternative but to go along. In 1907 President Theodore Roosevelt wanted to send our whole fleet of sixteen battleships on a good-will cruise around the world. Congress indicated that it would be unwilling to make available the funds for the purpose. President Roosevelt then announced that he had sufficient funds to send the fleet to the Pacific Ocean and that it would stay there unless Congress appropriated the funds to bring it back.

The President, in addition to deciding what he wants to do, must also persuade Congress and the public that what he proposes is the course that should be followed. Sometimes party interests and discipline are sufficiently strong so that the administration can count on a favorable vote in Congress. At other times, when congressional support is not assured, the President may carry his case directly to the people. President Wilson went on a speaking tour to muster support for the Versailles Treaty, and President Franklin D. Roosevelt used his fireside chats to gain public sympathy for lend-lease and other assistance to the allies.

The ultimate responsibility of the President cannot be shared with anyone else. As President Truman said, "The buck stops here." It was he, and he alone, who had to make the decision whether to use the atomic bomb on Hiroshima and whether to send troops to defend South Korea.

On the morning of October 16, 1962, the late President Kennedy saw for the first time the photographs giving unmistakable proof of the installation of Soviet missiles in Cuba. That afternoon he spoke in the State Department auditorium to newspapermen and radio and television broadcasters who had been invited to Washington some weeks before for a background briefing conference. He closed his remarks by quoting these lines from Robert Graves' translation of the poem "A Bullfight" by Domingo Ortega:

> Bullfight critics ranked in rows
> Crowd the enormous plaza full;
> But only one is there who knows
> And he's the man who fights the bull.

Although the audience appreciated the aptness of the quote, it was not to realize until nearly a week later what the President may have had in mind. It was he and he alone who had to make the decision as to what action the United States would take in regard to Cuba.

The President determines the role he plays in foreign affairs. Some have taken a very active part. Others have preferred to entrust the conduct of foreign affairs to the Secretary of State. Either system works so long as the President and the Secretary keep each other fully informed. This was not always the case under President Franklin D. Roosevelt. On a number of occasions he communicated directly with Winston Churchill and our wartime ambassadors in London, Moscow, and Chungking. Secretary of State Cordell Hull often did not learn until much later of the decisions taken.

THE CONGRESS

Congress provides the means for thorough discussion of merits and disadvantages in a proposed course of action and of reaching, usually through compromise and modification, a position which can command majority support. The Constitution gives the Congress three vital powers in the conduct of foreign relations.

The first is the advice and consent of the Senate required to approve treaties and confirm ambassadors. A classic example is the refusal of the Senate to give its concurrence to the Treaty of Versailles. As a result, the United States did not join the League of Nations.

Although the Senate nearly always gives its advice and consent to presidential nominations of ambassadors, its attitude on several occasions has led the President to withdraw the nomination. The hearings conducted by the Senate's Committee on Foreign Relations can be extremely embarrassing, as the individual nominated to be ambassador to Ceylon learned a few years ago when he was unable to name the Prime Minister of that country. President Eisenhower's nomination of Mrs. Clare Boothe Luce as ambassador to Brazil was confirmed by the Senate after somewhat acrimonious hearings. Her subsequent comment, however, that a particular senator must have been kicked in the head by a horse, aroused so much criticism that she deemed it advisable to resign.

The second main power is that of the purse. Like any business, foreign affairs cannot be conducted without funds, and it is Congress which appropriates them. Differences in opinion as to amounts needed, and particularly for the foreign aid program, result each year in a struggle between Congress and the administration, whether Republican or Democratic. The appropriations committees of the two houses thus have an important voice in determining the size and scope of a number of activities in the field of foreign affairs.

The third main power of Congress in the field of foreign relations is the passage of bills and resolutions. Some of them have charted new directions in foreign policy. Public Law 584 of 1946, introduced by and named after Senator

Fulbright, authorized the United States to finance student exchanges through the sale abroad of war surplus property. Senator Vandenberg's resolution in 1948 expressed the wishes of the Senate that the United States associate itself "with regional and other collective arrangements as are based on continuous and effective self-help and mutual aid, and as affect its national security." This resolution gave the administration the assurance it needed before undertaking discussions which resulted in the North Atlantic Treaty Organization (NATO). Public Law 480, passed in 1954, set up mechanisms for the disposal abroad of surplus agricultural commodities.

Committees of Congress frequently call upon persons with knowledge on specific subjects to provide them with the information they need to carry out their duties as legislators. When Congress is in session, a considerable portion of the time of the top officials in the Department of State, as well as in other departments and agencies, is spent appearing before congressional committees. In 1962 the Secretary of State met with members of Congress no fewer than 90 times—25 of these sessions representing formal appearances before committees. In addition some 87 other officers of the Department testified before congressional committees a total of 224 times and frequently visited Members of Congress to discuss questions of mutual interest. These appearances afford the administration a good opportunity to present its case, to explain what it is doing and why, and thus to build up support for its program. Witnesses have learned from experience that they must be well prepared. How searching congressional questioning can be was illustrated by the remark made by Senator Morse on June 13, 1963, in connection with hearings on foreign aid: "I want a breakdown of the figures and I also want to have presented clear proof as to why a reduction here or there would do serious damage to the security of the country."

In this country we know that the statements of a Member of Congress on foreign affairs represent his own views and not necessarily those of the government. This distinction is not so readily understood abroad. Statements by Members of Congress not infrequently are picked up by the local press abroad and by the Soviet propaganda apparatus and are used to give an erroneous impression of the attitude of the United States. While on a tour of Africa, one Senator remarked that the natives of that continent were not prepared to govern themselves. This comment aroused considerable resentment against the United States even though the Senator emphasized that he was expressing only his personal opinion. His repetition of the remark a few months later over a Washington, D. C., television program led ambassadors of African countries to protest to the Secretary of State and to the President, despite the fact that the executive branch has no authority over statements of the legislative branch.

Every administration seeks to establish a close working relationship with Congress and attempts to keep foreign policy matters out of domestic politics. This is difficult to achieve. Members of Congress have frequently expressed the opinion that they should be consulted before the administration makes up its mind on a particular course of action. Yet, because of the open nature of our society, consultation in advance can sometimes result in premature disclosure of the administration's thinking and to a weakening of its position if negotiations with other governments are involved. Since secrecy was so essential to the success of the measures the administration took following its discovery in October 1962 of Soviet missile bases in Cuba, key Members of Congress were informed of the President's intentions only shortly before he publicly announced them.

THE DEPARTMENT OF STATE

Organization and Operation. The Department of State is the official channel through which the American people conduct their relations with the other governments and peoples of the world. Its head is the Secretary of State, whose primary functions are to advise the President on foreign affairs, to supervise the activities of the Department of State and the Foreign Service in carrying out their responsibilities, and to work closely with other government departments and agencies having interest in foreign policy so that their activities contribute to overall U.S. objectives.

Next in command is the Under Secretary of State, who is in charge when the Secretary is away from Washington. A second Under Secretary concentrates on political matters. There are two Deputy Under Secretaries, one of whom specializes in general policy matters, the other in management and organization.

The work of the department is carried on by organizational units, each with a functional or geographic responsibility, under the direction of these officers:

The Counselor and Chairman of the Policy Planning Council.

The Legal Adviser.

The Director of the Office of International Scientific Affairs.

The Assistant Secretaries for the five geographic areas—Europe, Latin America, the Far East, Africa, and the Near East and South Asia.

The Assistant Secretaries for Public Affairs, Educational and Cultural Affairs, Congressional Relations, International Organization Affairs, Economic Affairs, and Administration.

The Administrator, Bureau of Security and Consular Affairs.

The Director of Intelligence and Research.

The bureaus are divided into offices. As an example, the Bureau of African Affairs has six offices, each of which has a definite area of responsibility, such as the Office of Northern African Affairs. Within the office one officer, known as the desk officer, is responsible for the conduct of our relations with a particular country, for example, the Officer-in-Charge of Moroccan Affairs. Usually he has served in that country and is considered an expert on it. Over his desk pass the department's communications to that country and the communications from our posts in that country to the department. The desk officer may suggest a course of action to meet a particular problem. Routine matters are ordinarily decided below the level of the assistant secretary. Important matters of basic policy may be submitted to the Secretary or to the President.

Many proposed actions governing our relations with a particular country concern more than one bureau in the Department of State and often other departments and agencies, and they must be consulted before a proposed course of action is carried forward. This process is known as "clearance." Thus, on one problem the interested bureau may seek clearance from the Bureau of Economic Affairs, the Department of the Treasury, the Agency for International Development, and the Export-Import Bank.

To cope with problems that are of continuing major concern to a number of departments and agencies, a new organizational device—the task force—has been used with considerable success. The Berlin Task Force brings together representatives of the departments and agencies concerned, including the White House, State Department, Defense Department, and the United States Information Agency (USIA). Through regular meetings it does the political, economic, military, and informational planning designed to cope with contingencies that might arise. The task force also discusses and approves instructions and guidelines to our diplomatic missions and military posts concerned with Berlin developments.

COMMUNICATIONS, BUDGET, AND PERSONNEL. The daily communications traffic between the Department of State and its more than three hundred overseas posts exceeds that of the Washington offices of the two major news services. The number of communications sent and received each workday averages 5,000. The department is kept informed constantly of events throughout the world.

Although its responsibilities are world-wide, in terms of both expenditures and personnel the Department of State is the next to the smallest of all the government departments. In 1790 Thomas Jefferson, our first Secretary of State, had a staff of five clerks, a part-time translator of French, and two messengers. Today total personnel is approximately 24,000, of which 7,000 Americans are in the United States and another 7,000 Americans and 10,000 foreign nationals are at our overseas posts. Only about 22 per cent of the total 32,000 civilian American government employees overseas work for the Department of State. About 58 per cent of this total are employed by the Department of Defense.

The top positions in the Department of State are filled by presidential appointees who may or may not be chosen from the career services. Most of the other positions in the department are filled by career employees either from the Civil Service, who serve in Washington, or from the Foreign Service. The 9,141 Americans (as of September 30, 1963) in the Foreign Service fall into three categories—Foreign Service Officers (3,768), Foreign Service Reserve Officers (1,343), and the Foreign Service Staff Corps (4,017).

Foreign Service Officers (FSO's) are the professionals who are in the Foreign Service as a career. Entrance is usually on the basis of competitive examination, both written and oral. The successful candidate is usually appointed, with the advice and consent of the Senate, as a Foreign Service Officer class 8. Through promotion he can progress to class 1 and the two grades above that, of career minister and career ambassador. The salary, as of January 1964, ranges from $5,795 per annum for class 8 to $19,650 for class 1. The ambassador at a major post receives $27,500 a year.

In the postwar years the demand for people with expert knowledge in specialized fields, such as labor, international finance, and petroleum, has been greater than could be supplied by the Foreign Service Officer Corps. Accordingly, persons with special talents may be appointed as Foreign Service Reserve Officers for limited periods of time.

The Foreign Service Staff Corps, over half of whom are women, provides clerical, administrative, and technical personnel—such as secretaries, code clerks, typists, and accountants.

More than 10,000 foreign nationals, hired locally by our posts after a careful security screening, provide continuity and an invaluable knowledge of the local scene. Their jobs, which do not deal with matters affecting the security of the United States, range from driving a car to typing of visas to research on markets for American products.

OTHER DEPARTMENTS AND AGENCIES

Four other agencies associated with the Department of State are responsible for specific aspects of foreign relations. Two of them are semi-autonomous agencies within the Department of State: the Agency for International Development (AID), which administers the foreign assistance program, and the Peace Corps, which provides voluntary skilled manpower to work with and train people in some 45 less developed countries. Their activities are discussed in chapter VI.

Two other agencies, the United States Information Agency (USIA) and the United States Arms Control and Disarmament Agency (ACDA), are separate from the Department of State but receive overall policy guidance from, and work closely with, the department. ACDA is concerned with formulating and implementing U.S. arms control and disarmament policy, as explained in chapter VIII.

USIA tells America's story abroad and seeks to make our national policies everywhere intelligible and, wherever possible, palatable. To achieve these purposes, USIA (known abroad as USIS—United States Information Service) uses the techniques of modern mass communications: press, radio, film, television, libraries, exhibits, the arts, and personal contact by its some 1,300 officers at approximately 240 overseas posts. Its global radio network, the Voice of America, speaks by short wave in 36 languages, 761 hours weekly, to an overseas audience numbering in the millions.

Other departments and agencies are also concerned with foreign affairs in matters which fall within their particular competence, as these examples will illustrate. The Department of the Treasury is concerned with policies and programs relating to the international financial and monetary field. The Bureau of Sport Fisheries and Wildlife of the Department of the Interior cooperates with Canada and Mexico on conservation measures. The Bureau of International Business Operations of the Department of Commerce is concerned with American participation in overseas trade fairs and sends trade missions abroad. The Civil Aeronautics Board rules on applications of foreign air carriers for landing rights in the United States and assists the Department of State in the negotiation of agreements with foreign governments for the establishment or development of air routes and services.

THE NATIONAL SECURITY COUNCIL

Because many units of the U.S. government are involved in the making of foreign policy, there is a need for coordination of effort at the highest level. Cabinet meetings used to serve this purpose, but after World War II the vast number of major foreign affairs problems made Cabinet consideration impractical. In order to improve coordination between the military and other departments, the National Security Council (NSC) was established in 1947 to advise the President with respect to the integration of domestic, foreign, and military policies relating to the national security. Members of the council are the President, the Vice President, the Secretary of State, the Secretary of Defense, and the Director of the Office of Emergency Planning. The Chairman of the Joint Chiefs of Staff and the Director of the Central Intelligence Agency are advisers. Other high officials may be invited to attend when the subject matter indicates that their presence would be useful.

The vitality of the National Security Council depends upon the use the President wishes to make of it. During the Truman and Eisenhower administrations, it met regularly and provided a channel, at least in theory, for bringing out into the open conflicting views so that the President could then decide which course of action to follow. President Kennedy preferred to consult, either individually or in groups, directly with the officials concerned with a particular problem. During the Cuban crisis he conferred with a group of officials some of whom served on the NSC and some of whom did not. This group came to be known as the Executive Committee of the National Security Council.

OUR OVERSEAS POSTS

More than three hundred posts overseas are the local offices of the United States government. Those in the capitals of other countries are known as diplomatic missions. An embassy is headed by an ambassador, a legation, by a minister. The ambassador, or the minister, is the President's personal representative to the head of state of the host country. Until 1893 we were represented by ministers, the lower ranking level of envoys. Since then, and particularly since World War II, we have carried on relations with most other countries at the ambassadorial level. As of July 1963, we had 105 embassies and only four legations, three of which were in the satellite states of Eastern Europe.

Consular posts are maintained in cities other than the capital. The more important ones are called consulates general and the others, consulates. They deal with the provincial and municipal authorities and concern themselves primarily with economic and commercial matters, looking after the welfare of American citizens and seamen, and issuing visas to foreigners wishing to enter the United States.

The most common diplomatic and consular titles are grouped as follows:

diplomatic	consular
ambassador	consul general
minister	consul
counselor	vice consul
first secretary	
second secretary	
third secretary	
attaché	
assistant attaché	

In many of our diplomatic missions, officers below the rank of counselor hold diplomatic and consular titles concurrently, for example, third secretary and vice consul.

The ambassador has the overall responsibility for the conduct of American policy in the country to which he is assigned and has authority to supervise not only the activities of the embassy and the consulates but also all other United States government activities within that country. The President may appoint anyone he chooses, subject, of course, to confirmation by the Senate. Over two-thirds of our present chiefs of mission have been appointed from the career service. The ambassador's primary job is the practice of diplomacy—the art of transacting business between his government and the government to which he is accredited. His success or failure depends primarily on how well he is able to influence, without improper intervention in local affairs, attitudes and actions by that government which do not run counter to our interests and hopefully run parallel to them. How freely he is able to operate depends upon the environment. In an Iron Curtain country our ambassador's contacts are severely limited. In a democracy he has a much broader scope. Through public talks, cultivation of all elements of society, including labor and students, and through visits to remote areas of the country, he tries to create a favorable impression of the United States which goes far beyond government circles. Where he can, without jeopardizing good relations with those in power, he becomes acquainted with opposition leaders. He should be able to recognize problems before they assume serious proportions and take measures necessary to prevent them from embittering relations between the two countries. The ambassador is not just an observer; to be effective, he must take an active role in coordinating the work of the embassy and other U.S. Government activities so that they all contribute harmoniously towards promotion of our objectives.

A typical medium-sized embassy is divided into five sections, each with several officers.

1. The *executive section* consists of the ambassador, his second in command, known as counselor of embassy, and probably two secretaries. The counselor assumes charge in the absence of the ambassador and during this period is known as "chargé d'affaires ad interim." In a large embassy (Paris, Rio de Janeiro, Tokyo) the second in command may

carry the title of minister or of counselor with the personal rank of minister.

2. The principal tasks of the several officers in the *political section* are to keep themselves informed on political developments within the country, report them to Washington with an analysis of their significance, discuss with their counterparts in the foreign ministry problems arising in the relations between the two countries, and present our points of view on matters coming up in the United Nations and other international bodies.

3. The *economic section* closely follows economic and commercial matters, reports developments to Washington, looks for trade opportunities for American business, and advises and assists Americans doing business in or with that country. If we are extending economic assistance to the country, the economic section works closely with the AID mission in planning and execution of programs.

4. The *consular section* is the one which most people know best. It issues passports to American citizens, assists them if they become involved with the local authorities, and takes charge, if need be, of funeral arrangements. The consular section issues visas to foreigners desiring to go to the United States and has the unpleasant task of refusing those applicants who are inadmissible under our laws.

5. The *administrative section* looks after the physical operation of the embassy—seeing that the building is heated, that the employees are paid, and that supplies and equipment are ordered.

Officers sent to the embassy to perform specialized duties are known as "attachés." Some of them, such as the scientific and geographic attachés, are selected by the Department of State. The commercial and labor attachés are selected with the concurrence of the Department of Commerce and the Department of Labor, respectively. Military and agricultural attachés are detailed by their respective departments subject to the approval of the Department of State.

The United States Information Agency (USIA) is responsible for the conduct of our information program abroad and in a typical medium-sized embassy may have several American and a number of local employees. Working as the public affairs unit of the embassy, USIA directs reading rooms and libraries; organizes classes in English, the exchange of students and professors, and film and music programs; sets up press conferences for visiting American dignitaries; sponsors appearances of American musicians and artists; issues publications; and supplies material to the local press.

If the country is receiving military assistance from the United States, there may be a military mission (usually known as the Military Assistance Advisory Group) to instruct personnel in the use and care of equipment. If the country is receiving economic assistance, there will probably be an AID mission. Although the missions and some of the attachés report on operating and technical matters directly to their own departments or agencies in Washington, they must keep the ambassador informed of their activities and follow his general policy guidance. The heads of the missions, the principal attachés, and the principal officers of the embassy meet regularly with the ambassador as a "country team" to discuss our policies in regard to that country and to coordinate their efforts in carrying them out.

THE TOOLS OF MODERN DIPLOMACY

We have described briefly the government apparatus both in Washington and abroad for the making and conduct of foreign policy. The extent to which we can shape actions abroad so that they flow in directions favorable to our objectives is the measure of the success of our foreign policy. The tools which we use in working toward our objectives are also the tools which other nations employ. Among them are:

NEGOTIATION. This will be successful only if both parties really want a solution, are willing to settle for something less than their original demands, and are reasonably assured that an agreement, if reached, will be observed. The Austrian State Treaty, which ended that country's occupation status, took eight years to negotiate, but it was in the interests of the Soviets as well as of the Western powers to withdraw their troops and provide for Austria's neutrality. Negotiations for a peace treaty with Germany have not been successful. The West has been unwilling to recognize the permanent division of Germany. The Soviet Union has been unwilling to consider reunification of the two zones based upon free elections which might mean the end of the Communist regime in East Germany.

THREATS. Chairman Khrushchev in a speech in 1960 said that

> . . . the United States is now not at such an unattainable distance from the Soviet Union as formerly. Figuratively speaking, if need be, Soviet artillerymen can support the Cuban people with their rocket fire, should the aggressive forces in the Pentagon dare to start intervention against Cuba.[1]

President Kennedy in October 1962, after the discovery of Soviet missile sites in Cuba, was much more direct. He announced that we would regard

> . . . any nuclear missile launched from Cuba against any nation in the Western Hemisphere as an attack by the Soviet Union on the United States, requiring a full retaliatory response upon the Soviet Union.[2]

ALLIANCES. The principle that an attack upon one member will be regarded as an attack upon all members of the alliance can make aggression too costly to contemplate. The protection afforded by the alliance also imposes obligations and restraints upon its members.

FOREIGN AID. As we have used it, it is for the purpose of assisting countries to maintain their independence and to become self-supporting. We will not extend assistance unless the recipient country is prepared to take meaningful steps toward that end. The Soviets use aid as a means to tie the recipient country more closely to the Communist bloc, thereby increasing Soviet political influence.

UNITED NATIONS. Every nation seeks to use the U.N. to further its interests. For the smaller nations it is a means of increasing their protection. In the Congo the U.N. served as a means of avoiding a probable direct confrontation of the Soviet Union and the United States.

TRADE. The policy of the United States, to which its allies in general adhere, is not to supply the Communist bloc with strategic materials and technology that might help develop

[1] Speech of 9 July 1960, quoted in *The New York Times*, 10 July 1960.

[2] Address to the nation, 22 October 1962. From *The Department of State Bulletin* (Washington, D. C.: U. S. Government Printing Office, 12 November 1962), p. 718.

its military strength. We have imposed a total embargo on trade with Communist China, North Korea, and North Vietnam, and also a total embargo on trade with Cuba with the exception, for humanitarian purposes, of medicines and foodstuffs. We have refused to sell arms to certain Middle Eastern and Latin American states when we feared the arms would be used for purposes of which we did not approve.

RETALIATION. After the Soviet Union restricted the movements of American citizens in its territory, we imposed similar restrictions on movements of Soviet citizens in the United States. Our object was to bring about the removal of the Soviet restrictions. When the United States increased the duties on imports of glass and carpets, an act of particular importance to Belgium, the Common Market retaliated by increasing its duties on certain chemicals supplied chiefly by the United States.

REACHING PEOPLE DIRECTLY. In the battle for men's minds many tactics are used—short wave broadcasts (which may be jammed), information programs, student exchanges, and cultural presentations.

III. COMMUNISM AND THE SOVIET UNION

How to cope with the aggressive activities of communism is our central problem. Sixty years ago a civil war in a country in Southeast Asia would have been a matter of only passing interest to the rest of the world. Today, almost inevitably, the great powers become involved and a local conflict becomes a cold war issue. Our relations with communism and the Soviet Union come up time and time again during the course of this book. Therefore, before proceeding further with a discussion of American foreign policy, we would do well to look at the nature of communism and the foreign policy of the Soviet Union.

Communism has three identities which to some extent operate independently of each other and yet are closely entwined:

1. As an ideology, with Marx and Lenin the high priests of the cult.
2. As a world-wide revolutionary movement, with Communist parties in countries throughout the world.
3. As states, with the U.S.S.R. as the first and foremost.

These interlocking identities are illustrated in the Soviet Union by the positions occupied by Nikita Khrushchev. He is not only Chairman of the Council of Ministers (a position equivalent to premier in Western usage), the highest executive and administrative organ of state power, but also First Secretary of the Central Committee of the Communist Party, the key position in the party apparatus.

MARX

Let us consider communism as an ideology. Its Bible is *The Communist Manifesto,* written by Karl Marx and Friedrich Engels and published in 1848. The *Manifesto* states:

> The Communists disdain to conceal their views and aims. They openly declare that their ends can be obtained only by the forcible overthrow of all existing social conditions. Let the ruling class tremble at a Communistic revolution. The proletarians have nothing to lose but their chains. They have a world to win.

In the *Manifesto* Marx and Engels propounded a philosophy of history—the struggle of opposing classes and the inevitable downfall of capitalism—upon which the Communist movement is based. For the true Communist it is just as valid today as it was a century ago. It is impossible to understand the movement without an understanding of Marx's thinking.

As a student in Germany he was greatly influenced by the German philosopher Hegel, whose theory of dialectics—the art of arriving at a truth through the clash of opposing views and arguments—stirred up heated discussions among German university students in the 1830's. Hegel maintained that any idea (thesis) contained within itself an opposite (antithesis) and that the clash of the two resulted in a new idea (synthesis), which in turn bred its own antithesis and so on. This meant that change was the rule of life and inevitable.

Marx believed that the production and exchange of goods are the basis of every social order and that any changes or revolutions are to be explained by changes in the method of production and exchange of products. This became known as the "materialist concept of history." To it Marx added Hegel's theory of dialectics to form the ideology known as "dialectical materialism." By this method he tried not only to explain the past but also to predict the future. He viewed history as having five stages, each based on a particular method of production—the original primitive-communal society, the slave state, feudalism, capitalism, and communism, the ultimate stage. The first four stages, Marx maintained, succumbed because they contained the seeds of their own destruction. One class within the society controlled the means of production and exploited the working class. The continual clash of interests between classes was responsible for all historical progress. Since communism will have no private ownership of the means of production and will therefore be a classless society, Marx argued that the dialectical process will then cease to operate.

The Communist Manifesto was followed by an enormous work of 2,500 pages called *Das Kapital* (Capital) on which Marx labored for eighteen years. The first volume was not published until 1867. To demonstrate his theory that capitalism was doomed, Marx set up what he considered to be an ideal capitalist society and then proceeded to show by his process of logic how it would destroy itself. Remember, though, he was writing a century ago, and his vivid imagination did not foresee the changed social environment that would permit capitalism to flourish in the United States and Western Europe. He did not even dream there could be such developments as a strong labor movement, a graduated income tax, ownership of large corporations by millions of stockholders; he could not conceive that man could ever act in any way except in furtherance of his own immediate materialistic interests.

Yet Communists today accept Marx's theses with the same fervor that the Nazis accepted *Mein Kampf*. Where changes during the past century would seem to negate the bases of Marxist thought, the Communists have interpreted the facts so as to prove the theory.

PROGRAM OF THE SOVIET COMMUNIST PARTY

Communist dogma as it is today can be found in *The New Program of the Communist Party of the Soviet Union,* adopted by the Twenty-Second Congress of the Party on October 31, 1961, at Moscow. The quotes in this chapter not otherwise identified are from the *Program*. Communism is defined as "a classless social system with one form of public ownership of the means of production and full social equality of all members of society." The party does not maintain that the Soviet Union has yet reached that stage, rather that it is still in the socialist stage and will need another three decades to reach "the highest form of organization of public life." In reading Communist writings, the term "socialism" should be construed as an earlier phase of communism, not, as democratic socialists use the word, an ideology which favors a representative government and a state capitalist economy.

The supreme goal of the party is to build a Communist society, not only in the Soviet Union, but throughout the world. Building a Communist society implies a social revolution, and any means to that end are to be employed—peaceful or violent. As the *Program* so succinctly puts it:

> Where the exploiting classes resort to violence against the people, the possibility of a non-peaceful transition to socialism should be borne in mind. . . . The success of the struggle which the working class wages for the victory of the revolution will depend on how well the working class and its party master the use of all forms of struggle—peaceful and non-peaceful, parliamentary and extra-parliamentary—and how well they are prepared for any swift and sudden replacement of one form of struggle by another form of struggle.

Why a revolution?

> The expropriated masses have no other prospect of acquiring property than the revolutionary establishment of the social ownership of means of production.

Who is to lead the revolution?

> The dictatorship of the proletariat and the leadership of the Marxist-Leninist party are indispensable conditions for the triumph of the socialist revolution and the building of communism.

From where will support come?

> . . . the Communist Party of the Soviet Union regards it as its duty to call on the peoples of countries to rally, muster all internal forces, take vigorous action, and drawing on the might of the world socialist system, forestall or firmly repel imperialist interference in the affairs of the people of any country risen in revolt and thereby prevent imperialist export of counter-revolution.

THE PREDICTED DOWNFALL OF CAPITALISM. Communists view the present period as one of struggle between two opposing social systems. This struggle is to end in the abolition of colonialism and the breakdown of imperialism. The revolting colonies will then join the socialist camp, and finally will come "the triumph of socialism and communism on a world-wide scale." They divide this struggle into three phases:

1. World War I and the Bolshevik revolution in Russia.

2. World War II and the succeeding Communist take-overs in Eastern Europe and China, North Korea, and North Vietnam.

3. the internal breakdown of capitalism and imperialism. The constant emphasis in the party's *Program* on the inevitable breakdown of capitalism and distorted descriptions of conditions in the United States make a Western reader feel as if he were being asked to look at an unreal world. Yet, the inevitability of the collapse of capitalism is the cornerstone of the Marxist ideology. If it doesn't die as it is meant to, communism's ideological foundation crumbles.

The *Program* states:

> Marxism-Leninism discovered the objective laws of social development and revealed the contradictions inherent in capitalism, the inevitability of their bringing about a revolutionary explosion and of the transition of society to communism.

Communist ideology holds that capitalism is doomed because the means of production belong to a numerically small class of capitalists and landowners. The masses of people own no means of production and therefore are obliged to sell their labor. Since a capitalist does not pay a worker full value for his labor, the extra amount he works, for which he is not properly paid, becomes the profit of the capitalist. Continued development of large-scale capitalism leads to the elimination of the small producers, to a large number of unemployed, and to a widening of the gulf between the haves and the have-nots. In control is a "financial oligarchy" which uses the state as a committee to manage its affairs.

> State monopoly capitalism combines the strength of the monopolies and that of the state into a single mechanism whose purpose is to enrich the monopolies, suppress the working class movement and the national-liberation struggle, save the capitalist system, and launch aggressive wars.

The Communists' views of capitalism—and particularly of the United States—would be laughable if they did not take these myths seriously as a base for action. In a way the repeated derogatory comments on capitalism found in the party's *Program* sound almost as if capitalism were being selected as the whipping boy for the shortcomings of Soviet communism. The following are some of the theses laid down as facts:

1. Capitalism as a system is inefficient, necessarily begets unemployment, has periodic financial crises, can't cope with new scientific and technical techniques, and has doomed bourgeois society to low rates of growth.
2. The world capitalist market is "partitioned by countless customs barriers and restrictive fences and split into exclusive currency and financial zones."
3. "Small farms survive at the cost of appalling hardships."
4. The workers lead a miserable life; "wages lag behind the daily material and cultural requirements of the workers and his family"; the "working class is suffering from mass unemployment"; "in spite of some successes in the economic struggle the condition of the working class in the capitalist world is, on the whole, deteriorating."
5. "A handful of millionaires and multimillionaires wield arbitrary power over the entire wealth of the capitalist world and make the life of entire nations mere small change in their selfish deals." They lead parasitical lives.
6. The relatively high standard of living in the advanced capitalist nations such as the United States rests upon "the plunder of the Asian, African and Latin-American peoples, upon non-equivalent exchange, discrimination against female labor, brutal oppression of Negroes and immigrant workers, and also upon the intensified exploitation of the working people in those countries."
7. "U.S. imperialism is in effect performing the function of world gendarme, supporting reactionary regimes and decayed monarchies, opposing democratic, revolutionary changes and launching aggressions against peoples fighting for independence. The U.S. monopoly bourgeoisie is the mainstay of international reaction."

Revisionism. The creed of communism is an intolerant one that cannot suffer deviations from dogma. This is understandable, because once any fundamental tenet of the faith is questioned, the validity of the whole ideology is imperiled. The Soviet Communists have been as harsh with those within their own camp who question any aspect of Marxist-Leninist dogma as they have with the capitalist enemy. They fear, above all, mounting nationalistic feelings from any satellite, because the people of that state might eventually place the interests of their own country above those of the U.S.S.R. For that reason, feeling has been strong about Yugoslavia's independent course.

> Right opportunism, which is a reflection of bourgeois influence, is the chief danger within the Communist movement today. The revisionists, who mask their renunciation of Marxism with talk about the necessity of taking account of the latest developments in society and the class struggle, in effect play the role of pedlars of bourgeois-reformist ideology within the Communist movement. The revisionists deny the historical necessity of the socialist revolution and of the dictatorship of the proletariat. They deny the leading role of the Marxist-Leninist party, undermine the foundations of proletarian internationalism, and drift to nationalism. The ideology of revisionism is most fully embodied in the program of the League of Communists of Yugoslavia.

Yet, Yugoslavia was welcomed back into the fold in December 1962, when this course appeared desirable for the Soviet Union's national interests. Communist China and Albania are now out of favor, because they oppose the rapprochement with Yugoslavia and other attempts by the Soviet Union to dictate policy for the whole of the Communist world.

The Soviet Communist Party is apprehensive about any country taking the road to communism by itself without direction from Moscow. This course obviously opens the way to straying from the party line and for placing national interest ahead of those of the international Communist movement. The struggle against all departures from Marxism-Leninism is considered a necessary condition for "the further strengthening of the unity of the world Communist movement and for the consolidation of the socialist camp."

IDEOLOGY VS. STATE

Communist ideology is certainly the motivating force behind the Communist states and eighty-seven Communist parties; but ideology and state are not one and the same. A major dispute took place in the Soviet Union after Lenin's death as to whether socialism should be built first in one country, the Soviet Union, as Stalin argued, or whether it had to be built simultaneously in a number of countries, as maintained by Trotsky. Stalin won the argument that communism needed a base of operations—that it had to be secure in one country before it could spread to others.

Although Communist ideology decries nationalism, there have been times when Moscow has acted much more like the capital of the Russian nation than the headquarters of the world Communist movement. The nonaggression pact with Nazi Germany shook the Communist parties in France, Italy, and elsewhere, and badly damaged the Communist cause in Western Europe. During the German invasion, the effective appeal to the Russian people was not to fight for world communism but to fight for Mother Russia. Moscow finds itself at times in the anomalous position of supplying aid to countries which have outlawed the local Communist party, as is the case in Algeria, Iraq, and the United Arab Republic. When a choice must be made, the Soviet Union has not hesitated to place its national interests ahead of those of international communism.

SINO-SOVIET RELATIONS AND PEACEFUL COEXISTENCE

Those who see every action of a Communist country as part of a coordinated conspiracy—Soviet missiles in Cuba coordinated with the Chinese Communist invasion of India —would be sorely puzzled at the press reports of the meeting in Rome in late 1962 of the Tenth Italian Communist Party Congress. Frol Kozlov, a Secretary of the Soviet Communist Party, publicly criticized Peiping for its role in the border conflict with India and called for a peaceful solution. He attacked those who ignored peaceful coexistence and adopted an "adventurist position which has nothing to do with Marxism." The Chinese delegate, Chao Yi-ming, denounced President Tito of Yugoslavia as a "servant of American imperialism . . . a 100 per cent traitor to the cause of world communism" and the head of a clique which has "brought capitalism back to Yugoslavia." Meanwhile in Moscow Chairman Khrushchev was warmly welcoming Tito with full honors and as a mark of special favor provided him and his wife with an apartment in the Kremlin.

The climax came with Chairman Khrushchev's speech on December 12, 1962, to the final session of the Supreme Soviet. He said the "so-called Marxist-Leninists" who criticized his Cuba policies were trying to get the United States and the Soviet Union at one another's throats and that those who called imperialism a paper tiger should remember that "the paper tiger has nuclear teeth." [1]

[1] *The Washington Post*, 13 December 1962.

In his speech to the Sixth Congress of the East German Communist Party on January 16, 1963, in East Berlin, Khrushchev made very clear that he fully appreciated the devastation a nuclear war would cause and his realization that the Chinese Communists (whom he really meant when he spoke of Albanian leaders) did not.[2]

> As regards Marxists-Leninists, they cannot conceive the creation of a Communist civilization on the ruins of world cultural centers, upon an earth deserted and poisoned by thermonuclear fallouts. And let us not forget that the question of socialism would cease to have any meaning at all to many peoples, because they would have physically disappeared from the surface of our planet.
>
> The Soviet Union . . . knows well the potentialities of these arms.
>
> As it is said, blessed is he who chatters about war and does not understand what he is chattering about. The Albanian leaders chatter much about rocket-nuclear war, but this does not disturb anybody. All know that, except for chatter, they have nothing to their name, and that they do not dispose of any real means. As you see, in these matters we have different positions and different responsibilities.

Since the Soviet Union, in 1960, cut off military aid credits and technical assistance to Communist China, the Chinese economy has gone from bad to worse. In the fall of 1962 Peiping could see Soviet missiles in Cuba while it had none, Soviet economic assistance going to Afghanistan, India, and the United Arab Republic when Communist China was receiving none, and, most humiliating of all, the possibility that Soviet fighter planes would be sent to India where Peiping had been skirmishing along the frontier since 1959.

There definitely is a crack in what had been termed the monolithic structure of communism. This is far more serious than disputes among allies of the Western alliances because our system is flexible enough to accept diversity. We are not governed by dogma that cannot tolerate any deviation from the party line. There has been much speculation about the causes of this schism; these are undoubtedly among them:

1. Peiping's distrust of Moscow, which goes back to the days when Moscow appeared willing to sacrifice the strug-

[2] *The Washington Post*, 17 January 1963.

gling Chinese Communists for its own national interests. Furthermore, the Soviet Union continues to occupy vast territories taken from China in the nineteenth century.

2. A difference in policy. While the Soviets have for several years been preaching "peaceful coexistence" and Khrushchev has been stating that he did not regard war with the capitalist nations as inevitable, the Chinese have taken a much harder line. They see no reason to seek any accommodation with the West and viewed as appeasement Khrushchev's withdrawal of missiles from Cuba.

3. A struggle for leadership which resulted in violent Chinese propaganda attacks on Yugoslav revisionism and strong support of Albania, which had defied the Moscow leadership.

4. Great difference in wealth. One could almost say that Communist China heads up the "poor" nations within the Communist camp while the Soviet Union heads up the "rich" nations. Communist China tried the Soviet tactic of extending foreign aid but curtailed it when Red Chinese leaders realized that the country could not afford it, and since then has criticized Soviet aid to India as doing nothing to promote the cause of communism.

5. The degree to which the Communist bloc should run the risk of the war in dealings with the West. Khrushchev has said, and has demonstrated, that he is aware of the horrors of nuclear war and wants to avoid it. The Chinese Communists seem much less concerned with this question, perhaps because of the small value they place on human life.

In his speech of January 6, 1961, to the Soviet Communist Party, in which he came out strongly for peaceful coexistence, Khrushchev did not, however, renounce the use of force. He said there were three types of wars—the general war, the limited war, and the war of national liberation. He eschewed general and limited war as instruments of Soviet policy but made clear that he considered it a Communist duty to aid those countries who wished to throw off the yoke of imperialism. This meant that the Soviets would be supporting so-called "third-party wars," such as in Laos and Vietnam, where someone else does the fighting. The Soviets, although aiding and abetting, are not directly involved but, where useful to discourage free world intervention, hold out the threat of stepping in.

SOVIET FOREIGN POLICY

Soviet Communist domination of the world is still the objective of Soviet policy. These appear to be the main policies directed toward that end:

1. Security of the Soviet Union, through:
   a. build-up of a powerful military machine with emphasis on research and development. The Soviet Union is spending proportionately a greater share of its resources than we are, and there are indications that the shoe is beginning to pinch. This is an expensive business, and Soviet resources are limited.
   b. concentration on space exploits. The successful launching of the sputnik in 1957 gave ample evidence of the great propaganda effect of space achievements in promoting the idea of Soviet scientific and military superiority.
   c. toleration on its borders of only friendly governments, preferably Communist satellites.
   d. elimination of American overseas bases capable of being used to mount an attack against Soviet territory; for example, the Khrushchev proposal to dismantle missile bases in Cuba in exchange for our abandoning military bases in Turkey.
   e. efforts to break up NATO and other Western defensive alliances.
   f. refusal to permit the reunification of Germany.
   g. paying lip service to disarmament but not signing a disarmament treaty if more than token inspection of Soviet territory is involved. We don't know the Kremlin's innermost thoughts on this matter but suspect that the Soviets may not want any disarmament treaty unless it tips the power balance in their favor.
2. Aiding the spread of communism by:
   a. aiding and abetting so-called "wars of liberation," such as in Algeria, Laos, and Vietnam.
   b. unwillingness to cooperate in any general efforts to bring peace to troubled areas—such as the Middle East and the Congo.
   c. encouragement of actions that would embarrass the West and promote unrest; for example, the extensive arms aid given Indonesia when it was threatening to take West New Guinea by force.
   d. supporting eighty-six other Communist parties. Those in non-Communist countries have as their objective the establishment of a Communist regime.
   e. keeping the movement "pure," that is, submissive, by op-

posing, when tactically possible, heresies such as in Red China and Albania.
f. strict control of frontiers of the Communist bloc to prevent escape of people; for example, the Berlin wall.

3. The development of her basic economy with particular emphasis on heavy industry necessary for an effective war machine. Since the death of Stalin there has been some attention paid to consumer goods, probably in the realization that the Soviet people are after all human and cannot be expected to sacrifice indefinitely without some prospect of better living standards for themselves. The development of a successful economy is also necessary if the under-developed countries are to be convinced that communism can provide a solution to their own problems.
4. Soviet participation in international trade. The growth of Soviet trade serves both political and economic ends. It makes possible the acquisition of machines and technology needed for the Soviet economy and, at the same time, treads on the toes of the West. The Soviets have now become a major supplier of oil for Italy, and are trying to lure other Western countries with the prospect of a vast market in the Soviet Union if they would only remove present restrictions on export of strategic goods to the bloc.
5. Aid to the less developed countries. This is the "soft sell" designed to show them that they need not depend on the West, that the Soviets are anxious and able to help them. From January 1, 1954, to June 30, 1962, $7.2 billion in credits and grants has been extended to twenty-six countries. Some newly independent countries, confused by Soviet propaganda, are unaware that before the Revolution, Russia was the fifth largest industrial power in the world. Communism appears to provide an easy blueprint for transforming a primitive society into an industrialized one in one generation.
6. Attempting to sow dissension among the countries of the West and to win the uncommitted by attacks on colonialism and imperialism.
7. Educational and cultural exchanges. An estimated four thousand students from the under-developed countries are now attending school in the U.S.S.R. The program of student and cultural exchange may be a disadvantage to the Soviets as it tends to open up their closed society and, on the basis of reciprocity, makes possible the introduction of Western cultural attractions and students.

Reports from the U.S.S.R. indicate that significant intellectual ferment is taking place. The de-Stalinization program, which has been tearing apart the image of the man who was regarded for years as infallible, has shaken the peoples' faith to the roots and has made them begin to question a system which heretofore they had blindly accepted.

U.S. POLICY TOWARD THE SOVIET UNION

Our fundamental policy toward the Soviet Union is five-sided:

1. Maintain a position of military strength.

2. Persist in trying to find ways of reducing tensions and reaching agreements where possible on points of conflict. Agreement is sometimes possible: for example, the Austrian State Treaty, the treaty on Antarctica, and the limited nuclear test-ban treaty. We are still trying to see if there is any common ground for reaching an understanding on disarmament and on Berlin.

3. Prevent the bloc from taking over any more territory. This means assisting threatened nations, such as South Vietnam, to maintain their independence.

4. Avoid contributing to the strength of the bloc by banning, together with our allies, the shipment to it of strategic goods.

5. Open up the Iron Curtain to ideas from the outside by encouraging travel and cultural exchange.

These points will be touched upon time and time again during the course of the succeeding chapters.

IV. DEFENSE—STRATEGY IN THE COLD WAR

Our proposed defense expenditures for fiscal year 1964 are $52.4 billion (nearly 10 per cent of our gross national product). We are pledged to the defense of forty-two nations; we are spending about $1.5 billion a year to provide defense assistance to friendly nations; and we maintain overseas more than 250 major military installations. The struggle between the free world and the Communist bloc, the cold war, has been the central fact of life for us since the end of World War II. The forms our defenses have taken directly reflect the concepts we have had of the best way to combat this threat. These concepts in turn have been directly related to our technological progress in the field of weaponry, to Soviet technological progress, and to Soviet tactics in the cold war. Perhaps a clearer picture will emerge in this discussion of defense if we divide the cold war into four periods, each characterized by our concept of how to deal with the Soviet Union and its satellites:

1945–47	Hope for cooperation
1947–52	Containment
1953–60	Massive retaliation
1961–	The appropriate response

HOPE FOR COOPERATION

At the close of hostilities in 1945, the United States had over twelve million men under arms; two years later, only two million. Our demobilization was rapid, perhaps too rapid. Consequently, the Soviets, with the largest army in the world, realized we presented no effective obstacle to their taking a free hand in Eastern Europe. The United States, however, along with Canada and the United Kingdom, possessed the knowledge essential to the use of atomic energy, and only the United States possessed the bomb. As long as we had the monopoly, we had no fear that any power would attack us directly. We realized, though, that this happy state of affairs—this relatively cheap and optimum security—would not last long, that it was only a question of time before other nations, particularly the Soviet Union, would discover how to make the bomb. We came to the conclusion that the only way to keep irresponsible hands from utilizing this dangerous knowledge was to place it under international control. In 1946 the United States proposed to the United Nations that all nuclear processes be brought under the control of an international authority. The Soviet Union opposed the plan. On September 23, 1949, President Truman announced to the American people that we had evidence that an atomic explosion had occurred in the U.S.S.R. This was the end of our monopoly and made essential a rethinking of our defense strategy.

CONTAINMENT

Meanwhile Soviet actions elsewhere were rapidly destroying any illusions we had that the Soviet Union would cooperate in setting up the type of postwar world we had envisaged. The Communist take-overs in Eastern Europe, the Communist-aided insurrections in Greece and the Far East, Soviet pressures on Iran and Turkey, and, finally, the Berlin blockade imposed in June 1948, showed that the Soviets intended to push wherever they saw a vulnerable point. Our problem then was how to stop them.

We adopted a policy of containment. Its premises were that the Soviet Union was weaker than the West, that Soviet policy was not intractable, and that Soviet society contained within itself the seeds of its own destruction. Containment would have the United States confront the Russians with counterforce at every point where they threatened the peace of the world. In other words, wherever the Russians applied pressure, we would apply counterpressure, very much like a fireman rushing to put out fires wherever they might occur. To make this policy effective required supporting countries throughout the world willing to fight to maintain their independence.

President Truman explained our rationale in his message to the Congress on March 12, 1947, recommending aid to Greece and Turkey.[1]

[1] "A Decade of Foreign Policy," *Basic Documents, 1941–49* (Washington, D. C.: Government Printing Office, 1950), p. 1255.

> We shall not realize our objectives, however, unless we are willing to help free peoples to maintain their free institutions and their national integrity against aggressive movements that seek to impose upon them totalitarian regimes. This is no more than a frank recognition that totalitarian regimes imposed upon free peoples, by direct or indirect aggression, undermine the foundations of international peace and hence the security of the United States.

These were the methods we were to use to accomplish that purpose:

1. Economic aid to rebuild war-shattered economies. Their prostration invited subversion.
2. Military aid to help friendly nations develop the capacity to resist aggression.
3. Military alliances, serving notice that an attack against one would be an attack against all and making possible joint defense planning and utilization of men and material.
4. Bases in strategic areas ringing the Soviet perimeter so that American military might could be made readily available.
5. A great increase in our defense budget.

By repelling Communist aggression wherever it might appear, we hoped that the Soviet Union could be made to realize that aggression did not pay. As long as we had exclusive possession of the bomb, we could have threatened to drop one on Moscow if the Soviets made one more move. This threat, however, unless we were really prepared to go through with it, would not be effective. In military terminology, was the deterrent credible? Anyone at all familiar with the American character and the American system of government simply could not believe that the President, or the Congress, or the American people could ever support the wiping out of thousands of civilians unless our very national existence were at stake. The memory of the horrors of Hiroshima was too fresh. After the Soviets acquired the ability to make their own atomic bombs, the argument against this use of the bomb as a deterrent was reinforced by the knowledge that the Soviets could retaliate in kind.

The Korean War was a test of the policy of containment and of our ability to follow it. Following the defeat of Japan in 1945, Soviet troops entered the north of Korea and American troops entered the south for the purpose of accepting the surrender of Japanese forces. The 38th Parallel was made the temporary line of demarcation between them.

The Soviets set up a Communist puppet government in North Korea and refused to cooperate with U.S. efforts to hold elections, under U.N. auspices for a democratic government for all of Korea. In June 1950 troops from North Korea invaded South Korea. The U.N. Security Council condemned the invasion; President Truman ordered the use of U.S. troops to support South Korea, and the U.N. Security Council asked the United States to designate a commander for all U.N. forces.

War is an instrument of foreign policy used to achieve a particular objective. If the objective in sending troops to Korea were to contain the Communist advance, then the action need only be a limited one—to push the North Koreans back of the 38th Parallel and go no further. Tempted by initial success, we pushed beyond the 38th Parallel, an action which implied the larger objective of unifying all of Korea. In doing so we faced the strong possibility that the Chinese Communists, feeling their vital interests threatened, would openly enter the conflict, as they did. If we went further and pushed beyond the Yalu River, the border between North Korea and China, then we faced the danger of open Soviet intervention. What started as a limited war with a limited objective, fought only with conventional weapons, could easily have developed into a major war, perhaps fought with nuclear weapons. For that reason President Truman refused to allow our forces to bomb Chinese supply lines beyond the Yalu River. The end result was a stalemate, as it obviously had to be. Many Americans were frustrated and bitter because they had expected a decisive conclusion, did not understand that the likely alternative to a limited war was an unlimited world war, and, consequently, although we had achieved our limited objectives, we viewed the outcome as something less than an American victory. And it had been terribly expensive.

MASSIVE RETALIATION

Military policy was one of the issues of the 1952 campaign. The Republicans advocated, in place of containment, an active, less costly policy that would roll back Communist power by peaceful means, liberate the Eastern European satellites, and make unnecessary further Korea-type wars. President Eisenhower's "new look" at military policy emphasized the collective strength of the free world and the use of that power to deter aggression by making it too costly to the aggressor. Building up the collective strength of the free world required carrying still further the previous policies of defensive alliances, military aid to our allies, and foreign bases from which our forces could operate. The "new look" took into account the advantages of the Communist bloc: (1) a contiguous land mass, (2) plenty of manpower, and (3) superiority in conventional forces. It saw as the free world's advantages: (1) air and naval power and (2) atomic weapons. If we were to continue the policy of meeting aggression by direct and local opposition, then the enemy could pick his time, place, and method of warfare. The Eisenhower military policy would reinforce local defense by massive retaliatory power and the willingness to use it at places of the free world's choice.

Secretary of State John Foster Dulles expressed the rationale:[2] "A would-be aggressor will hesitate to commit aggression if he knows in advance that he thereby not only exposes those particular forces which he chooses to use for aggression but also deprives his other assets of 'sanctuary' status." Reliance on atomic weapons meant building up the Air Force to carry them. It also meant a reduction in the number of men under arms and, for a few years, lower defense budgets. "More bang for a buck" was the way the press expressed the concept of a maximum deterrent at a bearable cost.

There were two main flaws in the theory of massive retaliation. The first concerned our willingness to use it. Were we really prepared to drop the bomb unless our most vital interests were threatened? Talk of rolling back the Iron Curtain, of liberating the satellites, was meaningless unless we were willing to commit ourselves militarily to that purpose. The revolt in Hungary showed that we were not. The second flaw became more and more apparent as the Soviets increased their nuclear capability. Any massive retaliation on our part would bring about massive retaliation from the Soviets.

The doctrine of massive retaliation was also not an effective counter to the change in Soviet tactics that occurred after Stalin's death in 1953. Soviet strong-arm methods gave

[2] "The Evolution of U. S. Foreign Policy," speech before the Council on Foreign Relations, 12 January 1954. From *Readings in American Foreign Policy*, edited by Robert A. Goldwin (New York: Oxford University Press, 1959), p. 485.

way to the "soft sell." The less developed nations found the Soviets willing to buy their surplus commodities, to lend them money at low rates of interest, to furnish them with economic and technical assistance, including hospitals and steel mills. This approach of winning rather than coercing agreement was potentially far more dangerous to the United States, for, if carried out with finesse, it could ease states into the Communist camp. Against this attitude of sweet reasonableness, massive retaliation made no sense.

Meanwhile, technology had not stood still. Jet planes exceeding the speed of sound had given way to missiles which could reach halfway around the world in fifteen minutes. By 1960 it appeared that, since both the Soviet Union and the United States had the capacity to shower nuclear missiles upon each other, neither side could afford to introduce nuclear weapons into any action except as a last resort. The question now was how to repel aggressive moves without resorting to nuclear retaliation.

In Moscow on January 6, 1961, Khrushchev explained the decisions that had been reached at the November 1960 Moscow meeting of Communist parties from eighty-one countries. He made explicit what had already been implicit in Communist tactics for many years. Although he talked of peaceful coexistence, he did not rule out so-called "wars of national liberation"—"uprisings . . . against decayed reactionary regimes." Communism could contribute to "third-party" struggles in places like Algeria, the Congo, and Vietnam without actually involving the Soviet Union and thus running the risk of retaliation. This decision to concentrate on wars of covert aggression was based on the Soviets' appreciation of our nuclear capability.

THE APPROPRIATE RESPONSE

In his message to the Congress of March 28, 1961, President Kennedy discussed defense policy and the budget and spelled out his philosophy of defense. These are the basic principles which guided his administration in determining the amount of money it should spend to insure our national security:

1. The primary purpose of our arms is peace; war is not our objective. We must maintain sufficient strength, however, to make any attack upon us unprofitable.

2. We will never make the first strike. Neither our psy-

chology nor our tradition would permit us to launch a Pearl Harbor type of attack. Therefore our security depends upon having weapons that would survive an enemy attack and make retaliation swift and certain.

3. Our arms must be adequate to meet our commitments and insure our security, even if this means spending over arbitrary budget ceilings. The Department of Defense is guided by this principle—assess military needs on the basis of the best possible defense posture and then satisfy those needs at the lowest possible cost.

4. The military, as it has from the founding of this country, must remain under civilian control.

5. We want to do everything possible to reduce the danger of accidental war or the unnecessary escalation of a small war into a large one. Nothing could be more dangerous than for other nations not to understand our intentions or for us not to understand their intentions. Underestimating a response can only lead to crises that too easily can become wars.

6. Our defense posture must be flexible. We must be able to respond with the appropriate weapon, not find ourselves meeting a challenge with no effective weapon except the atomic bomb and then being deterred from using it because of fear of starting a nuclear war.

THE ARMS TO MAKE POSSIBLE THE STRATEGY

These principles dictate our present-day military strategy. Since we will not make the first strike, our only hope of being able to retaliate in the event of a surprise attack is to rely on weapons that are hidden, are moving, or come from relatively invulnerable bases, such as:

1. Polaris. Nuclear-powered submarines can stay under water a long time; their atomic reactors require refueling only every several years. While submerged they can launch solid-fueled, nuclear-armed Polaris missiles and are thus practically invulnerable to surprise attack. The first five submarines carried missiles with a range of 1,200 nautical miles. Missiles on the newer submarines will have a range of 2,500 nautical miles. The first Polaris submarine was launched in November 1960, and as of November 1962 there were nine in operation. Our defense budget calls for a total of forty-one.

2. MINUTEMAN. This is a solid-fueled missile with a range of nearly 6,300 miles. It can be fired in less than 15 seconds. To be placed underground in protected or "hardened" sites in the United States, the missiles should be secure except from a direct hit. Present plans call for 800 Minutemen, at a cost of over $3 billion; an additional 150 are proposed. The first 20 Minutemen were declared ready for duty in December 1962.

3. BOMBERS. Until our missiles were completed and ready to go, our chief hope for deterring attack lay with the long-range bombers, B-47's, B-52's, B-58's. A sizeable percentage of the manned bomber force is either in the air or on a fifteen-minute ground alert. One of the continuing problems facing the Department of Defense is shifting from manned bombers to missiles. The B-52 and B-58 assembly lines were shut down in the summer of 1962; it may be that they are the last generation of bombers.

The RS-70 has been a favorite of the Air Force and many Members of Congress. This aircraft, which has yet to be flight-tested, is to have a speed of over 30 miles per minute. It would have the function, following a missile attack made by us, of examining targets and, if required, attacking them with short-range missiles. The Department of Defense believes that development of the RS-70 would not add sufficiently to our effectiveness to justify the vast sums required to bring the plane into production. Three experimental models are, however, on order.

The Skybolt is a solid-fueled missile with a nuclear warhead designed to be carried by a B-52 and launched up to 1,000 miles away from the target. It had been argued that Skybolt would prolong the usefulness of the manned bomber. In late 1962 the Department of Defense decided to drop the Skybolt program because it combined the disadvantages of the bomber with those of the missile. It promised to be far more expensive than originally planned, and its intended functions could be better performed by the Minuteman.

Polaris, Minuteman, and the manned bombers are among the chief weapons systems constituting the Strategic Retaliatory Forces. For fiscal year 1964, the sum of $7.3 billion in obligational authority is asked for them.

Essential to the effectiveness of these forces is advance warning of an enemy attack. A series of radar stations in Canada, Greenland, and the United Kingdom serves that purpose. We are now concentrating on a satellite system, the Midas, which in its orbit around the earth is able to detect missiles immediately upon launching and thus give up to 30 minutes of warning. Only the President can order our nuclear weapons into operation, and a great deal of attention is being given to making sure that no failure in procedures and communications could result in an accidental war.

Nuclear weapons are a deterrent against a nuclear attack on us, but they do not supply an answer to the nibbling away at the free world's security by guerrilla warfare, subversion, intimidation, and limited wars. Here, little is possible unless the countries directly threatened are willing to fight. If so, we stand ready to supply assistance. In these limited war situations, the need is for conventional rather than nuclear weapons. This has called for a build-up of ground forces, more and faster transport planes to put forces on the spot quickly, better conventional weapons, and the study and teaching of tactics to combat guerrilla tactics. All this costs a great deal of money. The key to victory in the so-called "wars of national liberation" is not military, however, for the threatened government must be persuaded to face the reasons for popular discontent and to take meassures to remove them as rapidly as possible.

ALLIANCES

The United States is committed to the defense of forty-two countries, as shown in the chart of collective defense arrangements on page 231.

RIO TREATY. The first treaty of collective defense was signed at Rio de Janeiro, in 1947. In this treaty, which included all twenty-one nations of the Americas, each state agreed that an attack against one would be considered as an attack against all, and each one undertook to assist in meeting the attack. This commitment at Rio was an outgrowth of the increasingly close cooperation that had prevailed among the states of the Americas since the days of Franklin Delano Roosevelt and particularly during World War II when a number of countries took collective action against Nazi Germany and its allies. The pact turned out to have particular value at the time of the Cuban crisis in the fall of 1962, and made possible the collective action of the states of the

Americas authorizing the quarantine of Cuba. Although the wording of the Rio Treaty was to have a strong influence on subsequent pacts, it should not be regarded primarily, as the others were, as induced by the cold war.

NATO. Only three years after the end of World War II, the aggressive actions of the Soviet Union and the subversive activities of local Communist parties convinced countries of Western Europe of the need to take common defensive action. The first step was the Brussels Treaty of 1948 (discussed in the next chapter), under which Belgium, France, Luxembourg, the Netherlands, and the United Kingdom pledged themselves to build up a common defense system. The next step was the formation, in 1949, of the North Atlantic Treaty Organization (NATO), in which the five Brussels pact countries were joined by five other European states, Canada, and the United States. Greece and Turkey joined in 1952, the Federal Republic of Germany in 1955.

The North Atlantic Treaty is an agreement among the signatory countries for collective self-defense and for joint action in the economic, political, and social fields. It is the cornerstone of the security of the free world, with a unified military command.

Although in principle the maintenance of peace and security is the task of the United Nations, by use of the veto power the Soviet Union had made the Security Council ineffective. It was obvious that we and the countries of Western Europe would have to look elsewhere for security. For the United States to join in an alliance in time of peace was a departure from the policy we had followed since the days of George Washington. We learned, however, through the experience of two world wars, that we would inevitably be involved in any conflict in Europe.

The groundwork for our entry into NATO showed the close collaboration between the administration and the Congress which is essential for a smooth-working foreign policy. Senator Vandenberg introduced a resolution to the effect that the Senate looked with favor upon "association of the United States, by constitutional process, with such regional and other collective arrangements as are based on continuous and effective self-help and mutual aid, and as affect its national security." On June 11, 1948, the Senate passed the resolution by a vote of 64 to 4.

The chief authority of NATO is the North Atlantic Council, which is composed of representatives of each of the fifteen member states. These representatives may be foreign ministers, or permanent representatives, or even heads of government. General Eisenhower was chosen as the first Supreme Allied Commander. This position has continued to be filled by American generals—Ridgway, Gruenther, Norstad, and now Lemnitzer. The position of Secretary General was first filled by Lord Ismay, then by Paul Henri Spaak, at present Foreign Minister of Belgium, and now by Dirk U. Stikker, former Netherlands Permanent Representative on the Council.

The basic problem of NATO is how best to defend the territory of its member states against Soviet aggression. A fundamental unresolved question is whether Western Europe can be successfully defended by conventional weapons alone, and, if so, whether the cost would be prohibitive. At the Council session held in Lisbon in 1952, the member governments decided that they should contribute a total of 50 divisions, 4,000 airplanes, and strong naval forces. Since then they have considerably reduced these goals.

The principle of NATO has been the equitable sharing among member governments of the financial burden and the contribution of men and matériel to one force under one command.

The strategy adopted by NATO was the so-called "forward strategy," which meant that any aggression must be resisted as far to the east as possible. This strategy, however, required the defense of Europe on German soil which, of course, would have been impossible for the long term without the military and political participation of Germany. So in the early years of NATO a main concern was to find a way of getting Germany into some form of common defense organization. There were many related political questions that had to be solved.

In late 1954, under the Paris agreements (discussed in the next chapter), the occupation of West Germany was ended, and the Federal Republic of Germany agreed to maintain on its territory forces at least equivalent to the strength of those stationed there at the time the agreement was signed. The Federal Republic of Germany adhered to the North Atlantic Treaty as of May 5, 1955, and nine days later, on May 14, the U.S.S.R. concluded the Warsaw Pact with its European satellites.

The Soviet Union's actions in 1955, 1956, and 1957—

repression of the Hungarian revolt, launching the sputnik, equipping their forces with tactical nuclear weapons, and their threats of nuclear destruction of European capitals—made necessary a rethinking of NATO's defense policy. Late in 1957 the NATO Council made the important decision to establish stocks of nuclear weapons in Europe and to put IRBM's (intermediate range ballistic missiles) at the disposal of the Supreme Allied Commander. The only country that had these missiles was the United States, and our Atomic Energy Act prohibited the transfer of nuclear weapons to any foreign power. The solution was to establish stockpiles in Europe under American control. Their use in a particular country would be regulated by agreement between that country and the United States. France was unwilling, and still is, to enter into this arrangement, and the result is that we do not maintain any nuclear weapons in France.

Some Europeans are concerned that the defense of Europe should rest so completely upon the United States and question whether Americans would run the risk of the destruction of Washington for the sake of Paris or London. This doubt strikes at the heart of NATO; its chief tenet is the indivisibility of the defense of the West. If there is a lack of confidence among members of NATO, then the alliance makes no sense. The United States has adequate stocks of nuclear weapons for the defense of the West. Nevertheless, both France and the United Kingdom have decided that independent nuclear capabilities are essential to their defense and prestige.

The United States believes the cause of common defense would best be served if our European allies concentrated upon building up their conventional forces, which are still short of agreed goals. Building an independent nuclear capability is fantastically expensive; ours costs about $15 billion a year, almost as much as all our European allies together spend on their total defense programs. Although we recognize that this is a decision which each nation must make for itself, two considerations alarm us.

The first is the proliferation of nuclear weapons. The more countries with nuclear capability, the greater is the risk of war and the more difficult to negotiate effective international arms control arrangements. The Russians above all fear German possession of nuclear weapons.

The second consideration concerns the strength of Western defense. Compartmentalizing NATO's nuclear strength weakens its overall strength. For the West's nuclear response to be effective there must be a single chain of command. Targets must be allocated to weapons in advance, and decisions must be made and executed promptly.

The United States has therefore taken the position that we would have no objection if our NATO partners wish to create a European strategic nuclear force but that it should be an effort of NATO rather than of individual countries and should be closely integrated with our own so that it could be jointly targeted and directed in a coordinated fashion.

Both France and the United Kingdom have exploded atomic devices. To our knowledge, they have not yet developed nuclear warheads or perfected the missiles needed to deliver them. For that reason, presumably, the French wish to continue testing. The present British and French nuclear capability consists, therefore, of being able to drop free-falling nuclear bombs from jet planes. Because of developments in ground-to-air missiles, it now appears that by the mid-'sixties planes will find it extremely difficult to penetrate the Soviet frontiers. Air-to-ground missiles such as Skybolt offered the possibility of extending the usefulness of jet planes.

In 1960 the United States entered into an agreement with the United Kingdom to make Skybolt missiles available, under certain conditions, if we proceeded with production. At the Nassau conference in December 1962, President Kennedy informed Prime Minister Macmillan of the reasons for our decision to cancel Skybolt. Several alternatives were offered. The Prime Minister decided to accept the third alternative, the sale of Polaris missiles to the U.K., with that country furnishing its own submarines and warheads. The submarines constructed under the agreement would be assigned as part of a NATO nuclear force and targeted in accordance with NATO plans. Perhaps the reason for the strong reaction in Britain against the cancellation of Skybolt was the clear demonstration of how dependent upon the U.S. was the U.K.'s supposedly independent nuclear deterrent, as the opposition Labour Party had maintained.

France was invited to participate in a multilateral Polaris force on the same basis as the U.K. At the press conference in January 1963, in which he made clear France's opposition to Great Britain's admission to the Common Market, General de Gaulle expressed his lack of interest in the Polaris force and emphasized his determination to proceed with France's independent nuclear force. Although dependent for delivery upon supersonic jet planes and insignificant in comparison to the strength of Soviet and American nuclear forces, its use could perhaps trigger an all-out war. This so-called "force de frappe" would therefore appear to give France far more leverage than the strength of her nuclear deterrent would appear to warrant.

In the summer of 1963 Great Britain, the U.S., and the U.S.S.R. reached agreement on a limited nuclear test ban treaty. All nations were invited to sign it, but France made clear that it was not interested in doing so because it still needed to test in order to develop its independent nuclear capability.

The question of how to handle the nuclear deterrent is the basic issue facing the NATO alliance. Upon its successful resolution depends the future of the Atlantic partnership. As yet answers have not been found to these perplexing questions which strike at the root of the problem:

How can we give our allies a voice in the use of nuclear weapons, taking into account that a decision must be made immediately in case of attack?

Before using the nuclear deterrent, should all the chiefs of state of the NATO countries be consulted? Should this process be too time consuming, as it appears to be, can the decision be delegated to a committee of several of them?; or left with the President of the United States, as is the case at present? Should a new supranational Atlantic political institution be created and given this power of ultimate decision?

Is there a satisfactory way of bringing our allies into positions of operational responsibility for nuclear weapons? If so, would they be willing to forego development of independent nuclear capabilities?

How do you make available nuclear-capable weapons to your allies and still insure that the decision to use them rests with only one authority? Can a surface fleet using Polaris missiles be satisfactorily operated by men of several different nationalities and native languages?

ANZUS, SEATO, AND BILATERAL DEFENSE TREATIES. As the chart on page 231 indicates, from 1950 through 1954 we signed a number of other treaties of collective defense with nations primarily on the Communist perimeter. There was a difference in the wording, however, between these treaties and the NATO and Rio treaties. Instead of using the formula —an attack on one would be considered as an attack against all—the formula used was that "each party recognizes that an armed attack on any would be dangerous to its own peace and safety and declares that it would act to meet the common danger in accordance with its constitutional processes." These treaties did not involve the merging of forces as practiced in NATO, but through joint high-level planning and joint maneuvers and standardization of certain equipment they go a long way toward insuring smooth cooperation during times of emergency.

CENTO. Iran, Pakistan, Turkey, and the United Kingdom are members of the Central Treaty Organization (CENTO), and the United States is an observer. For that reason CENTO is not shown on the chart of collective defense arrangements. Although not a full member of the Council of CENTO, the United States is, however, a member of major committees and contributes an equal share to the international staff and budget and a large share of military and economic assistance.

BASES

Through agreements with friendly nations, many of them linked to us by defense treaties, we now have over 250 major military installations outside of the United States. They include naval bases, training facilities for the Army and Marine Corps, supply depots, communications facilities, air fields, and sites for guided missiles. They are essential to a military establishment with world-wide responsibilities and with forces maintained abroad, such as the 250,000 man Seventh Army in West Germany and the Sixth Fleet in the Mediterranean with 50 ships, 30,000 men, and 200 aircraft. Bases have more than a purely military function. They are a strong indication of U.S. involvement in the defense of a particular ally. If we had accepted the Soviet proposal made during the Cuban crisis that the Soviets would remove their missiles from Cuba in exchange for closing down our missile bases in Turkey, the Turks might well have concluded that we were no longer willing to assist in the defense of their country and had decided that they were expendable.

The fast pace of military technology has, however, reduced the importance of air and guided missile bases. Until a few years ago, our bombers lacked the range to reach Soviet territory from air fields in the United States. By using overseas bases our bombers could have reached the U.S.S.R. and thus make credible our nuclear deterrent. In addition to one base each in Guam and Puerto Rico, we were able to obtain through agreements with the governments concerned these bases abroad for the use of the Strategic Air Command (SAC): United Kingdom–4, Spain–3, Morocco–3 (from which in accordance with the desires of the Moroccan Government we withdrew in December 1963); and Canada–2. SAC's long-range bombers now have the range to launch an attack from the United States.

We have had missile installations abroad in only three countries—in the United Kingdom, sixty Thor IRBM's; in Italy, two squadrons of Jupiter IRBM's for a total of thirty; and in Turkey one squadron of Jupiters. These missiles, liquid-fueled, take longer to launch than the newer solid-fueled missiles and are in unprotected sites. Extensive discussions with the United Kingdom, Italy, and Turkey resulted, in 1963, in the decision to remove these obsolescent missiles and assign their tasks to submarines with Polaris missiles.

V. CLOSER ASSOCIATION—
EUROPE AND THE ATLANTIC COMMUNITY

Our defense, as outlined in the preceding chapter, is the first of the five major components of our foreign policy. The second is a closer association of the more industrialized democracies of Western Europe, North America, and Asia (specifically Japan) in promoting the prosperity and security of the entire free world. This chapter examines the core of this closer association—the relationship between Europe and North America.

The concept of Atlantic partnership is based on the following premises:

1. War in Europe destroys peace in America. We learned this in 1917 and relearned it in 1941. Both times, one of the fundamental causes of war was the conflict between the interests of France and Germany, a conflict compounded by a long history of bitterness and mutual mistrust. If the economies and objectives of the two nations can be inextricably woven together, they then lose not only the motive but also the independent means to wage war. The interests of the United States and Western Europe are so close that a threat to the freedom of Western Europe is also a threat to the freedom of the United States. The security of the two regions is indivisible.

2. The United States, Canada, and Western Europe have a common heritage and share the same ideals. Their major objectives should be the same.

3. Many of the great problems the United States faces are international. One nation, no matter how powerful, cannot resolve them entirely on its own.

4. The industrialized countries of the free world have far greater power and resources than the Communist bloc and, if they can find unity of purpose, are capable of solving the mutual problems of defense, trade, assistance to the less developed countries, and the balance of payments.

5. To make possible this partnership, Western Europe must progress from a group of nation-states to a community capable of speaking with one voice and acting with one intent. This community would be even more effective if Great Britain formed part of it.

Let us look at the Atlantic partnership in two stages. The first is the European Community—embracing the relationship of the European states to one another, to their colonies, to the United Kingdom, and to the institutional framework which may eventually bring political unity. The second stage is the Atlantic Community—the partnership between an enlarged European Community and North America.

PRINCIPAL EUROPEAN ORGANIZATIONS
(with year of entry into force)

Country	OEEC (1948) & OECD (1961)	NATO (1949)	CE (1949)	WEU (1948)	*European Community* ECSC (1952)	EEC (1958)	Euratom (1958)	EFTA (1960)
	(Original members indicated by *x*; subsequent members by year of joining.)							
Austria	x							x
Belgium	x	x	x	x	x	x	x	
Denmark	x	x	x					x
France	x	x	x	x	x	x	x	
Germany	x[a]	'55	'51	'55	x	x	x	
Greece	x	'52	'49			'62[c]		
Iceland	x	x	'50					
Ireland	x		x					
Italy	x	x	x	'54	x	x	x	
Luxembourg	x	x	x	x	x	x	x	
Netherlands	x	x	x	x	x	x	x	
Norway	x	x	x					x
Portugal	x	x						x
Spain	'59							
Sweden	x		x					x
Switzerland	x							x
Turkey	x	'52	'50			'63[c]		
U.K.	x	x	x	x				x
Canada	x[b]	x						
Japan	'63							
U.S.	x[b]	x						

a—Western Germany was represented through October 1949 by the commanders of the Allied Occupation zones.
b—Canada and U.S. were associate members of OEEC but are full members of OECD.
c—Associate member.

The European Community

Since the end of World War II Europe has taken a number of steps leading not only to greater unity but also to a bewildering assortment of organizations. The following chart lists the principal organizations and their membership. The impetus toward unity has come from two sources—external and internal. The external impetus has been the willingness of the United States to extend economic assistance to Europe and to join in arrangements for collective defense.

STEPS TOWARD UNITY—EXTERNAL IMPETUS

MARSHALL PLAN. World War II left Europe a shambles. The general state of exhaustion, despair, and cynicism offered little hope for a quick rebuilding of cities and factories but did provide fertile ground for the growth of Communist parties. If Europe were to recover quickly, outside help was needed. In his now famous speech at Harvard University in June 1947, General George Marshall, then Secretary of State, proposed that the United States extend economic aid to Europe. General Marshall made clear, however, that the countries of Europe would have to reach agreement on their requirements and on a common program to place Europe on its feet. Although the offer was extended to all Europe, the Soviet Union and its satellites declined to participate in what came to be known as the Marshall Plan.

In order to carry out their part in determining distribution of United States aid, the recipient countries formed the Organization for European Economic Cooperation (OEEC). The OEEC proved itself an effective organization. It was able to enlist the cooperation of its members in removing a number of impediments to European trade, such as quantitative restrictions on imports, export subsidies, and the difficulties in exchanging the currency of one European country for another. The European Payments Union (EPU) was set up in 1950 to provide a mechanism for the free exchange of currencies. By 1959 most of the currencies of Western Europe were freely convertible.

NATO. The North Atlantic Treaty Organization, discussed in detail in chapter IV, came into effect in 1949.

STEPS TOWARD UNITY—INTERNAL IMPETUS

Efforts in the past to unify modern Europe were either confined to theoretical speculation or to attempts by force (Napoleon and Hitler). After World War II the desirability of closer union was becoming increasingly apparent to a number of European leaders for these reasons, among others—

1. Pooled national efforts could speed economic recovery.
2. Protection against external aggression.
3. To give Europe a much larger voice in world affairs than possessed by the individual states.
4. As a guard against possible future German aggression by interweaving the economies of the countries of Europe.

Two schools of thought claimed the best way toward unification. The first, the federalists, advocated the establishment of a federal political organization and assumed that economic integration would follow. The second school, the functionalists, argued for cooperation in limited fields for limited purposes, such as economic or military. They believed that one step at a time was the surest road to political unification.

THE COUNCIL OF EUROPE. The council was the result of the federalist approach, developed from a meeting at The Hague in May 1948, attended by some eight hundred European leaders, including Winston Churchill. A year later ten nations, subsequently joined by others, signed the statute setting up the Council of Europe. Its institutions are a committee composed of the foreign ministers of the member governments, a consultative assembly of members chosen by the national parliaments from among their own members, and a secretariat. The aim was to achieve "a greater unity for the purpose of safeguarding and realizing the ideals and principles which are their common heritage and facilitating their economic and social progress." Matters of defense do not fall within the council's scope. Since the council can only advise, the principal result of its deliberations has been to acquaint Europeans with common problems and possible solutions to them.

In 1952, at the urging of the Consultative Assembly of the Council of Europe, the charter of a European Political Community was drafted. The concept lacked, however, sufficient governmental and popular support to advance any further.

The functional approach to European unity has produced more tangible results.

BENELUX. In January 1948 a customs union came into effect between Belgium, Luxembourg, and the Netherlands.

WESTERN EUROPEAN UNION (WEU). By the Brussels Treaty of March 1948, the Benelux countries, France, and Great Britain agreed to collaborate for collective self-defense and for economic, social, and cultural matters. Should any of the contracting parties be the object of an "armed aggression in Europe," the other signatories would afford the attacked party "all the military and other aid and assistance in their power." The treaty, with a duration of fifty years, provided for the creation of a supreme body in WEU, known as the Consultative Council, consisting of the five foreign ministers. Under it was a Western Defense Committee consisting of the defense ministers. The Soviet blockade of Berlin, which began in June 1948, emphasized the need for a wider defense system. Through the formation of NATO in April 1949, collective defense became the responsibility of a larger body backed by the strength of the United States.

WEU did, however, provide a politically acceptable method for rearming Germany. The Communist attack on South Korea in 1950 strengthened the growing conviction of NATO members that the successful defense of Europe required resisting aggression as far to the east as possible and that this "forward strategy" required the use of German territory and, consequently, the participation of Germany in collective defense arrangements and its rearming. But how was Germany to be permitted to rearm in the face of widespread fear of resurgent German militarism? The merging of the armed forces of the countries of Western Europe, including Germany, seemed to offer a solution.

Long and difficult negotiations resulted in the signing of a treaty in 1952, by Belgium, France, Germany, Italy, Luxembourg, and the Netherlands, setting up the European Defense Community (EDC). EDC envisaged "a common army constituted without discrimination among the participating States." The national armies would be fused under a supranational command.

When the French National Assembly in 1954 refused to approve EDC, another formula had to be found for the rearming of Germany. At Paris in October 1954 agreements were reached and arrangements made which brought about the following:

1. Germany and Italy joined the Western European Union.
2. Germany joined NATO and placed all its military forces under NATO command. (On May 26, 1952, France, the U.K. and the U.S. signed contractual agreements to end the

occupation status of West Germany when the Federal Republic was integrated into the Western European defense community.)

3. The Council of Western European Union was given some powers of decision over the German military contribution and control of armaments.

4. Chancellor Adenauer declared that Germany would not manufacture atomic, biological, or chemical weapons. He also accepted the condition that Germany would not produce long-range missiles, guided missiles, strategic bombers, and larger warships except with the approval of the Council of Western European Union by a two-thirds vote.

5. WEU announced that it would work in close cooperation with NATO and, to avoid duplicating the military staffs of NATO, would rely on NATO for information and advice on military matters.

EUROPEAN COAL AND STEEL COMMUNITY (ECSC). Even before the military integration of Germany into Europe was being considered, a small group of European leaders came to the conclusion that Western Europe could fulfill its potential as a leader of the free world only through close economic integration followed by political unity. It was obvious that a united Europe would be an impossibility as long as France and Germany continued to distrust each other. After the defeat of Nazi Germany, the Allied Powers were determined that never again should Germany be in a position to use its industrial capacity for the purpose of waging war. The Allies soon realized, however, that setting limits on German industrial capacity and dismantling German factories did not provide an answer to this problem. In May the French Foreign Minister, Mr. Robert Schuman, proposed a far better solution—a joint authority to look after the whole of the French and German coal and steel production and to be open to other European countries.

The Schuman plan, as it came to be known, provided for a single market for coal, steel, iron ore, and scrap; the abolition of trade barriers for these commodities; and the development of rules of fair competition. If these basic industries could be closely integrated without relation to national frontiers, then neither France nor Germany would have the means of waging war against each other. The French Foreign Minister extended invitations to discuss this proposal to Belgium, West Germany, Italy, Luxembourg, the Netherlands, and the United Kingdom. All but the United Kingdom accepted. Their discussions resulted in the formation of the European Coal and Steel Community, which came into effect on January 1, 1952. The High Authority, the executive body of the ECSC, was the first common European authority (independent of governments) empowered to make decisions in its field. The rise in steel production of the six member countries from 42 million metric tons in 1952 to 73 million in 1961 is evidence of the effectiveness of the ECSC.

EEC AND EURATOM. The success of the ECSC led the six member states to consider further measures of economic cooperation. Negotiations over a period of several years resulted in the signing at Rome in 1957 of two basic treaties, both of which were to enter into force on January 1, 1958.

The first treaty set up the European Economic Community (EEC), better known as the Common Market. Over a twelve year period, the six member states were to work towards full economic union through abolishing trade barriers between them, setting up a common external tariff, and making possible the free circulation of labor, capital, and services. They would seek to reach common policies on foreign trade, transport, and agriculture and would coordinate policies in a large number of other economic fields. The rationale of the Common Market was that the abolishment of trade barriers, which had split Europe into small protected markets, would make possible large-scale manufacturing based on mass production methods and, as a result, would raise living standards and speed technical progress in an expanding economy.

The second treaty, signed at Rome in 1957, set up the European Atomic Community (Euratom) for the purpose of helping to develop a peaceful nuclear energy industry in Europe.

WHAT THE COMMON MARKET HAS ACCOMPLISHED

The timetable set forth in the Treaty of Rome for accomplishment of Common Market goals has not only been met but in some cases exceeded. By July 1963 customs duties between the member states had been reduced by 55 per cent for agricultural products and by 60 per cent for industrial products. Quota restrictions on industrial products have been abolished. The objective of free movement of persons, services, and capital is rapidly being approached. Thousands of Italians are working in Belgian and German mines and factories, and in all countries except Italy there is an acute shortage of skilled labor.

As internal tariffs have come down, a common external tariff has been erected. It applies to almost all items imported from the rest of the world and is an average of the national tariffs. Trade among the six members during the first four years of operation increased 84.5 per cent for manufactured products, 34 per cent for raw materials. Trade with countries outside the Common Market also increased. U.S. exports to the EEC increased by 45 per cent between 1958 and 1961, and in 1962 totaled $3.6 billion. The Common Market is the largest single trading bloc in the world—$64 billion of trade in 1961 compared to total U.S. trade of $37 billion.

All in all, this Community of 170 million people has made amazing progress. The European working man is earning more than ever before and for the first time is able to consider buying automobiles, television sets, and refrigerators. Real income per capita in Western Europe is, however, only about half that in the U.S.

AFRICA AND THE COMMON MARKET

The Treaty of Rome of 1957, setting up the Common Market, provided that colonies and former colonies of the Six could acquire associate membership based on the following three main features:

1. The six EEC countries would gradually abolish all quotas and tariffs on imports from the associated overseas countries.

2. The associated countries would, in general, abolish duties on imports from the EEC but might impose duties to protect infant industries.

3. The EEC set up a development fund to aid the associated countries.

France had insisted upon provision for associate membership because of the very close economic ties it had maintained with its colonies and former colonies. The French had regarded their colonies as an extension of France itself and considered the ultimate objective of the relationship to be complete equality in citizenship and political representation. Trade between the colonies and France was conducted in a closed circuit. All colonies were part of the franc zone, with the local franc freely convertible to the French franc. The French were prepared to make up budget deficits if necessary and allowed the colonies to sell their tropical products in France at guaranteed prices often above the world market. Thus, the French colonies were insulated from direct competition in world markets. Upon gaining independence they would have faced grave economic distress if France had not continued to pour in governmental capital and to provide an assured market for their products.

Seventeen French-speaking African states and Somalia have accepted associate membership in the Common Market.

THE UNITED KINGDOM AND THE EUROPEAN COMMUNITY

In the summer of 1961 the United Kingdom decided to apply for membership in the Coal and Steel Community. This action was a reversal of British policy, which traditionally had sought to steer clear of close involvement in continental affairs. Great Britain had turned down invitations to become a charter member of the Coal and Steel Community and the Common Market since it doubted the practicability of the two communities, did not at that time wish to tie itself to the close political association implicit in membership, and did not see how it could accept membership without weakening its ties with the Commonwealth.

To counter the possible loss of their export markets within the Common Market area, the United Kingdom, Austria, Denmark, Norway, Sweden, Portugal, and Switzerland organized the European Free Trade Association (EFTA). EFTA, known colloquially as "the Outer Seven" in contradistinction to "the Inner Six," is not a common market but a free trade association. The convention setting up EFTA went into effect July 1, 1960, and provided that the participating countries would progressively reduce and eventually eliminate tariffs and other barriers to trade among themselves but would keep their own external tariffs and be free to bargain separately with other countries. This was a purely economic union which was not to lead to a political union. The United Kingdom hoped that eventually some way might be found to merge the Inner Six and the Outer Seven into some cooperative arrangement. The countries of the EEC showed little interest in doing so, however, because such an arrangement would not have promoted their main objective of closer political union.

When it became increasingly apparent to the United Kingdom that the growth of its trade and economy was not keeping pace with that of the EEC, it decided to apply for membership. The United Kingdom saw three main obstacles to membership: (1) its commitments to the members of EFTA, (2) its domestic agricultural policy, and (3) its responsibilities to members of the Commonwealth, particularly as chief consumer of their agricultural exports.

The countries of EFTA, however, also saw advantages in belonging to the Common Market and, depending upon the U.K.'s admittance, were planning to seek either full or associate membership.

In contrast to the continent's policy of high support prices for farm products, Great Britain, the world's largest importer of foodstuffs, has traditionally set low prices and supported its farmers by subsidies. Imports from the Commonwealth have either entered free of duty or with a Commonwealth tariff preference. New Zealand's economy, for example, depends upon export of agricultural products, and over half of its export trade (91 per cent of its butter and 94 per cent of its lamb and cheese) is with the United Kingdom. If the U.K. had joined the Common Market, it would have had to apply (in the absence of a special arrangement) the common external tariff against New Zealand while permitting eventual free entry to products from EEC countries.

Associate membership in the Common Market for those Commonwealth countries heavily dependent upon Great Britain for their exports was expected to relieve some of the economic difficulties they would have faced had Britain joined the EEC. The United Kingdom and the Six had long and difficult bargaining sessions on that subject. Several of the African Commonwealth countries opposed association on political grounds. They argued that association would tend to make them dependent upon trade with the EEC, would hinder African unity, and would involve them in the cold war. Yet failure to join might have exposed them to loss of the British market for their tropical products and to resultant economic distress.

Although the economic obstacles to Great Britain's joining the Common Market were great, progress was made to resolve them. Then, at a press conference in January 1963, General de Gaulle abruptly revealed that France would oppose Great Britain's application on political grounds. The import of the General's remarks was that the U.K. was not sufficiently European in outlook to subordinate its Commonwealth ties, that its membership in the European Community would make more difficult the political organization of Europe as contemplated by General de Gaulle, and perhaps most telling of all, that, because of Great Britain's close relationship to the United States, British membership would mean introducing an American presence into European political affairs.

That same month France and Germany signed a treaty of cooperation which stated: "The two governments will consult before any decision on all important questions of foreign policy and in the first place on questions of common interest, with a view to reaching as far as possible an analogous position." A treaty which ordinarily would have been hailed as the end of a long history of rivalry and bitterness between these two neighbors was therefore looked upon with some misgivings by other members of the EEC as leading to an inward-looking Europe, in which France, supported by Germany, would be dominant. General de Gaulle's insistence on maximum French independence in foreign affairs and defense and his stated preference for a system of political unity on the continent in which each participating national state would retain the essentials of national sovereignty ran counter to the idea of supranational authority contemplated by other members of the EEC.

Because of the feeling in Germany, a preamble was added to the treaty before it was submitted to the German parliament for ratification. This preamble set forth German adherence to the principles of close cooperation between Europe and the United States, common defense within the Atlantic alliance, and the admission of Great Britain and other countries to a United Europe.

The Atlantic Community

The rate of progress of the countries of Western Europe toward unity has been set back, at least for the time being, by the exclusion of Great Britain from the EEC. The way in which Europe evolves is, however, a question which the Europeans themselves must decide, and their decision will in turn be important in determining the relationship between Western Europe and the United States in the context of partnership in an Atlantic community. The military, economic, and political ties between the two areas are closely interwoven. In the previous chapter we examined the military relationship. Let us now look at the economic relationship.

Economic collaboration between the United States and Western Europe falls into three broad areas—trade, assistance to the less developed countries, and monetary policy.

One of the principal means for working together on common economic policies is the Organization for Economic Cooperation and Development (OECD). The OECD is an outgrowth of the Organization for European Economic Cooperation (OEEC), which was set up in 1948 to coordinate the economic plans of the European nations receiving Marshall Plan assistance. The OECD, which came into being in 1961, provides a means for the major industrial nations of the free world to discuss common economic problems, such as the rate of growth and assistance to the less developed nations. Canada and the United States are members; Japan was invited to join in July 1963.

TRADE

At the beginning of the great depression of the 1930's it was thought that by raising United States tariff rates more purchases of American products and consequently more jobs for American workers would result. The Congress, in passing the Smoot-Hawley Act of 1930, raised the tariff to new heights. Other countries soon retaliated by erecting high tariffs of their own; international trade was reduced to a trickle, and more and more men were thrown out of work. No country benefited from the process. We learned the hard way that it was to our advantage, and to the advantage of other countries, to promote the growth of international trade.

After the Smoot-Hawley Act, our first legislative attempt to open up the channels of trade was the Trade Agreements Act of 1934. It authorized the President to reduce tariffs by 50 per cent by negotiating with other countries for reciprocal reductions in their tariffs. Subsequent legislation allowed the

President to make further reductions through negotiation. Three principles have governed U.S. trade policy. The first is the progressive lowering of tariffs. The second is the elimination of quantitative restrictions—the limiting by a country of the amount of a certain import it will accept, for example, so many yards of a certain type of textile and no more. The third element is nondiscrimination—we will not give any country special trading advantages nor accept discrimination against our exports except under specified circumstances. "Most favored nation treatment" is open to all countries which can qualify. Exceptions to this practice have been rare.

Negotiation with one country at a time, however, was a slow cumbersome process. For this reason, the General Agreement on Tariff and Trade, better known by its initials as GATT, was negotiated at a conference in Geneva in 1947. This is an international, multilateral contract under which countries accept a code of practical rules for fair trading in international commerce and agree to cooperate in lowering trade barriers. GATT brings together representatives of all its participating countries. They simultaneously negotiate in pairs; the chief supplier of a particular product generally bargains with the chief consumer. Once the two reach agreement, the lower duties become a part of the GATT tariff schedules. The nations that belong to GATT account for approximately 80 per cent of the world's trade.

Under the Trade Agreements Act, the United States concluded tariff-reducing negotiations with fifty-four countries. In recent years, however, we found that legislative restrictions and the percentage tariff reductions already made under the Act left us less and less with which to bargain. It became apparent that American exports to the Common Market would be at an increasing disadvantage as internal rates among the Six were progressively lowered. For example, an American concern may be able to sell to Germany a particular chemical at a cheaper price than its principal competitor, an Italian manufacturer. Yet, as the common external tariff is applied and the internal tariff rates between Italy and Germany go down, the Italian firm may be able to undersell the American.

President Kennedy decided that, if trade between the United States and the Common Market and the rest of the free world were to continue to grow, he required far broader authority to bargain than contained in the Trade Agreements

Act. He would have to be able to reduce tariffs across the board, not just on an item by item basis, and by a substantial percentage. The Trade Expansion Act, which Congress passed in October 1962, gives a President the power to:

1. Reduce tariffs up to 50 per cent of the July 1, 1962, level.
2. Reduce tariffs, or even eliminate them, on those commodities in which the United States and the European Economic Community jointly account for 80 per cent of the world trade. (Intra-EEC trade and intra-Communist bloc trade are excluded from the measurement of world exports.)
3. Eliminate tariffs on tropical products not produced in the United States in substantial amounts.
4. Reduce tariffs more than 50 per cent on agricultural commodities if the President determines this would expand our exports of those commodities.
5. Eliminate all duties set at 5 per cent or less of the import price as of July 1, 1962.
6. Provide federal benefits as high as $61 a week for as long as seventy-eight weeks for workers who lose their jobs because of lower tariffs and provide for retraining assistance.
7. Increase duties to a rate not more than 50 per cent over the rate existing on July 1, 1934, under certain circumstances.

The Trade Expansion Act contains several provisions to strengthen the hand of the President in dealing with foreign import restrictions. He may, for example, impose duties or other import restrictions on the products of any country which establishes or maintains unjustifiable import restrictions against U.S. agricultural products. It is not our intention or expectation, however, to engage in a trade war. We are much more interested in what the European Economic Community can mean in a much larger context if it adopts outward-looking policies.

ECONOMIC ASSISTANCE

The second field of economic cooperation envisaged by the Atlantic partnership is assistance to the less developed areas of the world. We have already noted the aid the European Community is giving to former colonies in Africa. In the next chapter we shall look at the U.S. foreign assistance program. Our thesis, briefly put, is that economic assistance to the less developed areas is very much in the interests of the free world, that the United States, however, has carried a disproportionately large share of this burden, and that it is now time that the other industrialized democracies contributed in proportion to their resources.

MONETARY POLICY

The U.S. dollar, backed by almost 40 per cent of the free world's monetary gold stocks, is used around the world. The world payments system is, in fact, based upon the interchangeability of gold and the dollar at a fixed price and confidence in the stability of other leading currencies. A foreign government knows that at any time it may present dollars to the U.S. Treasury and receive in return gold at the fixed rate of $35 an ounce.

The U.S. balance of payments is the financial record of transactions which take place between the United States and the rest of the world during a particular period of time. If the United States pays out fewer dollars than it receives from abroad, it will have a surplus in its international accounts, known as a favorable balance of payments. If it pays out more than it receives, it will have a deficit in its international accounts, or an unfavorable balance of payments. From 1950 on, with the exception of 1957, the United States has been running a deficit in its international accounts, averaging for calendar years 1950 through 1957 almost $1.3 billion a year. From 1958 on, the deficit has been much larger—$3.5 billion in 1958, $3.7 billion in 1959, $3.9 billion in 1960, $2.4 billion in 1961, and $2.2 billion in 1962. (In the past two years, however, special government transactions—foreign prepayment of U.S. Government loans, advance payments for military equipment, and foreign purchases of U.S. Treasury non-marketable, medium-term securities—have significantly reduced the deficits. Without these special transactions, the deficit in 1961 would have been $3 billion and in 1962, $3.6 billion.)

The net outflow of dollars which the deficit represents may be held by foreigners or turned into their central banks, which may purchase gold from the U.S. Treasury. Gold purchases have been largely responsible for the decrease in our gold stocks from nearly $23 billion in 1957 to less than $16 billion by May 1963.

Private and government transactions account for the flow

of dollars abroad. Among private transactions are imports of goods and services (including expenditures of American tourists in foreign countries), investments (either direct, such as the building of factories, or portfolio, such as purchase of stocks and bonds of foreign companies), and short-term capital movements (such as deposits placed in a foreign bank to benefit from a higher rate of interest than paid in the United States).

The two principal government activities resulting in an outflow of dollars are our military expenditures abroad and aid to foreign countries. (A sizeable percentage of these expenditures flows back to the United States, however, in the form of purchases of U.S. goods and services.)

Among the principal transactions accounting for a flow of dollars to the United States are foreign purchases of American goods and services (including expenditures by foreign tourists in the U.S. and income on U.S. investments abroad) and foreign investments in the U.S.

The United States sells to other countries more goods and services than it buys from them. Exports of goods and services exceeded imports by $5.4 billion in 1961 and $4.3 billion in 1962.

Although we are the richest nation in the world and although the annual deficit in our balance of payments may seem small in comparison to our gross national product, the United States cannot sustain a sizeable deficit each year which eats away its gold stocks and consequently causes loss of confidence in the dollar. There are a number of possible ways to tackle this problem. Each way, however, would have some repercussion on U.S. receipts because it would reduce the amount of dollars owned by foreigners which they use to purchase U.S. goods and services or to invest in the United States. Preventing Americans from traveling abroad for any purpose would save us nearly $2.5 billion a year (provided other countries didn't take retaliatory measures); prohibiting Americans from investing abroad might save us $2.8 billion a year; eliminating our overseas military bases, bringing all troops back to the United States, and cutting off military and economic aid would perhaps save us $4 billion annually. None of these steps would, however, serve our long-run interests. Either we would have to impose totalitarian controls upon our citizens or abdicate the responsibilities we feel must be carried for the well-being of the free world.

An American economy moving ahead at full steam would go far toward solving our balance of payments problem. The administration hopes that the tax reduction may supply the necessary incentive. An accelerating American economy would not only induce much U.S. investment capital to stay at home but would also attract investment capital from abroad. Other administration actions to meet the problem include:

1. Raising interest rates to attract short-term capital.
2. Proposal for placing a tax on the purchase of foreign securities so as to discourage their purchase by Americans.
3. Through tariff reduction negotiations under the Trade Expansion Act, increasing American exports.
4. In the aid programs, tying in loans and grants abroad to the purchase of American goods and services.
5. Further economies in government operations overseas, particularly those for defense purposes, and continuation of the special transactions to help finance the deficit.

The actions we can take alone are only part of the picture. Surpluses have for the most part been accruing to the industrial countries of Western Europe. Their cooperation is needed, as balance of payments problems are international, if a satisfactory permanent solution is to be found. They have already been extremely helpful in checking the outflow of dollars from the United States by prepayment of obligations owed us, placement of military orders in the U.S. and payment in advance for them, and purchase of U.S. Treasury securities. A long-run solution requires further cooperation and on two fronts. The first is the assumption by the countries of Western Europe of a far larger share of the expenses incurred for the common defense and for aid to the less developed countries. The other front lies in their adopting certain trade and financial measures, such as elimination of remaining barriers to American exports, reducing their high interest rates which have been responsible for the furnishing by the U.S. capital market of an excessive amount of the world's capital requirements, and taking measures to encourage the building up in their countries of more adequate capital markets.

IN CONCLUSION

A number of institutions exist through which Western Europe and North America now work together. Although these institutions are primarily economic or military in purpose, working together on economic or military matters inevitably involves political considerations and tends to strengthen political ties. As President Kennedy summed it up in his speech in Frankfurt, Germany, on June 25, 1963:[1]

> Our defenses are now strong, but they must be made stronger. Our economic goals are now clear, but we must get on with the performance. And the greatest of our necessities, the most notable of our omissions, is progress toward unity of political purpose.

[1] *The Department of State Bulletin*, (Washington, D. C.: U. S. Government Printing Office, 22 July 1963), p. 122.

VI. ECONOMIC AND MILITARY ASSISTANCE

Our present programs of economic and military assistance began with lend-lease in World War II. Since then every president and every presidential candidate has been for foreign aid. Congress has voted the annual appropriations but in recent years with increasing reluctance. Why? Because the program has had only the lukewarm support of the American people. Although a Gallup poll in early 1963 showed that 58 per cent favored foreign aid, an increase from the 51 per cent of March 1958, few people understand why aid is given or the concept behind the amounts expended. This confusion is not surprising, for there is a vast difference in concept between the Marshall Plan aid for a devastated Europe and today's aid for the less developed countries. Too often foreign aid has been "sold" to the Congress and to the public solely as a means of combatting communism rather than as an act that also springs from our own convictions and principles. In this chapter we will examine the "whys" and "hows" of aid and its role as a key element of our overall foreign policy.

WHY AID?

A nation, like an individual, develops best in a friendly environment. Thus the security of each nation in the free world depends to a degree on the security of every other. Our security was diminished when China, North Vietnam, the northern provinces of Laos, and Cuba fell under Communist domination. Our programs of military and economic assistance are intended to make less likely a similar fate for other countries. By assisting countries that seek to maintain their independence and to become self-supporting, we improve the odds for the survival of our own free institutions.

Military and economic assistance are closely linked. A nation is vulnerable not only to direct pressures but also to conditions of economic and social misery which invite Communist exploitation. Providing arms, training, and, in some cases, budgetary assistance can give a nation the strength to stand up to outside pressure and to put down internal subversion. Reasonable security and a stable government are preconditions to economic and social improvement.

Following World War II, military assistance to our NATO allies and economic assistance under the Marshall Plan were given for very clear purposes—to protect Europe from the threat of Soviet aggression and to help Europe get back on its feet through rebuilding its war-devastated industry and agriculture. There was a strong possibility that a prostrate Europe without hope would turn to communism. Our effort was dramatically successful; it gave Europe the security and the push which enabled it not only to recover from the war but to achieve a standard of living far higher than it had ever known. Europe's strength and prosperity contribute directly to our own security and prosperity.

We have now undertaken a program of aid to the less developed nations of the free world because we think it in our national self-interest and because we feel it morally right. We have two choices. The first is to tell them that their problems are not ours and that they need not look to us for help. One billion people who have been getting poorer and poorer in comparison to Americans are not going to remain passive. They know enough about the rest of the world to realize that misery does not have to be their lot and that of their children. They want change, and they want it in a hurry. If help were not forthcoming from the West, it most likely would be from the Soviet bloc. We would face the prospect that within a decade we, as well as our more prosperous allies, would find ourselves isolated in a Communist world. The $6 billion a year that we would have saved on aid would be peanuts in comparison to the additional expenditures we would feel compelled to put out for defense.

The second choice is one that comes much more naturally to us. It means accepting the role of a responsible citizen in a community, being concerned whether there are hospital facilities for all, whether there are enough school rooms for the children of the town, whether everyone has food and shelter.

A stable world will never be possible as long as the gap between the rich nations and the poor nations continues to grow wider. Our efforts must be directed to starting wherever possible the cycle of sustained growth which, combined with social justice, is the cornerstone of any country's strength and independence. A successful aid program should result in not only creating a much better relationship between the developed and the less developed, but also in bringing about a much closer partnership among the industrialized nations.

We should be very clear about our objective. It is "a peaceful world community of free and independent states—free to choose their own future and their own system, so long as it does not threaten the freedom of others." If aid to a particular country is not going to contribute to that objective, then we shouldn't give it. As long as we stick to that concept, we should have few political quarrels with the governments of recipient countries. This does not mean that we intend to finance a developing country's adoption of communism. We are confident that a country which is free and independent will not make that choice. No country receiving substantial American aid has. It does mean, though, that we should not use aid as a club to demand a vote favorable to our side in the United Nations. Naturally, we prefer helping those who think the way we do, but their position in the long run is of value to us only if they agree out of conviction, not if they agree because of expectation of favors. This is what Western missionaries discovered in China years ago. A person hungry enough would let himself be baptized in return for rice, but a "rice Christian" remained one only as long as he was hungry.

THE LESS DEVELOPED NATIONS

We made the choice to aid the less developed countries without fully realizing the size of the task. Quick success was possible in Europe because there already existed an economy that didn't have to be built from scratch—educational, financial, and commercial institutions that functioned, a supply of trained manpower, and a sense of direction on the part of the people themselves. This is not the case with most of the less developed countries.

To make progress in closing the gap between the developed and less developed countries, investment capital is needed. This can only come from three sources: a country's export earnings if they are substantially greater than the amount of its imports, as is the case of some oil-producing countries of the Persian Gulf; external aid, public or private; and forced savings, requiring the government to assume complete control of the economy, as in the U.S.S.R., so as to channel earnings not into consumers' goods but into productive plant.

A number of countries were able to finance the beginning of their development schemes from export earnings during the Korean War boom in basic commodity prices. Since then, however, the prices of the basic commodities have drifted downwards while the prices of the manufactured goods which the less developed countries need to buy have gone up. During the past decade, while exports of the industrialized countries doubled, exports of the less developed increased by only one-third. Indeed, a number of Latin American countries are today earning less from exports than they were ten years ago. Sixteen of them derive more than half of their export earnings from one or two commodities—Brazil and Colombia from coffee, Bolivia from tin, Honduras from bananas.

Until ways can be found to enable the less developed countries to increase their export earnings, their development as free societies will depend upon external aid. The demand for aid is large, and the supply is limited. The United States has learned from experience that it is necessary to have criteria by which to measure competing demands, having in mind that the main purpose of economic aid is to enable the recipient eventually to achieve self-sustaining growth. By dividing recipient countries into three groups, we can make a rough judgment as to what should be the nature and extent of U.S. participation in their development.

In *Group I* there are about thirty countries which show prospects of making substantial economic and social progress in the next few years. Over 90 per cent of all development lending is to this group. Although U.S. economic assistance averages only 3 to 4 per cent of the countries' national incomes, this amount is typically 20 per cent of their own expenditures for development and, together with aid from other sources, can make the difference between progress and stagnation. Group I can be divided into three subgroups:

1. countries such as Venezuela, Mexico, Jamaica, Israel, Greece, and the Republic of China, which are approaching self-sustained growth;

2. countries such as India, Pakistan, Colombia, and Nigeria, which are further from a state of self-sufficiency but which are following relatively effective development policies and making substantial progress;

3. countries with potential for development but which have not yet shown sufficient readiness to help themselves. U.S. assistance will be keyed to the effort these countries put forth.

In *Group II* the purpose of assistance is to discourage external aggression and to put down internal subversion. A nation disrupted by guerrilla warfare can hardly concentrate on a long-range goal of economic development. Only seven countries are now in this group. For those located on the edge of the Sino-Soviet land mass, such as South Vietnam, military assistance is a major part of the aid contribution.

Group III contains those countries, forty-seven of them, in which U.S. assistance is limited or secondary. For most of these recipients, the United States is a minor contributor in a program in which the former colonial powers or international institutions play the dominant role, such as in Africa. For some of the countries in this group, limited aid programs provide an alternative to dependence on Communist bloc aid. In some instances aid programs enable us to use strategic facilities or to exert an influence toward the development of freer institutions.

THE MECHANICS OF THE OPERATION

There are many types of economic assistance. The choice for a particular country depends upon its degree of economic development. A country which already has an industrial plant and skilled manpower, and has shown itself able to use its resources intelligently, obviously has different requirements from a newly-independent country with practically no factories, few educated or trained people, and little experience in self-government or in managing its resources. For the first country, a loan to enable it to buy heavy industrial equipment might be the most effective contribution. In the case of the second country, the greater need will be for schools and roads. A large injection of capital is not helpful, because the country does not yet have the human resources to enable it to use capital to good advantage. More important to it than money is knowledge. The transfer of that knowledge should be the first goal of any program of assistance.

Economic aid is extended either in the form of money (and there are several ways of doing this) or food.

MONEY. Money may be supplied for specific purposes such as building a dam, constructing roads, or providing budgetary support (enabling the recipient nation when in financial straits to meet its obligations). Financing may be done through:

1. Development loans, repayable in dollars over a period of up to fifty years. Most development loans, which go to those countries already well along the path toward modernization, are used to finance imports of essential commodities such as machine tools, farm equipment, and steel.
2. Development grants, to be used principally by countries in the early states of growth, for those projects which are essential but are not going to yield a direct monetary return. Most development grants finance technical assistance programs in such fields as health and education.
3. Supporting assistance. The primary purpose is not development but to defend our interests in the cold war, to
    a. help countries support their own military effort,
    b. maintain base rights,
    c. prevent economic instability which would threaten U.S. political interests,
    d. prevent exclusive dependence on Sino-Soviet aid.
4. Voluntary contributions to international organizations.

FOOD. In 1954 Congress passed the Agricultural Trade Development and Assistance Act (Public Law 480, generally referred to as PL 480). The act authorizes the sale of surplus agricultural products to friendly countries for their own currencies. Up to 10 per cent of these payments is reserved for the use of the United States in that particular country; the balance may be used for local currency grants or loans. PL 480 also permits the giving of surplus stocks for famine relief; surplus stock may also be donated to voluntary organizations, such as Church World Services and CARE, for distribution to the needy overseas.

These are the channels through which our government conducts economic assistance operations:

1. *The Agency for International Development (AID)* came into existence in 1961 and took over the functions and most of the personnel of its predecessor, the International Cooperation Administration (ICA), which previously had

been known as the Foreign Operations Administration (FOA), before that as the Mutual Security Agency (MSA), and before that as the Economic Cooperation Administration (ECA). Although the name changed, the essential nature did not. Incorporated into AID was the principal loan-making partner of ICA, the Development Loan Fund (DLF).

2. *The Peace Corps* was established in 1961. Congress defined its purpose as follows:

> . . . to promote world peace and friendship through a Peace Corps, which shall make available to interested countries men and women of the United States qualified for service abroad and willing to serve, under conditions of hardship if necessary, to help the peoples of such countries and areas in meeting their needs for trained manpower, and to help promote a better understanding of the American people on the part of the peoples served, and a better understanding of other peoples on the part of the American people.

In July 1963 the Peace Corps had almost five thousand volunteers and was operating in some forty-five countries.

3. *The Department of Agriculture,* working closely with the Department of State and AID, makes available surplus foods under PL 480.

4. *The Export-Import Bank (Eximbank),* a government agency, makes loans to enable the borrower to buy American exports. Loans are repayable in dollars.

5. *International organizations:*

a. those U.N. organizations concerned with supplying relief and technical assistance, such as the Expanded Technical Assistance Program, the Special Fund, the United Nations Children's Fund (UNICEF), and certain specialized agencies;

b. those U.N. specialized agencies in the business of lending—the International Bank for Reconstruction and Development (IBRD), the International Finance Corporation (IFC), and the International Development Association (IDA);

c. Inter-American Development Bank (IDB), established in 1959 by the Latin American countries and the United States for projects in this hemisphere. The IDB administers a Social Welfare Fund, financed by the United States, for projects such as sanitation and education, desperately needed but not bankable because there is no prospect of a direct monetary return.

Our present aid program is based on the following principles:

SELF-HELP. Sustained aid will go to those countries making serious efforts to help themselves. This means a proper devotion of public resources to the development effort, tapping the energies of the entire population, foregoing luxuries, establishing proper standards of public honesty, and levying taxes on their own citizens comparable to those asked of the American taxpayer.

LONG-RANGE PLANNING. The nation seeking aid should have specific goals and priorities on what must be done to reach those goals. Development planning must include good budgeting, equitable tax measures, improvement of health, education, and transportation, and encouragement of private enterprise. If a nation is unable to draft its own development plans, it can call on AID or one of the international organizations.

LONG-RANGE COMMITMENTS. In order to induce nations to take the risks involved in a development program, the United States must be able to commit loan funds for more than one year. Prior to the aid legislation of 1961, Congress had not authorized commitments of funds beyond one year.

SOCIAL PROGRESS. A nation will not advance along democratic lines if the people do not have a stake in the advancement. Such was the case of Cuba. Although its economy showed a significant growth rate, the poor were not getting the benefits. A tenant farmer who must turn over to an absentee landowner a large part of his crop is not greatly interested in improved methods of farming. In many countries land reform is essential; in others, tax reform to iron out some of the vast inequalities between the very rich and the very poor; in nearly all, better housing and education.

FREE WORLD COOPERATION. This is a job the United States cannot and should not do alone.

COST

The United States has spent more than $100 billion for economic and military foreign assistance. During the past decade the annual expenditures have been between $5 billion and $7 billion. About half this amount is appropriated by the annual foreign aid appropriation bill (known as the Foreign Assistance Act) and the balance by other acts.

Each year the administration presents to Congress its proposed economic and military assistance programs and requests funds for those programs falling under the Foreign

Assistance Act. Congress must take two actions—authorize the programs and then appropriate the funds for them. Inevitably the funds appropriated are considerably less than the funds authorized, which in turn are less than what the President requested.

U. S. Aid, by Region—1946–62
(millions of dollars)

TOTAL FISCAL YEARS 1946–1962

PROGRAM	Near East & S. Asia	Latin America	Far East	Africa	Europe	TOTAL All Regions
Economic—Total	12,703	6,184	13,729	1,730	28,866	66,455
Loans	5,744	4,690	1,904	680	10,588	23,695
AID Programs	7,038	1,313	7,415	1,106	15,235	33,571
Social Progress Trust Fund	—	224	—	—	—	224
P. L. 480	3,967	771	1,185	377	1,853	8,355
Export-Import Bank Long-term Loans	801	3,361	708	179	2,458	7,506
Other Economic Programs	897	514	4,421	68	9,320	16,798
Military—Total	5,144	641	8,108	116	15,840	30,678
GRAND TOTAL	17,847	6,824	21,837	1,845	44,706	97,133

Source: Agency for International Development, Statistics and Reports Division

U.S. Aid, by Region—Fiscal Year 1962
(millions of dollars)

FISCAL YEAR 1962

PROGRAM	Near East & S. Asia	Latin America	Far East	Africa	Europe	TOTAL All Regions
Economic—Total	2,027.9	1,233.7	725.7	500.0	272.9	5,084.4
Loans	1,292.7	918.5	243.5	204.5	177.1	2,836.2
A.I.D. Programs	1,123.0	478.2	367.6	315.5	16.4	2,508.2
Social Progress Trust Fund	—	224.4	—	—	—	224.2
P. L. 480	819.2	156.5	250.8	109.7	180.0	1,562.7
Export-Import Bank Long-term Loans	83.1	253.9	103.1	67.6	76.5	584.2
Other Economic Programs	2.6	120.7	4.2	7.2	—	204.9
Military—Total	264.9	132.0	597.9	23.9	425.8	1,526.2
GRAND TOTAL	2,292.8	1,365.7	1,323.6	523.9	698.7	6,610.6

Source: Agency for International Development, Statistics and Reports Division

PRIVATE INVESTMENT

Although assistance on a government-to-government level may be crucial to a country's development, it will not be successful without private investment, both foreign and domestic. One of the principal functions of government aid is to make possible the conditions that will attract private capital. Obviously a businessman's motive in investing is to make a profit. He is not going to invest in a country, even his own, if he has doubts about its stability. For this reason American businessmen have placed most of their direct, long-term investments abroad (about $40 billion in all) in the modern industrialized countries.

AID is trying to encourage the investment of private capital in the less developed countries. Among its methods are government loans for well-conceived private projects, acquainting private businesses with development opportunities, and insuring investments against specific risks.

Private investment is not, however, a one-way street. One of the principal tasks of our aid program is to encourage countries receiving aid to do the things necessary to attract private investment. Expropriation without compensation is not one of them. The aid bill provides that a country expropriating American private property has six months in which to take appropriate steps toward compensation; if it doesn't, aid will be cut off. Thus in February 1963 assistance was cut off to Ceylon, where American gas stations had been taken over without compensation.

THE SINO-SOVIET ECONOMIC OFFENSIVE

Foreign assistance has proved to be an effective instrument of United States foreign policy. The clearest tribute to its effectiveness has been the adoption by the Soviet Union of the same tools we had been using.

The Soviets have always regarded the people of the less developed countries as potential recruits to communism, but they drastically changed their recruitment tactics about the time of Stalin's death in 1953. Prior to that time, and particularly in the years 1948–1950, Moscow encouraged the local Communist parties to follow a militant line with the objective of overthrowing existing governments by force. Communist-led insurrections in Burma, Malaya, and the Philippines were unsuccessful, as was an attempted take-over in Indonesia. These actions had the result of alerting the less developed nations to the dangers of communism, forcing many of them to turn to the West for military aid, and tarnishing the image of the Soviet Union as a peace-loving nation.

By 1955 the Soviets were well embarked on a much more subtle approach, that of wooing the less developed nations by good-will missions of high Soviet dignitaries, red-carpet treatment in Moscow for African and other leaders, scholarships for students, trade agreements, and programs of military and economic assistance. Their minimum objective was to insure that a less developed country took a neutral stand on East-West disputes. The next steps were to orient its economy toward the Soviet bloc, influence its leaders toward acceptance of the Communist point of view, and finally, when the country was sufficiently softened up, bring about its digestion into the Soviet system through a local Communist party take-over. Foreign aid was a tool to be appraised not on its own merits but on the extent it contributed to the Soviet Union's political objectives.

The bloc offers aid where it will do it the most political good and is particularly quick at stepping in when there has been a strain on a country's relations with the United States or one of its allies. Thus, when the United States decided in 1955 not to contribute to the financing of Egypt's proposed high dam at Aswan, the Soviet Union offered its services and was accepted. Bloc aid in 1962 went to twenty-nine free world countries.

Military aid went mainly to Afghanistan, Cuba, Egypt, Iraq, Indonesia and Syria. Commitments to Guinea, Mali, and Yemen, although smaller, are of major significance in relation to the size and requirements of these countries. Military aid, of course, is also a very good way of insuring close ties with the armed forces and particularly with the ambitious younger officers.

Two-thirds of the bloc economic aid has gone to Afghanistan, Cuba, Egypt, India, and Indonesia. As in the case of military aid, lesser amounts have gone to a number of other countries, where it has still had a significant impact on their economies.

Like aid, the Soviet state directs trade where it will do the most good politically. The bloc takes advantage of the disposal problems some countries have had with their one-crop economies such as Burma's rice, Egypt's cotton, Iceland's codfish, and Uruguay's wool. A Soviet offer to buy a country's surplus is hard to resist, particularly if the contract is long-term and the price attractive. It later discovers the disadvantages. It accepts payment in bloc credits good only for bloc goods, and these goods may not be as cheap or as good as it could buy in the open market. It finds that its usual markets can be disrupted by such tactics as Soviet sales of Egyptian cotton on the world market at cheaper prices. It learns that bloc purchases are not in fulfillment of long-term normal needs but can be shut off like a faucet if the bloc wishes to apply pressure for political ends.

Nearly all the bloc aid funds have gone into projects such as a steel mill, oil refinery, dam, sports stadium, or hotel that can be pointed to as examples of bloc aid. Little has gone into the intangibles such as education. The purpose of bloc aid is, of course, to further bloc aims—either to win a country into the Communist camp, as was attempted in Guinea, or to stir up trouble for the West, as in the case of Indonesia.

Although so far none of the free world countries receiving bloc aid have gone into the Communist camp, Guinea in 1961 appeared headed that way. Guinea had accepted grants and credits from the bloc, including Communist China, of $125 million, was host to 1,500 bloc personnel, and sent 40 per cent of its exports to the bloc. Then blunders in the Soviet aid program were accompanied by blunders in Soviet diplomacy. In December 1961 President Sékou Touré accused the Soviet Ambassador of fomenting student demonstrations against the government and demanded his recall. Since then Guinea has shown much more interest in building up its relations with the West.

The Soviets have been able to create great tension in Southeast Asia by supplying military equipment to Indonesia far in excess of that needed for defense. With this strength, Indonesia adopted an aggressive position toward the Dutch in regard to West New Guinea and toward Malaysia over its Borneo territories.

The United States is not opposed to the acceptance by the less developed countries of bloc aid if they do not put themselves in a position of complete dependence upon it. Certainly a country as vast as India and with its enormous requirements can benefit by accepting aid from both the West and the East as long as it is careful to prevent political penetration. Peaceful competition of this type is welcome.

VII. UNITED NATIONS

"Get the U.S. out of the U.N. and the U.N. out of the U.S." This slogan, used by certain right-wing organizations in the past few years, shows a lack of understanding of the United Nations. The U.N. performs functions which need to be performed; and, if the U.N. did not exist, it would be in the highest interest of American foreign policy to create it.

FOUNDING OF UNITED NATIONS

During World War II the Allied Powers realized that, if the peace, when won, were to be maintained and some system of general security were to be established, there would have to be a world security organization. Fifty nations which had fought together against the Axis Powers met in San Francisco on April 25, 1945, for the purpose of drafting the charter of such an organization. China, the United Kingdom, the Soviet Union, and the United States were the sponsoring powers. The fifty nations reached agreement and signed the Charter on June 26, 1945. Although not a participant, Poland signed shortly thereafter, thus making fifty-one charter members of the international organization known as the United Nations.

CHARTER

The purposes and principles of the U.N. are spelled out in the Charter. Article I of the Charter sets forth these purposes:

> 1. To maintain international peace and security, and to that end: to take effective collective measures for the prevention and removal of threats to the peace, and for the suppression of acts of aggression or other breaches of the peace, and to bring about by peaceful means, and in conformity with the principles of justice and international law, adjustment or set-

tlement of international disputes or situations which might lead to a breach of the peace;

2. To develop friendly relations among nations based on respect for the principle of equal rights and self-determination of peoples and to take other appropriate measures to strengthen universal peace;

3. To achieve international cooperation in solving international problems of an economic, social, cultural, or humanitarian character, and in promoting and encouraging respect for human rights and for fundamental freedoms for all without distinction as to race, sex, language, or religion; and

4. To be a center for harmonizing the actions of nations in the attainment of these common ends.

In brief, the United Nations set as its targets not only the prevention of war but the elimination of those conditions which breed war.

STRUCTURE

This chapter examines the effectiveness of the United Nations in moving toward these targets and its actions in relation to American interests. Before discussing performance, let us first look more closely at what the U.N. is and what it does. Its structure is complex. The principal organs are as follows:

1. *The General Assembly* is composed of all the member states, 112 as of early 1964. It may discuss and make recommendations on matters within the scope of the Charter; elects, by itself, or in combination with the Security Council, all nonpermanent members of other U.N. organs; receives reports of the activities of all other U.N. organs except the International Court of Justice; and decides on the budget. Each regular session usually begins on the third Tuesday in September and lasts about three months. New officers are elected for each session, including the president, the thirteen vice presidents, and the chairmen of the seven principal permanent committees, each concerned with a broad field of activity such as economic and financial or administrative and budgetary matters. The General Assembly may establish other committees for special purposes such as peaceful uses of outer space and effects of atomic radiation.

2. *The Security Council* is composed of eleven members, five of which are permanent—China, France, U.S.S.R., U.K.,

and U.S. The Security Council has primary responsibility for maintaining the peace and security and for taking action in case of aggression. Decision on all except procedural matters requires the affirmative vote of seven members including the permanent members. Thus, a negative vote of any of the five permanent members can veto action.

3. *The Economic and Social Council (ECOSOC)* is responsible for carrying out the U.N.'s tasks in improving economic and social conditions throughout the world. ECOSOC is composed of eighteen member states elected for three-year terms. Its decisions in general are subject to confirmation by the General Assembly. One of the council's main tasks is to coordinate the work of the thirteen U.N. specialized agencies. To accomplish its work, ECOSOC has set up a system of commissions, committees, and special bodies, concerned with such subjects as human rights, narcotic drugs, technical assistance, and child welfare.

There are four regional economic commissions with headquarters in Geneva, Switzerland; Santiago, Chile, Addis Ababa, Ethiopia; and Bangkok, Thailand. Their function is to bring together the countries in each area to cooperate in meeting their mutual economic problems. One group, the Economic Commission for the Far East (ECAFE), has undertaken a regional project for the development of the lower Mekong River in Southeast Asia. A project like this could not be undertaken by one country alone, since the lower Mekong is of great importance to Thailand, Laos, Cambodia, and Vietnam.

4. *The Trusteeship Council* assists the General Assembly in carrying out its responsibilities for the trust territories. Eventual self-government or independence is the aim, with the consequent liquidation of the trusteeship system. The trust territories are those areas which have been placed under U.N. trusteeship by agreement between administering countries and the United Nations and consist of those territories formerly mandates of the League of Nations or those detached from enemy states as a result of World War II. Events are rapidly reducing the work of the Trusteeship Council; of the eleven original trust territories, all but three have now achieved independence.

The Trusteeship Council is composed of those nations administering trust territories and an equal number of those who do not. The council receives annual reports from administering powers, sends out special missions to examine the territories, receives petitions from the inhabitants, and holds hearings—such as on the future of French Togoland.

5. *The International Court of Justice* is the principal judicial organ of the U.N., and all U.N. members are automatically parties to the Statute of the Court. The function of the court is to decide, in accordance with international law, any disputes submitted to it by states and to render advisory opinions at the request of the General Assembly, the Security Council, or other organs authorized by the General Assembly to request opinions. The court sits at The Hague and is permanently in session except for judicial vacations.

6. *The Secretariat* serves as executive agent for the other U.N. organs. It is headed by the Secretary General, who is appointed by the General Assembly on the recommendation of the Security Council. He may bring to the attention of the Security Council any matter which in his opinion may threaten the peace. He has been charged by the U.N. with peacekeeping tasks in the Middle East and in the Congo, with field missions in Korea and India-Pakistan, with preparing background material for various U.N. bodies, and with making the physical arrangements for their meetings. Helping him perform these tasks are the some six thousand international civil servants in the Secretariat. They are appointed by the Secretary General and are solely responsible to him.

THE SPECIALIZED AGENCIES

Before the creation of the United Nations there existed several agencies established by intergovernmental agreement for the purpose of promoting international cooperation in specific fields. The U.N. Charter authorized the Economic and Social Council to coordinate the activities of these agencies within the United Nations framework. In addition, the United Nations can create new specialized agencies to further its economic and social goals. There are now thirteen specialized agencies:

International Telecommunication Union (ITU)
Universal Postal Union (UPU)
World Meteorological Organization (WMO)
International Labor Office (ILO)
International Monetary Fund (IMF)
International Bank for Reconstruction and Development (IBRD)

International Finance Corporation (IFC)
International Development Association (IDA)
Food and Agriculture Organization (FAO)
United Nations Educational, Scientific, and Cultural Organization (UNESCO)
International Civil Aviation Organization (ICAO)
World Health Organization (WHO)
Intergovernmental Maritime Consultative Organization (IMCO)

Membership is open to any member of the U.N. and to nonmembers if approved by a sufficient number of members. Not all the members of the United Nations belong to all the specialized agencies; for example, the U.S.S.R. is not a member of the International Bank, the International Civil Aviation Organization, or the Food and Agricultural Organization; whereas the Federal Republics of Germany and Switzerland, while not members of the U.N., belong to many of the specialized agencies.

The work of the specialized agencies covers many fields and seldom makes the headlines. The quiet, continued cooperation of the member governments has, however, made possible facilities and services we take for granted—such as world-wide delivery of mail and jet flights across the Atlantic. To give an idea of the scope and importance of the work of the specialized agencies, I am going to describe the work of three of them: the International Bank, UNESCO, and the World Health Organization.

INTERNATIONAL BANK FOR RECONSTRUCTION AND DEVELOPMENT (IBRD). Coming into being in 1945, it has its headquarters in Washington. Its purpose is to assist the development of territories of member countries through investment of capital for productive purposes. The IBRD obtains its funds through subscriptions of members and through sale of bonds. Most of the loans of the bank, already over $5 billion, have gone for electric power, transportation, communications, and industry. India has been the bank's biggest customer, mainly for the modernization and expansion of its railways. In addition, the bank has offered technical advice on development programs and has used its good offices to bring about a settlement by the United Arab Republic of the claims of the shareholders of the Suez Canal Company and a settlement of the Indus waters dispute between India and Pakistan.

United Nations Educational, Scientific, and Cultural Organization (UNESCO). Founded in 1946, it has its headquarters in Paris. By promoting collaboration among nations in the fields of science, education, and culture, UNESCO aims not only to increase understanding among nations but to enrich the intellectual and material lives of their citizens. In pursuit of this aim, its activities have been far-ranging: the campaign against illiteracy through extension of primary education and training of teachers; scientific research and exchange of information for the development of natural resources in the arid zones, particularly in the Middle East; the promotion of a Universal Copyright Convention to give world-wide protection to authors, already adhered to by a number of countries including the U.S. and the U.K.; exchange of art and cultural exhibits, particularly between the East and the West; book translations; and enlisting the help of a number of countries in saving the relics of Nubian art and the temples of the Nile Valley which will be flooded when the United Arab Republic completes its Aswan High Dam.

World Health Organization (WHO). WHO has the task of bringing the advantages of medical science to people all over the world. Founded in 1948, it has its headquarters in Geneva. The U.S.S.R. and eight members of the bloc withdrew in 1949-50; later Russia and some of the others resumed membership. WHO has set up a procedure for standardizing scientific names for drugs, has issued a pharmacopoeia containing physical and chemical properties for pharmaceutical products, and has set up quarantine regulations which have been adopted by most of its members. It is best known, however, for its efforts in combating communicable diseases, principally malaria, tuberculosis, and yaws. In 1955 WHO began a world-wide effort to stamp out malaria—the largest cooperative health campaign in history, affecting almost seventy countries in which almost 800 million people live. As a direct consequence of this campaign, the number of people suffering from malaria dropped from an estimated 250 million in 1955 to an estimated 140 million in 1961. WHO also maintains an epidemic-warning service, which has made possible the preparation of serums in time to combat influenza epidemics, and a widespread technical assistance program to build up public health services.

HUMANITARIAN ACTIVITIES

U.N. activities in the humanitarian field include control of the international distribution of narcotic drugs; the Universal Declaration of Human Rights, which has been used as a standard of moral principles to censure Soviet action in Hungary and Communist Chinese action in Tibet; and the convention on genocide. Of the widest interest, however, are those humanitarian activities caring for refugees and children.

UNITED NATIONS RELIEF AND WORKS AGENCY FOR PALESTINE REFUGEES (UNRWA). As a result of the fighting in Palestine between Arabs and Jews and the emergence in 1948 of the state of Israel, more than three-quarters of a million Arabs left their homes in Palestine and fled to the neighboring Arab countries of Jordan, Lebanon, Syria, and the Gaza Strip of Palestine (under Egyptian administration). Israel would not permit them to return; the Arab states were unwilling to resettle them in their territories, and the refugees themselves demanded the right to return to their homes or compensation for the property of those who elected not to return. The United Nations set up a temporary agency to take care of what it then regarded as a temporary relief problem. When no quick solution appeared possible, the General Assembly in 1949 created UNRWA to provide relief and works projects in cooperation with the host governments.

UNRWA has maintained camps for the refugees and supplied them with food, health and social services, schooling, and some job training. The agency is a special body within the U.N., and its functions and continued existence depend upon the will of the General Assembly. Its funds do not come from the regular U.N. budget but entirely from voluntary contributions. The budget for the fiscal year ending June 30, 1963, was $40 million; the United States pledged $24.7 million. The fate of these Palestinian refugees is one of the tragedies of modern times, particularly because the countries which should be most concerned with their plight have been unable to agree on any constructive steps.

THE OFFICE OF THE U.N. HIGH COMMISSIONER FOR REFUGEES (UNHCR). Established in 1951, pursuant to a resolution of the General Assembly to provide legal and political protection to refugees and to seek permanent solutions, the Arab refugees cared for by UNRWA are not within its scope. UNHCR has been active in assistance to other refugees throughout the world—including those from World War II still in displaced persons camps in Europe who by reason of health or handicap have not been employable, those who fled from Hungary at the time of the uprising, European and Chinese refugees who fled from China to Hong Kong, Tibetans in Nepal, and Angolans in the Congo.

THE UNITED NATIONS CHILDREN'S FUND (UNICEF). UNICEF was established in 1946 as an emergency agency to supply food and clothing for children in countries devastated by the war. In 1950 the emphasis shifted to programs of long-term benefit for children in the less developed countries. Among its programs UNICEF supplies powdered milk for schools, treats trachoma, aids vocational training of youth, and supports institutes for treatment and training of physically handicapped children. Contributions to UNICEF are voluntary. In 1961 over one hundred countries contributed $27.8 million, of which the United States gave $12 million. In addition to voluntary contributions by governments, private funds have been raised by sale of Christmas cards and through the popular Halloween "Trick or Treat" campaign.

ATOMIC ENERGY, DISARMAMENT, AND OUTER SPACE

PEACEFUL USES OF ATOMIC ENERGY. In order to provide a clearing house for the exchange of research and experience in the peaceful uses of atomic energy, the *International Atomic Energy Agency (IAEA)* came into being in 1957. It is charged with making sure that the assistance it offers and the materials it distributes are not used for military purposes. The IAEA has concentrated on bringing the benefits of the use of atomic energy to the less developed countries and has done this through training personnel, research into peaceful applications, providing experts and materials, and making health and safety regulations. It is neither an organ of the United Nations nor a specialized agency but an autonomous body affiliated with the U.N. It has seventy-seven members and headquarters in Vienna.

Disarmament. Explored in detail in another chapter, it is significant that nearly all the talks on this subject have been conducted in forums sponsored by the United Nations.

Outer Space. In 1959 the General Assembly unanimously voted to create the U.N. Committee for the Peaceful Uses of Outer Space. The resolution noted the applicability of international law, including the U.N. Charter, to outer space and celestial bodies; it declared that outer space and celestial bodies are free for exploration and use by all states in conformity with international law and are not subject to national appropriation; it asked the Secretary General to maintain a public registry of launchings of space vehicles into orbit; it proposed study of measures to advance the state of atmospheric science and technology and to develop weather forecasting facilities; and it proposed study of ways in which satellites could be used for the benefit of global communications.

Adlai Stevenson, our Representative to the United Nations, well summed up the importance of this resolution: [1]

> There is a right and a wrong way to get on with the business of space exploration. In our judgment the wrong way is to allow the march of science to become a runaway race into the unknown. The right way is to make it an ordered, peaceful, cooperative, and constructive forward march under the aegis of the United Nations.

PEACEKEEPING

The maintenance of peace and the prevention of war was certainly the primary purpose for which the United Nations was set up, and the Security Council was given the primary responsibility. The council's success in carrying out this task depended, however, on whether the five permanent members would have sufficient identity of purpose to reach agreement among themselves. It soon became apparent that Soviet objectives and the objectives of the other four powers were far from the same. As a result, the Security Council has been effective only in those few cases when the Soviets shared our views—as in the 1947 cease-fire between the Dutch and the Indonesians and the first three resolutions on the Congo —or when the Soviets boycotted the Security Council, mak-

[1] Source: Department of State.

ing possible the resolution to send troops to support the Republic of Korea.

It was originally planned that the five permanent members would supply the troops for peacekeeping activities, and a Military Staff Committee, composed of their representatives, was attached to the Security Council. Differences among the five permanent members, however, have prevented the conclusion of the agreements envisaged under Article 43 of the Charter to furnish troops. Consequently, the Military Staff Committee has held only *pro forma* meetings since 1948. When the U.N. has sent troops, it has, in all cases except that of Korea, called upon the smaller nations, less identified with the cold war, to supply them. In the case of Korea, the United States at the request of the Security Council supplied the U.N. Command.

Although it probably would be desirable to have a permanent force upon which the U.N. could call, political and financial considerations have so far not made this feasible. In each emergency, the Secretary General has had to improvise, to request nations to supply troops, and to worry later how the nations furnishing them would be reimbursed.

Because of the veto in the Security Council, much of its peacekeeping function has been assumed by the General Assembly. This was facilitated by the "Uniting for Peace Resolution" adopted by the General Assembly in September 1950, over bitter Soviet opposition. The resolution provides that if the Security Council is prevented from taking action by lack of agreement of its members in any case where there appears to be a threat to the peace, breach of the peace, or act of aggression, the General Assembly shall consider the matter immediately and may be called into emergency special session within twenty-four hours' notice on the vote of any seven members of the Security Council or of a majority of the U.N. members. This is an excellent example of the flexibility of the U.N. Charter. When most of the members are willing to do so they can adapt the rules to avoid being rendered impotent. The General Assembly, however, unlike the Security Council, can not impose sanctions; it can only recommend them.

In its role as guardian of the peace, the United Nations' record has been mixed. On the positive side:

1. The U.N. attitude in 1946 prompted the Soviet Union to decide it would be wise to withdraw its troops from

Azerbaijan, the province of Iran which it had occupied during World War II.

2. When the U.N. condemned three Balkan nations in 1947 for assisting the Greek rebels and sent observers to the area, American efforts to bring the civil war in Greece to a close and end Communist infiltration were expedited.

3. In 1949 the U.N. brought about an end to fighting between the Dutch and the Indonesians and the granting of full independence to Indonesia.

4. Under the auspices of the Secretary General, the thirteen-year-old dispute between Indonesia and the Netherlands over West New Guinea was settled in 1962, with the U.N. assuming control over that territory until it was transferred to Indonesia on May 1, 1963. Not later than 1969 the inhabitants are to vote whether they wish to be independent or to remain with Indonesia.

5. The U.N. in 1948 helped to bring about a truce in the fighting between the Jews and the Arabs, assisted Israel's emergence as a nation, and since then has maintained truce observation machinery on Israel's borders to prevent incidents from flaring up into serious fighting.

6. Since 1948 the U.N. has been concerned with the dispute between India and Pakistan over Kashmir. Although it brought about a truce and maintains military observers along the cease-fire line to prevent renewed fighting, it has not yet found a way to bring about a permanent settlement.

7. U.N. collective action, in which the United States played the leading role, stopped Communist aggression in Korea. Peacekeeping teams are still patrolling the armistice line.

8. U.N. action stopped the fighting in Suez in 1956. The U.N. Emergency Force (UNEF) assisted in the orderly withdrawal of forces and has since then been policing the Israeli-Egyptian frontier from the Gaza Strip to the Gulf of Aqaba.

In other instances the United Nations has not been effective. In the case of Hungary, intervention would have meant the possibility of conflict with the Soviet Union. In the case of India's seizure of Goa, the feelings of many members on colonialism outweighed their commitment to the principle of the peaceful settlement of disputes.

The operation in the Congo has been the severest test the United Nations has yet faced. Because it well demonstrates the difficulties which new nations face and because its outcome was crucial to the future of the United Nations itself, the Congo is the subject of a separate chapter.

SPECIAL PROBLEMS

There are a number of problems of special interest to the United States in its relationship to the United Nations.

FINANCES. The annual regular budgets of the United Nations and its specialized agencies total less than $200 million; voluntary contributions for special programs have been running somewhat over $200 million a year. In addition, there have been special assessments for peacekeeping in the Middle East and the Congo. The U.N. has encountered severe financial difficulties because certain members have refused to pay these assessments. The Soviet bloc refused to pay for either the Middle East or the Congo; most of the Arab states refused to pay for the Middle East; and Belgium, France, Portugal, and South Africa refused to pay for the Congo.

In July 1962, the International Court of Justice ruled that a member's failure to pay the assessed contributions for the peacekeeping operations could result in its losing the right to vote in the General Assembly under Article 19. The General Assembly accepted this ruling in December 1962. It would have applied to the Soviet Union as of January 1, 1964, if by then it had paid nothing toward the Middle East and Congo operations.

REPRESENTATION OF CHINA. Chou En-lai, the Prime Minister of Communist China, has stated the conditions which would have to be met if Communist China were to accept a seat in the United Nations:

> The United Nations must expel the Chiang Kai-shek clique and restore China's legitimate rights, otherwise it would be impossible for China to have anything to do with the United Nations.

These words mean the expulsion of a founding member, the Republic of China, and, in view of Peiping's repeated demands concerning its "legitimate rights," acquiescence in Communist China's design to conquer Taiwan and its 12 million people and thereby to overthrow and abolish the independent government of the Republic of China.

The question then is not just whether Communist China should be admitted to the United Nations but whether it should represent China. The United States believes that any decision on this matter should be governed by these realities:

1. The total suppression of all liberties on the Chinese mainland, the mass executions, and the two million Chinese refugees in Hong Kong indicate that the Chinese Communist regime does not represent in any meaningful way the 700 million people in whose name it purports to speak.

2. At the San Francisco conference in 1945 leading to the establishment of the United Nations, there was considerable discussion as to the qualifications for membership. Should all nations be automatically eligible (the principle of universality) or should membership be subject to certain qualifications? The conference decided that original members belong "by right" and that new members would have to fulfill the qualifications set forth in Article 4 of the Charter:

> 1. Membership in the United Nations is open to all other peace-loving states which accept the obligations contained in the present Charter and, in the judgment of the Organization, are able and willing to carry out these obligations.
>
> 2. The admission of any such state to membership in the United Nations will be effected by a decision of the General Assembly upon the recommendation of the Security Council.

Communist China already has a record of aggression and hostility towards its neighbors in Korea, Tibet, India, and Southeast Asia and has repeatedly announced its intention to take Taiwan by force. Chinese leaders have time and again made clear that they do not believe in "peaceful coexistence" but are dedicated to the forcible overthrow of non-Communist states. For that purpose, Communist China has maintained training centers for guerrilla warfare to train young men from Asia, Africa, and Latin America in sabotage and guerrilla tactics for eventual use in their own countries. Communist China has emphasized its reliance, as a matter of policy, on the use of force. Neither its actions nor its words qualifies Communist China as a "peace-loving" state within the meaning of the Charter. Communist China has given no indication whatsoever that admittance to the United Nations would in any way cause a change in its ways.

3. The Republic of China is a founding member of the United Nations, has performed honorable service in that

organization, and maintains effective jurisdiction over 14,000 square miles and 12 million people. Both in size and population it is larger than two-thirds of the present U.N. members.

The question of Chinese representation has been raised in various ways since 1950, not only in the major organs of the U.N., but in subsidiary bodies and specialized agencies. In October 1962 the General Assembly rejected a Soviet draft resolution to seat Communist China in place of the Republic of China by a vote of 42 in favor, 56 against, and 12 abstentions. Significantly, eight of the African countries which had abstained on this issue in 1961 voted against it in 1962. The real issue was becoming clearer—whether members of the United Nations would violate their own Charter to make room for a regime whose creed and actions were diametrically opposed to the letter and spirit of the Charter.

THE "TROIKA" PROPOSAL. The Secretary General is appointed by the General Assembly on the recommendation of the Security Council. Seven council members, including the five permanent members, must agree on the recommendation. The powers and responsibilities of the Secretary General have been expanded over the years; for example, the broad mandates given him by the General Assembly at the time of the Suez crisis in 1956 and by both the Security Council and the Assembly in the Congo situation in 1960. This development became increasingly unpleasant to the Soviets when they found that Secretary General Hammarskjold's Congo policy was not in accordance with their wishes. The only way they saw to block it was to destroy the effectiveness of the office. Accordingly, Soviet Premier Khrushchev, on September 23, 1960, at the Fifteenth General Assembly, proposed that the office of Secretary General be abolished and replaced by three men, a "troika" named after the Russian sleigh pulled by three horses, representing "the military bloc of the Western powers, socialist states, and neutralist countries." The three men would have to be in agreement before any decision could be taken. Khrushchev's purpose, of course, was to make it impossible for the executive machinery to take any action of which the Soviets did not approve. The Soviets at the same time announced their decision to have no further dealings with Mr. Hammarskjold.

The "troika" proposal received little support from countries other than the Soviet bloc, and presumably would have remained dormant until Mr. Hammarskjold's term of office expired on April 10, 1963, and the question arose of selecting his successor. Unfortunately, that question came up much sooner than expected. Mr. Hammarskjold was killed on September 18, 1961, when his plane crashed in Northern Rhodesia. The Soviets let it be known that they would agree to no single individual as Secretary General. When they realized, however, that the U.N. members, including those from Africa and Asia, would not buy the "troika" proposal or any of its variations, they backed down. On November 3, 1961, U Thant, Burma's Representative to the United Nations, was appointed by the General Assembly as Acting Secretary General for a term of office ending April 10, 1963. U Thant informed the Assembly that he intended to include among his advisers both an American, Ralph Bunche, and a Russian, Georgy Arkadev.

U Thant's energetic and quiet way of tackling problems—the Cuban crisis, peaceful solution of the Indonesian-Dutch dispute over West New Guinea, the $200 million U.N. bond issue, and the situation in the Congo—as well as his outspoken views on nuclear testing, disarmament, and aid to the less developed countries, has won him the confidence of the members. On November 30, 1962, the General Assembly, unanimously on the unanimous recommendation of the Security Council, elected U Thant for a full five-year term starting, in response to his own desires, from his original appointment in 1961.

CONNALLY AMENDMENT. Cases come to the International Court of Justice if the nations involved in a dispute 1) agree to submit it, 2) are parties to a treaty providing for referral of disputes to the court, 3) have agreed in advance to accept the court's jurisdiction over certain questions. At the time of the drafting of the Statute of the Court there was much discussion as to whether it should have compulsory jurisdiction in all international legal disputes. As a compromise, a clause was included in the Statute of the Court giving a member state the option of stating whether it would accept compulsory jurisdiction in cases involving interpretation of a treaty, any question of international law, a breach of international obligations, and the nature of reparation to be made for such a breach.

The United States Senate accepted compulsory jurisdiction under the optional clause, but with a reservation: the United States itself would determine whether a specific dispute was or was not within its domestic jurisdiction. This self-judging reservation—known as the Connally Amendment—in effect nullified our acceptance of the court's compulsory jurisdiction. Since then a number of resolutions have been introduced seeking its repeal.

This self-judging reservation is not consistent with a meaningful acceptance of compulsory jurisdiction and greatly undermines our efforts to persuade all states to bring their disputes to the International Court. For that reason, the Department of State is in favor of repeal of the reservation. Several states which had self-judging reservations have already acted to delete them, namely the U.K., France, India, and Pakistan.

In 1946, when the Senate Foreign Relations Committee, of which Senator Connally was chairman, was considering the optional clause, the committee unanimously recommended favorable action upon a resolution supporting the principle that the court itself should decide what cases came within its jurisdiction.

WHAT DOES IT ALL ADD UP TO?

This account of the United Nations and its many subsidiary agencies and affiliated bodies illustrates the diversity and breadth of its activities. Nearly every problem with any international implications, whether it be an attack by one state against another or the outbreak of a flu epidemic in the Far East, comes to the attention of the United Nations. And it's a good thing. The world is so closely tied together that it is essential to have some place where matters of interest to many countries can be discussed and action taken under a Charter which reflects our concept of the rule of law.

We must be realistic as to what the United Nations can do and what it can't do. It can certainly cope with nonpolitical problems such as health and welfare, when the question is one of working out a solution to a mutual problem and all interested nations want a solution. It can be helpful in mediating and serving as a "third man" when the parties are willing. It cannot resolve disputes between the major powers, for example, regarding Berlin, when lack of a common aim provides scant common ground for negotiation. Yet ventilating problems before other nations helps to shape public opinion throughout the world. "A decent respect to the opinions of mankind" often exerts a moderating influence, even on the Soviet Union, as we have already seen in its change of attitude toward cooperation in outer space and in giving up the "troika."

This function of talking without arriving at a conclusion has led to the charge that the United Nations is only a debating society. This same charge has frequently been made against our own Congress and overlooks the fact that congressional debates are one of the best means we have of informing the public of the issues of a particular proposal. The same is true in the United Nations, only the audience is far larger.

A by-product has been the liberal education given some of the diplomats of the new nations in democratic practice and parliamentary procedures as well as in the attitudes and objectives of other members. After listening to the discussion of the Soviet charges against the Secretary General for his conduct of the Congo operation and Khrushchev's assertion that there was no such thing as "a neutral man," they must have questioned any previously held opinions that the cold war was just a struggle between two superpowers which did not really concern the smaller nations. It should have become obvious that the United States was able to pursue its interests in the world within the framework of the U.N. Charter, whereas the Soviet Union was not.

The United Nations offers an unparalleled opportunity for private negotiation and informal, unpublicized exchanges of views between delegates. These preliminary discussions are essential when several nations cooperate in sponsoring a particular resolution and usually result in the toning down of extreme positions. It gives the United States, just as it gives every other member, an opportunity to point out our position on a particular subject and, even more important, to explain the reasons why.

The United Nations is also a place for action, and, as we have observed, this action ranges all the way from fighting malaria in Latin America to sending troops to the Middle East. The two ingredients for effective political action are a Secretary General willing and able to make and carry out decisions, and support of the Secretary General by a majority of the member states, including one or more of the major powers. In the case of the Congo, the support of the United States was crucial to the operation.

The rise in membership in the United Nations from 51 in 1945 to 112 in 1964 has certainly changed the nature of the organization and has worried some of its strongest supporters, who fear that the United States might be outvoted on a crucial issue. The new nations, it is true, now outnumber the old, and by far the largest number are in Africa. Twenty-three new nations in Africa became members of the U.N. in the period between January 1, 1960, and December 31, 1962. A look at their voting record, however, does not show that they vote as a bloc. They came closest to it on the issue of colonialism, on which they share the same deep and emotional views. The likelihood of resolutions being passed, however, that would run counter to the best interests of the United States is slim and for two reasons. The first concerns the organization of the United Nations. No measure can pass the Security Council if any of the five permanent members oppose it. In the General Assembly, a two-thirds majority vote is required to decide important questions. It is extremely unlikely that the United States would ever have difficulty in mustering the necessary blocking third on issues involving peace and security. Moreover, only the Security Council, where we have a veto, can take decisions binding on U.N. members. Except on budgetary matters, the General Assembly has authority only to recommend. The second reason has nothing to do with structure but with our own philosophy. We believe in the fundamental freedoms, and so do the new nations; so thus far we have yet to encounter a two-thirds vote against us on any question of direct and major concern to the United States. As long as our positions are sound, are reasonably responsive to the new nations' intense feelings on colonialism, and are in conformity with the principles of the Charter, we have small cause for concern.

VIII. NUCLEAR TESTING AND DISARMAMENT

Until the nuclear age the power of a major country lay primarily in its industrial capacity rather than its existing armed forces and its military equipment. Nations took time to mobilize, and wars dragged on for years. The nation, or group of nations, which could best harness its industrial power to the war effort was generally the victor. Although the attack on our fleet at Pearl Harbor was a serious blow, it destroyed only weapons at hand and did not impair our capacity and our ability to produce replacements.

Technology since World War II has changed the whole nature of war. In an age of missiles with nuclear warheads, what now counts is not a nation's capacity to mobilize its industrial might but the number and effectiveness of the weapons it has on hand. We have thus equated our feeling of security with our estimate of whether or not our supply of nuclear weapons was bigger and more powerful than that of the Soviet Union. The drive for more armaments has been to maintain a position of comparative strength. An arms race, however, in addition to being a voracious consumer of money and scientific manpower, heightens each contender's concern for his own security and may make tempting the idea of a "preventative" nuclear attack. As more and more nations develop nuclear military adaptability, as they are bound to do unless appropriate arms control and disarmament measures are adopted, more and more fingers, including probably some irresponsible ones, will be able to pull the trigger. For these reasons the United States has believed that arms limitation and reduction would make for a safer world. To that end, we have been willing to continue tedious and frequently frustrating conversations with the Russians on this subject.

Although attempts were made after World War I to control armaments, they did not have behind them any great sense of urgency. That came with the nuclear age. In 1945 only three nations—Canada, the United Kingdom, and the United States—possessed the knowledge essential to the use of atomic energy, and only the United States possessed the bomb. We realized the inevitability of the spread of atomic knowledge and the resultant danger to the world, and we concluded that the safest thing to do was to place it under international control.

A resolution of the United Nations General Assembly in January 1946 established a Commission on Atomic Energy and charged it with making specific proposals for the exchange of scientific information for peaceful ends, the control of atomic energy to the extent necessary to insure its use only for peaceful purposes, the elimination of atomic weapons, and effective safeguards such as inspection. Bernard Baruch, our representative to the Commission, in June 1946 presented our proposals—based on the report of a group (the Acheson-Lilienthal Committee) appointed by President Truman early in January. The premise underlying our proposals was that international inspection of national atomic activities was not of itself sufficient to safeguard the security of individual nations. Therefore, we suggested the creation of an international authority which would own all the raw materials, carry on the "dangerous" operations, and would license and inspect the "nondangerous" operations (peaceful uses) which would be in national hands. The United States offered to turn over its technical know-how to this authority. After the system of international ownership and control had come into effect, existing bombs were to be destroyed and no further bombs were to be made.

The Soviet Union proposed that nations should continue to own explosive atomic materials and to own, operate, and manage facilities for using these materials, and that control should be limited to international inspection of facilities, the existence of which the government concerned would report to the international authority. Although the General Assembly in 1948 overwhelmingly approved the American plan, the Soviet Union remained adamantly opposed.

In September 1949 the Soviet Union exploded its first bomb. The United Kingdom exploded its first atomic device in October 1952; France exploded its first in February 1960. Canada did not attempt to develop a bomb.

Competition in the field of atomic weaponry has been a major element of the cold war. The participants, however, have realized that this competition could lead to disaster. They accordingly have held, within the U.N. framework, numerous discussions on arms reduction and on the related question of the cessation of nuclear testing. Although we have the advantage in nuclear weapons, the Soviets have greater conventional land forces. Obviously, neither side has been willing to accept proposals that might put it at a comparative disadvantage.

The testing of nuclear devices is essential to the development of weapons. Therefore, a first step toward placing some control over the nuclear threat in particular and the arms race in general was a ban on nuclear testing.

NEGOTIATIONS ON NUCLEAR TESTING

The world became seriously concerned with the problem of fallout in 1954, following extensive nuclear tests in the atmosphere by both the Soviet Union and the United States. National leaders and U.N. resolutions urged that the nuclear powers—the Soviet Union, the United Kingdom, and the United States—cease testing. Although both the Soviet Union and the West made several proposals to this effect, the conditions attached to them and mutual distrust prevented any real progress toward agreement.

In March 1958, after completing a series of tests, the Soviet Union announced that it would cease testing so long as other nations did likewise. Since the United States was about to begin an announced series of tests, we considered the Soviet offer as a move to embarrass the United States before a world public opinion which was becoming increasingly worried about nuclear fallout. In April 1958 President Eisenhower, in a letter to Chairman Khrushchev, stated that, since the Soviet Union had rejected the American proposal to end weapons production and reduce stockpiles, the United States would continue to test for defensive purposes. The President proposed, however, that joint technical studies be undertaken on the problems involved in supervising and controlling agreements on the suspension of testing and other disarmament measures. Chairman Khrushchev accepted the proposal to consider the technical problems of a nuclear test ban. Subsequently, a meeting was held in Geneva that summer. Communist bloc and Western scientists agreed that it was technically feasible to set up a detection system to monitor a test ban and recommended a global network of control posts for this purpose.

The Soviet Union, the United Kingdom, and the United States agreed then to enter into negotiations for the suspension of nuclear weapons tests. To facilitate these discussions, the U.K. and the U.S. offered to stop testing for one year and did so by the opening of negotiations on October 31. Although the Soviet Union did not take up the offer, it ceased testing in early November. Thus a nuclear test ban did come into effect, not by agreement, but by self-imposed actions of the nuclear powers. This so-called "moratorium" on testing would last just as long as any one of the three wished to make it last.

For nearly five years the Soviet Union, the United Kingdom, and the United States discussed the cessation of nuclear testing. There have been three principal forums:

1. The Conference on the Discontinuance of Nuclear Weapons Tests opened in Geneva on October 31, 1958, and continued, with some interruptions, until January 29, 1962;
2. A subcommittee under the aegis of the 18-Nation Disarmament Conference opened in Geneva on March 14, 1962;
3. The meeting of representatives of the three governments in Moscow, from July 15 to 25, 1963, resulted in agreement on a limited test ban treaty.

As negotiations got under way in October 1958, the objective of the three parties was a total ban on all nuclear tests in the four testing environments—the atmosphere, outer space, underwater, and underground. Any agreement was to be policed by an effective control system based on the recommendations made earlier at the East-West experts' meeting. Yet, the difficulties in the path of reaching a comprehensive agreement became quickly apparent—particularly the Soviet Union's evident reluctance to accept adequate verification of a total ban.

On April 13, 1959, after the conference had spent months in inconclusive debate on the subject of inspection and control, President Eisenhower and Prime Minister Macmillan proposed a ban on tests in the atmosphere up to an altitude of 50 kilometers. This proposal (which did not require on-site inspection because atmospheric explosions could be detected by national detections systems) was the first effort by the U.K. and the U.S. to reach an agreement that would provide half a loaf when the whole loaf seemed unattainable. Chairman Khrushchev, however, rejected the proposal because it "does not solve the problem" of a complete prohibition of all nuclear testing.

So negotiations continued on a comprehensive ban. Although progress was made in hammering out many articles of a treaty which would end all testing, the inspection issue continued to bar the way to any final agreement.

Then, on August 30, 1961, the Soviet Union announced its decision to resume testing, alleging that an increasingly aggressive policy on the part of the U.S. and its NATO allies made this action necessary. Two days later the Soviet Union set off the first nuclear device in an intensive series of tests. On September 3, President Kennedy and Prime Minister Macmillan, disappointed at the Soviet action, urged Chairman Khrushchev to agree immediately "not to conduct nuclear tests which take place in the atmosphere and produce radioactive fallout." They asserted that existing means of detection would be sufficient to detect atmospheric tests and would not require an international control system. Six days later the Soviet Union rejected this plea. Chairman Khrushchev made it clear that the Soviet Union would not agree to a moratorium on nuclear tests until general and complete disarmament had been achieved and France had stopped testing. On September 15 the United States exploded the first nuclear device in a new underground test series.

At the end of three years of talks we had not reached any agreement. During this time, however, the U.S. learned a great deal about both technical and political matters.

On the technical side, we undertook a vast research program aimed at improving the detection and identification of nuclear tests. We hoped that this program, called Project Vela, would lead to a simplified policing system. We learned that scientific developments would permit existing detection systems lying outside the Soviet Union to determine whether tests were made in the atmosphere, space, or underwater. For example, atmospheric testing can be checked by positive identification of radioactive dust or cloud samples which drift beyond the borders of the area in which the test was made.

Underground testing presents a more difficult problem. While underground disturbances can be detected by a network of stations outside the U.S.S.R., not all of these disturbances can be identified either as earthquakes or nuclear explosions. Both set off shock waves which can be picked up on seismographs, the same instruments used to measure the intensity of earthquakes. By coordinating the readings of a number of seismographs in various places, we can determine the approximate center of the source of the shock waves. If the center is a populated area, we can conclude that the shock waves quite likely resulted from an earthquake. On the other hand, the center of the shock waves may be an area in which it would be feasible to set off an underground nuclear explosion. Although we have made progress in our ability to discriminate between earth tremors resulting from explosions and those resulting from earthquakes, the only way to check on certain disturbances of a suspicious nature is to conduct on-site inspections. A group of inspectors must go to the location of the blast as revealed by the seismographs. Inspection might require drilling into the ground for samples of earth and rock and then examining the samples to see if they are radioactive.

Technical discussions bogged down on the need for on-site inspection and the procedures for carrying it out. The Soviets maintained that on-site inspection was unnecessary and blocked the setting up of any effective system for policing underground tests.

From a political point of view, it did not seem that the Soviets really wanted an effective ban, but merely one which they could use to carry out clandestine underground tests while the U.K. and the U.S. were not testing. Doubts about the Soviet Union's intentions were further increased when we proposed, and the Soviet Union rejected, the idea of a partial ban without provision for international verification machinery.

By the beginning of 1962, prospects for a test ban were dim. Both sides had been conducting nuclear tests, and the Soviet Union took the position that the issue could no longer be considered separately from the whole question of disarmament. So, the three-power discussions recessed, and the matter was turned over to the same three powers in a subcommittee of the recently established 18-Nation Disarmament Committee, which began its deliberations in March 1962 in Geneva.

Although the situation had not changed, in August the U.K. and the U.S. submitted two draft treaties. The first banned nuclear weapons tests in all environments and called for a limited number of on-site inspections. The second banned tests in the atmosphere, in outer space, and underwater and left inspection up to each of the parties concerned. In October 1962 Ambassador Arthur Dean, our chief negotiator at the Geneva talks, said: [1]

> The Soviet Government is apparently determined at this time to continue nuclear testing or else it is unwilling or unable to accept a test ban for some political reason which the Soviet leaders do not wish to divulge.
>
> Mr. Chairman, there is no solid reason apparently in anything that Soviet spokesmen have said to explain why this whole past year has been frittered away without substantial progress in negotiating a comprehensive test ban treaty.

In December 1962 Chairman Khrushchev wrote President Kennedy that, although the Soviet Union considered national means sufficient to detect all tests, it would, in order to make agreement possible, allow two or three on-site inspections in the Soviet Union. President Kennedy, while welcoming the Soviet change of position, declared that the United States considered that a larger number of inspections, perhaps eight to ten, was necessary to safeguard against secret underground testing. Through the first months of 1963 Soviet, U.K., and U.S. representatives met in Washington, New York, and Geneva to bridge the difference between the three on-site inspections the Soviets were willing to accept and our eventual figure of seven. These efforts ended in a stalemate.

On June 10, 1963, in a speech at The American University in Washington, D.C., President Kennedy proposed a reexamination of our attitude toward the cold war, in which the United States and the Soviet Union "are both caught up in a vicious and dangerous cycle in which suspicion on one side breeds suspicion on the other and new weapons beget counterweapons." He then made two important announcements bearing on the test ban:

1. Chairman Khrushchev, Prime Minister Macmillan, and the President had agreed that high-level discussions would begin shortly in Moscow, looking toward early agreement on a test ban treaty.

2. To demonstrate good faith, the President pledged that the United States would not conduct nuclear tests in the atmosphere so long as other states did not do so.

The proposed discussions in Moscow took on added impor-

[1] Statement made to Committee I (Political and Security) of the U. N. General Assembly, 26 October 1962. From *The Department of State Bulletin* (Washington, D. C.: U. S. Government Printing Office, 26 November 1962).

tance on July 2 when Chairman Khrushchev, in a speech in East Berlin, stated that the Soviet Government was willing to conclude an agreement banning nuclear tests in the atmosphere, in outer space, and underwater. He made it clear that agreement on a total ban was unlikely, saying: [2]

> We have long realized that the Western powers need international inspection, not to control the discontinuance of tests, but to penetrate by any means various regions of the Soviet Union for intelligence purposes. Thus, it is not an issue of control over the discontinuance of tests, but essentially the legalization of espionage.

We can only guess at the motives of the Soviet Union in finally expressing a readiness to consider a limited test ban treaty. Testing nuclear weapons and trying to keep up with the United States in the arms race was becoming increasingly costly, perhaps prohibitively so, and was diverting funds badly needed in other sectors of the Soviet economy. Failure in food production indicated that the Soviet Union might even have to buy grain from abroad; the only sources were the capitalist countries. The rift between the Soviet Union and Communist China was becoming wider, and one of the main points at issue was Khrushchev's pursuit of the policy of peaceful coexistence with the West. Yet the confrontation with the United States over Cuba showed how frighteningly easy it was to come to the brink of nuclear warfare. All these factors, and Khrushchev's awareness that the alternative to peaceful coexistence was mutual disaster, undoubtedly influenced the Soviet decision.

THE LIMITED NUCLEAR TEST BAN TREATY. In mid-summer 1963 talks began in Moscow. Representatives of the Soviet Union, the United Kingdom, and the United States initialed a treaty banning tests in the atmosphere, in outer space, and underwater. The treaty bans only those tests which we ourselves can police. Underground explosions are permitted as long as the radioactive debris remains within the country where the explosions took place. Each party undertakes not to encourage or participate in any tests elsewhere which, under the terms of the treaty, it could not undertake in its own territory. Any party may propose amendments, but no amendment can take effect unless approved by a majority of

[2] *The Washington Post,* 3 July 1963.

all parties to the treaty, including the original three. The treaty is open to all states for signature. It enters into force after its ratification by the original parties and the deposit of their instruments of ratification. Any party can withdraw from the treaty, upon three months' notice, if it decides that extraordinary events have jeopardized its supreme interests.

After the treaty was signed in Moscow on August 5 by the three foreign ministers, the U.S. Senate held extensive hearings on it and on September 24 gave its concurrence by a vote of 80 to 19. After signature by the President and ratification by the Soviet Union and the United Kingdom, the treaty came into effect as of October 10, 1963. As of that date, over one hundred other countries had signed. Notable among those not subscribing were Communist China, Cuba, and France.

The advantages of the treaty may be summarized as follows:

1. It will virtually eliminate the radioactive pollution of our atmosphere from nuclear tests.

2. It will inhibit the spread of nuclear weapons. The more countries that have them, the greater the danger of a nuclear war. Most of the countries with the capacity and incentive to develop nuclear weapons over the next ten years signed the treaty. Permitting only underground tests makes more difficult and expensive the development of nuclear weapons. France has tested atomic devices and is already a nuclear power. Communist China has not yet tested a nuclear device. Although neither signed the treaty, any atmospheric tests they might conduct would almost certainly bring down upon them universal public disapproval.

3. Although the treaty is not in itself a disarmament measure, by limiting nuclear weapons testing it will slow down the frantic pace of the arms race.

4. The preamble to the treaty expresses the determination of the original signers to continue their efforts to end all test explosions. The treaty can serve as a first step toward greater cooperation between the Soviet Union and the West and thereby open up avenues to arms limitation and reduction.

5. The treaty will tend to maintain our generally acknowledged lead in nuclear weapons for a longer period than under conditions of unrestricted testing.

DISARMAMENT NEGOTIATIONS

While efforts were being made to stop nuclear tests, a number of proposals were also advanced to halt other facets of the arms race. In 1953 President Eisenhower made his "atoms for peace" proposal to the United Nations General Assembly. The nuclear powers were to turn over supplies of nuclear materials to an international agency which would use this material for peaceful purposes. In 1957 the International Atomic Energy Agency was set up for this purpose. President Eisenhower made another proposal in 1955 to the heads of government meeting in Geneva. His "open skies" plan, designed to reduce mutual fear between the United States and the Soviet Union, proposed that the two countries exchange blueprints of their military establishments and permit aerial inspections of each other's territory. The Russians did not show enthusiasm for either of these ideas. Although they reluctantly joined the International Atomic Energy Agency, they eventually turned down the mutual inspection plan.

Although during the decade of the fifties disarmament was discussed by the heads of government, the foreign ministers, the U.N. General Assembly, various committees of the U.N., and Western and Communist bloc scientists, no agreement was reached. In 1961 a thorough review of the disarmament question undertaken by the Kennedy administration resulted in two major steps. The first was to consolidate our activities in the disarmament field. Congress passed legislation creating the U.S. Arms Control and Disarmament Agency, the first of its kind to be created by any government, and gave it the specific responsibility of developing new approaches to disarmament.

The second step was to discuss with the Russians a resumption of general disarmament negotiations which had collapsed in 1960 when the Communist bloc nations walked out of the 10-Nation Disarmament Conference. The two countries were able to agree on a statement of principles designed to serve as a guide for future negotiations. Since they represent apparent common ground and were unanimously adopted as a United Nations resolution on December 10, 1961, they are worth examining:

1. ". . . establishment of reliable procedures for the peaceful settlement of disputes . . . (and) to strengthen institutions for maintaining peace."
2. ". . . agreed manpower for a United Nations peace force . . . (to) deter or suppress any threat or use of arms in violation of the purposes and principles of the United Nations."
3. ". . . disarmament . . . in an agreed sequence, by stages . . . (and) balanced so that at no stage . . . could any State . . . gain military advantage."
4. ". . . strict and effective international control . . . (to) provide firm assurance that all parties are honoring their obligations . . . the nature and extent of such control depending on the requirements for verification . . . in each stage."
5. ". . . an International Disarmament Organization . . . assured (of) unrestricted access without veto to all places as necessary for the purpose of effective verification."

The U.S.S.R did not accept the U.S. position that verification procedures should apply not only to forces disbanded or destroyed but also to the agreed levels of retained forces and armaments.

By the middle of December 1961 the U.S. and the U.S.S.R. were able to announce their agreement on the composition of a new disarmament negotiating forum. In addition to the five Communist countries and the five Western countries which had discussed the question in 1960, eight new nations were named to represent the major geographic areas of the world—Brazil, Burma, Ethiopia, India, Mexico, Nigeria, Sweden, and the United Arab Republic.

The 18-Nation Disarmament Committee began its work in March 1962 with only seventeen nations represented. France decided not to participate; its absence was marked by an empty chair. The objectives of the conference were two-fold: to fill in the outline of a treaty for complete and general disarmament and, without awaiting agreement on this task, to seek specific agreements which could be put into effect without delay.

In response to the first objective, both the United States and the Soviet Union presented detailed plans. The United States plan was entitled "Outline of Basic Provisions of a Treaty on General and Complete Disarmament in a Peaceful World" and that of the Soviet Union "Treaty on General and Complete Disarmament Under Strict International Control." Although both documents propose a three-stage program for the reduction and eventual elimination of national military establishment, they vary considerably in their approach to this objective.

The U.S. program is designed to permit the nations of the world to stop the arms race at an agreed time, to freeze the military situation as it then appears, and then to shrink military establishments to zero. All armaments and armed forces would be cut by approximately one-third of the initial size in each of the program's stages in order to keep the relative military positions of the parties as closely as possible to what they were at the beginning. At the same time peacekeeping machinery would be developed to make sure that, as national arms are scaled down and eventually eliminated, international peace and security will be fully and fairly safeguarded.

The Soviet Union's program places its emphasis on reducing selected categories of armaments, claiming that the threat or danger of nuclear war is directly linked to their possession. In the first stage, it seeks the elimination of the means of delivering nuclear weapons, and in the second stage, the total elimination of nuclear weapons. Reduction of other arms and armed forces is to take place during each of the three stages to assure their total elimination by the end of stage three. The Soviet plan also advocates reliance upon a strengthened United Nations to keep the peace during and after the disarmament process.

Efforts to develop a compromise program for general and complete disarmament have borne little fruit. Although the U.S. and the U.S.S.R. have made some slight modifications in the plans they introduced, their approaches from diametrically opposed points of view have yet to find common ground.

As it became clear that little headway was being made by concentrating on the ways and means of achieving total disarmament, emphasis was increasingly placed on the second objective—finding one or several measures on which agreement could be reached and which might have some effect on lessening the risk of war by accident, miscalculation, or surprise attack. This shift in emphasis has led to the establishment of a direct communication line between the White House and the Kremlin for use in times of crisis and a resolution adopted unanimously by the U.N. General Assembly in October 1963 calling upon all nations to refrain from placing nuclear weapons in orbit or stationing them in space or on any celestial body.

The pace of disarmament depends primarily upon the state of relations between the two nuclear giants—the Soviet Union and the United States. Both are aware of the awesome responsibility of possessing the means to destroy each other, and both are aware that the surest way of preventing World War III is to agree on some form of disarmament.

IX. THE SATELLITE STATES, YUGOSLAVIA, AND GERMANY

The preceding five chapters have examined the five major elements of our foreign policy. The remaining seven chapters concern the implementation of our policy in various areas of the world.

Of crucial interest to the Soviet Union is the area bordering its frontiers on the west. From this direction have come the invasions of Russian territory, notably Napoleon's march to Moscow and Hitler's thrust as far as Stalingrad. The Soviet Union is determined to have on this border, and as far west as possible, only friendly states, preferably Communist satellites. Our policies toward Central and Eastern Europe are of strategic concern to the Soviet Union, which views them in much the same light as we regard Soviet activities in the Caribbean.

THE SATELLITE STATES—POLAND IN PARTICULAR

What should be our policy toward the satellite countries? Should we assume that all persons behind the Iron Curtain are Communists, that all Communists are the same, and that the Soviet bloc has no internal differences and strains? Should we confine our activities to talk of eventual liberation and resolutions deploring the fate of captive nations? Should we cut off trade and other contact with them and thus reinforce their isolation from the free world? Our policy under all four postwar administrations has followed the idea that any breaks in the cohesiveness of the bloc would be to our interest and that the best way to encourage dissidence was to demonstrate to the people of these countries that there was an alternative to the Soviet system. This has meant keeping avenues of communication open and encouraging the exchange of goods and persons.

We too often assume that conditions in all satellite nations are the same and that they are all completely subservient to the Kremlin. This is not the case. Although a revolt in a satellite country would be quickly crushed by Russian arms, as happened in Hungary, each state has considerable latitude in its own internal affairs. A traveler visiting Prague and then Warsaw can see these differences immediately.

Poland in particular enjoys a measure of autonomy which, while limited, is nevertheless unique within the bloc. The people still retain strong national sentiments, a basic antagonism toward Russian domination, and an orientation toward Western civilization. Only a small part of the agricultural land has been collectivized. The rest is still in the hands of individual peasant farmers. In Warsaw, one can buy Western newspapers and magazines. Writers and artists have far greater freedom of expression than elsewhere behind the Iron Curtain. Western diplomats and travelers in Poland find that the people are not afraid of talking to them and are remarkably outspoken in expressing their opinions.

United States policy has been not to slam the door in the face of these expressions of an independent position. To the contrary, we have tried to encourage closer relations with the West. For that reason, we have sold surplus agricultural commodities to Poland. From 1947 through February 1, 1963, the total was $477.3 million. More than $61 million in credits have also been extended through the Export-Import Bank for the purchase of equipment and materials, agricultural commodities, and poliomyelitis vaccine. The United States has been able to arrange visits of American scholars and artists and other representative persons and groups and to provide exhibits and films which help the Polish people to understand our policies on world problems, our national aims, and the realities of life in the United States.

Obviously, the effects of these activities will only be noticeable over a long period of time. Unfortunately, an amendment incorporated into the Trade Development Act of 1962 which deprives both Poland and Yugoslavia of tariff treatment under the most favored nation clause had a negative effect. Although Polish exports to this country are less than $50 million a year, payment of higher customs duties will cut down on the amounts they will be able to sell to us and, in return, buy from us. When citizen action groups bring pressure on American stores not to sell merchandise originating in Communist countries, thereby greatly cutting down the sale of Polish hams in the United States, our objectives are not promoted. If the government is to be able to take advantage of ferment within the satellite countries, it must have room to maneuver. Actions which close the door to closer relations with the satellites can only limit their freedom of choice. As President Kennedy pointed out on October 14, 1962, in a speech in Buffalo: [1]

> We need more flexibility in our economic arsenal. Too often our hands are tied by a rigid statutory perspective of the Communist world. Everything is seen in terms of black and white. Nations are either for us or against us—either completely under Soviet domination or completely free. But this is not the case.
>
> There are varying shades, even within the Communist world. We must be able to seize the initiative when the opportunity arises, in Poland in particular and in other countries as time goes on behind the Iron Curtain.

YUGOSLAVIA

Only one country has shaken loose from the Soviet bloc and gotten away with it—Yugoslavia, in the summer of 1948. It was not that Marshal Tito ceased to believe in Communism. Far from it. He did insist, however, that Yugoslavia should be allowed to develop in its own way, free from the dictates of the Kremlin. He would not accept the Stalinist concept that communism could have only one voice. 1948 was the year of the Berlin blockade: a succession of Communist victories in the civil war in China; intense activities of Communist insurgents in the Philippines and Malaya; the Communist take-over in Czechoslovakia; and a bitter civil war in Greece, with Yugoslavia serving as one of the principal bases of operations for the Greek Communist forces. President Truman saw this break as an opportunity and decided to proceed cautiously to encourage and assist. In the summer of 1949 Tito closed the frontier to the dissidents in Greece, an action which contributed to the end of the civil war a few months later. In 1954 he reached agreement with Italy on the status of Trieste. Yugoslavia's independent course also led the way for Albania's defiance of Moscow, which was to become one of the main points of friction between Moscow and Peiping.

[1] *The New York Times,* 15 October 1962.

There is no doubt that Yugoslavia is a Communist state and that Tito is a dictator. Communism in Yugoslavia, however, has developed in a way far different from that in the Soviet Union. A halt was called to collectivization of farms, and the economy made room for considerable individual enterprise. The economy is a mixture of planning and the free market. The clothes the people wear and the number of private automobiles is evidence of a higher standard of living than in other countries of Eastern Europe. Nevertheless, the country is still not able to feed itself and is running a substantial deficit in its balance of payments. Less than 25 per cent of its trade is with the Communist bloc. The balance is with the West. Engineers, technicians, and managers are receiving their training in the West.

Western aid, of which the United States has contributed over $2 billion, enabled Tito to pursue a course independent from Moscow, but did not insure that the position he took in international affairs would necessarily follow that of the West. Although Yugoslavia voted in the U.N. against the Soviet troika proposal, on many other issues it has voted with the Communist bloc, as have the neutralist countries, and frequently it has seemed that Tito was trying to line up the nonaligned nations to support Soviet policies.

Nevertheless, this independent course has been a bone in the throat of the Kremlin. Yugoslavia is not a member of the Warsaw Pact. Since 1948 it has been supplied with arms by the West, and it is consequently dependent upon the United States for spare parts for its airplanes.

Since the break in 1948, there have been recurrent attempts at a rapprochement between Moscow and Belgrade. Relations between the two capitals were closer in 1963 than they had been for fourteen years, principally because the Kremlin recognized that only through persuasion could Tito be brought into closer alliance with the bloc.

Four U.S. administrations have followed the policy of aiding Yugoslavia, although not without some misgivings and increasing opposition from Congress and the public. This has been evidenced by protests against the sale to Yugoslavia of outmoded jets and against the training in the U.S. of Yugoslav pilots, the proposed boycott by the International Longshoremen's Union of Yugoslav ships, organized boycotts against purchase of Yugoslav products, the narrow margin by which an amendment that would have barred aid to Yugoslavia was defeated in Congress, and, finally, the provision in the Trade Expansion Act denying most favored nation treatment to Poland and Yugoslavia.

To the Yugoslavs, therefore, our policies have seemed far from consistent. On the one hand we were extending aid, while on the other, we were treating it as a member of the Communist bloc and putting obstacles in the way of its exports to the United States. Our basic objectives at times have been lost sight of in the controversy over methods used to carry them out. Supplying military equipment and training personnel may have been just as alarming to Moscow as the supplying of Soviet equipment to Cuba appeared to Washington.

From 1961 on, United States aid to Yugoslavia has been greatly reduced and now consists principally of surplus agricultural products. The Administration is keeping its policy toward Yugoslavia under constant review. It realizes aid cannot change ideologies but can make possible an independent course of action. Yugoslavia is a constant reminder to the satellites and to the neutralists that there is a freedom of choice.

BERLIN AND GERMANY

On May 7 and 8, 1945, the German High Command surrendered all forces under its control "unconditionally to the Supreme Commander, Allied Expeditionary Forces, and simultaneously to the Supreme High Command of the Red Army." Eighteen years later, although the Allies had terminated the state of war, there was still no peace treaty with Germany. In practice, there was not one Germany; there were two; and there was not just one Berlin, but two.

The Federal Republic of Germany, better known as West Germany, is a thriving, prosperous nation of fifty-three million people enjoying one of the highest standards of living in Europe. It is a member of NATO, of the European Economic Community, and of many other international organizations, except for the U.N., which tie free nations together. Its people have full political freedom and elect their representatives to parliament.

The so-called "German Democratic Republic," better known as East Germany, with a population of 16 million, enjoys the distinction of being perhaps the only country in the world with a declining population. Over three million East Germans "voted with their feet" by fleeing to the West.

The government was put into power not by public vote but by the Soviet Union. Twenty-two Soviet divisions in East Germany put down the revolt in 1953 and keep the government in power.

Whereas a barbed wire fence divides Germany, a wall divides Berlin, an enclave 110 miles within the Soviet zone. In West Berlin, comprising the American, British and French sectors, live 2.25 million people. Allied military forces in Berlin total only 11,000, of which 6,500 are American. West Berlin is the largest industrial center between Paris and Moscow. Every day 30,000 tons of food, raw materials, and articles are brought in, and every day 4,000 tons of industrial machinery, light bulbs, cigarettes, textiles, shoes, and other articles manufactured in the city are shipped out to West Germany. The traffic is handled by 13 freight and 12 passenger trains each day, trucks on the access highways, and 700 barges a month from West Germany. In 1961, 723,000 people arrived and 871,000 departed by air. Since the end of the Soviet blockade in 1949, the production of West Berlin has risen sixfold. Two hundred thousand West Berlin citizens own their own automobiles.

East Berlin, the Soviet sector, has 1.1 million people and is utilized by the Soviet puppet regime as the capital of East Germany. Nowhere in the world is the contrast between two regimes more sharply defined. Food is still rationed in East Berlin, and consumer articles are scarce. There is little new construction and none of the gaiety and vibrancy of the other part of the city, just over the wall.

A divided Germany and a divided Berlin exist today because the U.S.S.R. has refused to make any sort of arrangement with France, the U.K., and the U.S. which would make possible a peace treaty with representatives of all the German people selected in free elections or by some other means of real self-determination. The Soviets are unwilling to permit elections, because they know they would lose. A reunified Germany would push the Iron Curtain 200 miles farther to the east.

The division of Germany and Berlin goes back to wartime arrangements made by the Allies—the United Kingdom, the United States, and the U.S.S.R. In 1944, before any of the Allied troops reached Germany, an agreement was made to divide the country into three zones of occupation and, since Berlin would be within the Soviet zone, to provide for the occupation of the capital by all three powers and to divide it into three sectors. At the Yalta Conference (February 4–11, 1945) it was decided that France should have a zone of occupation and be admitted to the Allied Control Council. No specific provisions were made for access to Berlin, although this was implicit in the right of the occupying powers to be there. At the Potsdam Conference (July 7 to August 2, 1945) the heads of state agreed that local government in Germany was to be developed immediately on democratic principles and that Germany was to be treated as a single economic unit.

Because of the fortunes of war, American troops were able to sweep into central Germany much faster than had been anticipated, and by the time of the German surrender occupied about half the area making up the Soviet zone. Meanwhile, the Soviet troops had reached Berlin first and occupied the city. In accordance with an exchange of letters between Truman and Stalin, American troops withdrew from the Soviet zone and occupied the American sector of Berlin on July 1. During their ten weeks of sole occupation of Berlin, the Soviets systematically removed most of the still usable machinery, buses, subway trains, and telephone exchanges.

The next three years saw a steady deterioration in the German economy and a worsening of relations between the Western Allies and the Soviet Union. No agreement could be reached on treating Germany as an economic unit; the Russians would not consent to free movement of people and goods among the zones and currency reform. On March 6, 1948, when it became obvious that the Soviets did not share our objectives for Germany, the U.K. and the U.S., joined later by France, agreed to fuse their zones and on June 18 replaced the Reichsmark by a new currency, the Deutschmark. The Soviets walked out of the Allied Control Council for Germany (March 20, 1948), and the Kommandatura, the four-power governing body for Berlin (June 16, 1948), and imposed road and rail restrictions on Allied traffic to Berlin. The Soviets introduced a new currency into their zone and sector, and the Allies then introduced the Deutschmark into West Berlin. Communist riots took place in front of City Hall on June 23, 1948. The following day the complete blockade of Berlin began. In November the Soviets formally split the city and set up a rump municipal government for East Berlin. The great majority of the representatives to the Berlin parliament, who had been elected on October 20, 1946 (when the Communists polled less than 20 per cent of the vote), moved to West Berlin.

Through eleven long months this city of 2.25 million people was supplied entirely by air, an amazing feat which the Soviets had considered impossible. On the record day 15,000 tons were brought into West Berlin and planes landed at the rate of one every 40 seconds. It was expensive, and seventy Allied airmen lost their lives in the process, but it forged a strong bond between the courageous people of West Berlin and the West. When the Soviets realized that the blockade was not going to accomplish their purpose, they agreed in May 1949 to lift it.

During the next several years, two separate German governments developed and were incorporated into the economic and military structures of the two opposing camps. In West Germany, a parliamentary council drafted a provisional constitution; in August 1949 the people voted in the first free general election since 1932; and the Federal Republic of Germany came into being. That same year, the Soviets set up a puppet regime in East Germany and declared East Berlin its capital. In 1950 the Soviet Union began arming East German forces. In May 1952 at Paris the Western powers signed contractual agreements ending the occupation status, to take effect when the Federal Republic joined the European Defense Community. The Western powers, however, retained the right to station forces in West Germany. In 1954 the Federal Republic agreed to join NATO and the Western European Union. It undertook to limit its armaments and not to manufacture atomic, biological, or chemical weapons and not to produce missiles, bombers, or large warships without two-thirds approval of the Council of the Western European Union. It placed all its armed forces under NATO—the only member of NATO to do so.

The signing of the Austrian State Treaty on May 15, 1955, gave hope to some that a similar treaty might be concluded for Germany. Several meetings of foreign ministers and the summit meeting of chiefs of state at Geneva in July 1955 failed, however, to bridge the difference between the Soviet demand that unification be accomplished through agreement between East Germany and West Germany and the West's insistence that an all-German government be chosen through free elections.

In November 1958 Chairman Khrushchev began the second Soviet assault on the freedom of Berlin. He demanded the withdrawal of Western troops, declared null and void all agreements with the West on the status of Berlin, and threatened, if agreement were not reached within six months, to sign a separate peace treaty with the East German regime and to turn over to that puppet government control of access to Berlin. The West replied that it would undertake no discussions under duress. A conference of foreign ministers was held, however, in May 1959 in Geneva. The Allies reiterated their right to be in Berlin. The right of access to Berlin stemmed from the rights acquired by the occupying powers at the conclusion of World War II, and unilateral denunciation by the Soviet Union could not alter these rights.

At Geneva the Allies proposed a peace plan for Germany in four stages, providing for free elections in Germany and the progressive scaling down of Soviet and Western military forces. The Soviets said the Western plan contained no basis for negotiation and proposed instead separate peace treaties with West Germany and East Germany, the withdrawal of Western troops from Berlin, the creation of a so-called "free city," and the withdrawal of Soviet forces from Germany, Berlin, and Hungary, if NATO powers withdrew to their national borders and dismantled bases on foreign territory. In short, the Soviet proposal would have insured the permanent division of Germany and would have made exceedingly difficult the defense of Western Europe. Removal of American bases abroad, which has been a cardinal objective of Soviet policy, would place U.S. forces at least 3,000 miles away, while Soviet forces, even if withdrawn to the borders of the Soviet Union, would be only a few hundred miles away. The conference broke up without producing any results. Khrushchev, however, in spite of his threat to sign a peace treaty with East Germany within six months, let the deadline go by without taking any action.

In September 1959 Chairman Khrushchev visited the United States. In May 1960 the U-2 incident (American reconnaissance plane shot down over the Soviet Union) gave him an excuse to call off the summit meeting scheduled that month in Paris. Khrushchev indicated that no further negotiations would take place until there was a new administration in Washington. In June 1961, President Kennedy and Chairman Khrushchev met in Vienna in an encounter which the President later characterized as somber. At this meeting, Chairman Khrushchev launched the third assault on West Berlin. President Kennedy's reaction was to ask Congress for an increase of $3.2 billion in the defense budget to make possible an increase in the strength of the armed forces and to procure more conventional weapons.

Perhaps through years of bitter experience the East Germans have developed a sensitivity to Soviet intentions. In July 1961, 30,000 East Germans fled to the West—twice the usual number. During the first twelve days of August 22,000 escaped. On August 13 the Communists sealed off their sector in Berlin and a few days later began building a wall of cement blocks along the sector boundary.

As Khrushchev himself pointed out, West Berlin was indeed a bone in his throat. Here was a living demonstration 110 miles behind the Iron Curtain of what a free society could accomplish. Thirty to fifty thousand East Germans daily visited West Berlin and could see with their own eyes the contrast between the two systems. West Berlin radio and television stations were penetrating deep into the Communist bloc. The increasing number of refugees from East Germany was draining that country of doctors, engineers, and those of most value to the East German regime. Khrushchev either had to throttle West Berlin or else face the collapse of his East German creation. Since the building of the wall, Soviet policy has been directed towards forcing the West to accept East Germany as a state. No non-Communist government has so far done so. The Soviet tactics have been to try to force recognition of East German authority. The harassments may seem petty but are important. That is why we have refused to show East German police at control points on the access routes to Berlin the credentials which we are prepared to show Soviet soldiers. Any recognition at all of the East German alleged right to control the access routes would then mean a recognition of their right to stop the traffic. Although we are prepared at any time to discuss with the Soviets ways and means of solving the German problem, we do not intend to lose by negotiation our right to remain in Berlin and have free access to it. If necessary, we will fight to maintain those rights. Unless we are prepared to risk war, we can be sure that the Communists will win the struggle not just for Berlin but for all of Europe.

X. AFRICA

Although ancestors of 10 per cent of our population came from the so-called "Dark Continent," only in recent years have most Americans begun to consider Africa in terms of its people. Before then, we thought of Africa in terms of elephants, lions, and diamonds; if we thought of people at all, it was of the explorer, the white hunter, and the colonial administrator with his seat of power in London, Paris, Brussels, or Lisbon. The forces of nationalism, however, have produced changes, the ultimate effects of which we are just now beginning to perceive. In 1951 there were only four independent states in the whole continent of Africa; in the beginning of 1964 there were thirty-five, and more are to come. With these changes has come an awareness of the diverse peoples of Africa. Men with names such as Habib Bourguiba of Tunisia, Sékou Touré of Guinea, and Julius Nyerere of Tanganyika are not only remaking Africa but are playing important roles in international events.

GEOGRAPHY AND NATURAL RESOURCES

Africa is a vast continent of 11.6 million square miles, more than enough to hold the fifty United States and leave room for India, mainland China, and all of Europe except the Soviet Union. At its greatest extent, Africa is almost as broad as it is long—4,700 miles from Dakar on the Atlantic to the Horn of Africa on the Indian Ocean and 5,000 miles from Algiers on the Mediterranean to Capetown on the south Atlantic. The largest country, the Sudan, is ten times the size of the state of Oregon. Perhaps we can best comprehend its diversity if we view the continent as these five major geographic units:

1. *Arab-Berber North Africa,* the coastal region between the Mediterranean and the Sahara;

2. *The Horn of Africa*—the high Ethiopian plateau and the hot, arid land of Somalia;

3. *Savanna Africa*—the series of sand and grasslands states running along the bottom of the Sahara;

4. *Rain-forest Africa,* which stretches from just below Dakar in Senegal to a little below the mouth of the Congo River;

5. *Highland Africa*—the chain of mountains, high plateaus, and fertile valleys starting with the highlands in northern Kenya and running south through Tanganyika, the Rhodesias, the higher parts of the Portuguese territories, and on to Capetown.

The estimated 265 million people of Africa speak almost a thousand languages or dialects, and their cultures range from stone-age to very modern. Of this total, only 2.5 per cent are of European stock. The countries range in population from Nigeria with more than 40 million people to Gabon with less than half a million. About 16 per cent of the people are Christians, 40 per cent Moslem, and 44 per cent pagan or animist.

Africa is potentially rich. It produces commercially all but four of the fifty-three most important minerals and metals and accounts for most of the world's production of industrial diamonds, three-fourths of its cobalt, one-half of its gold, one-fourth of its copper, and one-fifth of its uranium and manganese. Newly drilled wells in Libya and Algeria are already producing significant quantities of oil, and much of the rest of Africa has not even been prospected. In terms of water which could be harnessed for power, Africa is pre-eminent. It has potentially 40 per cent of the world's hydroelectric power, but has developed less than 1 per cent. Africa's economy depends essentially upon agriculture, its major exports being peanuts, cocoa, coffee, wine, palm products, and sisal.

COLONIZATION

For centuries the area south of the Sahara was unknown to Europeans. The erroneous assumption was therefore made that Africa, except for the ancient Egyptians and the Arab states of the Mediterranean coast, really had no history. Such was not the case. In the Middle Ages, for example, there were flourishing kingdoms in the Western Sudan—successively, Ghana, Mali, and Songhay. It was no accident that two modern African states, seeking continuity with the past, took the names of the first two of these ancient empires. Further south, in the present-day Rhodesias and Mozambique, the Zimbabwe culture built irrigation works and stone forts, organized states, and traded with India.

In the fifteenth century the Portuguese made successively longer voyages down the west coast until Vasco de Gama rounded the Cape of Good Hope and reached India in 1498. Merchant adventurers established posts to trade in gold, ivory, ebony, and ostrich plumes, and soon enlarged their activities to include the most valuable commodity of all—slaves. By the time the traffic ended in the nineteenth century, at least 15 million Africans had been shipped to the New World.

Not until the middle of the nineteenth century did Europeans acquire detailed knowledge of the interior of Africa. The activities of explorers, missionaries, and traders, and the treaties of commerce and protection they negotiated with tribal chiefs laid the basis for the great colonial empires. The carving out of empires was a haphazard process; the boundary lines usually ignored not only geographic but ethnic considerations. Thus the Somalis found themselves under five different jurisdictions and the Bakongos under three—Portuguese Angola, the Belgian Congo, and the French Congo. The territory inside these boundary lines was subdivided into administrative areas, as in French West Africa, and these administrative lines have become the illogical boundaries of the newly independent states.

The colonial system was the vehicle by which most Africans met the modern world. It provided common languages, economic systems, roads and transport, and health and sanitation—but all in a spotty fashion tailored to the requirements of the colonial powers rather than to the needs of the inhabitants. Many conditions in Africa today are to a large extent an outgrowth of the policies of the colonial powers. Belgium, France, Great Britain, and Portugal were the major colonial powers. Spain has a few small colonies. Germany lost its African possessions in World War I. Those held by Italy became either independent or U.N. trust territories at the close of World War II. The United States has never had any African territories.

The colonial powers were united in their belief in the superiority of the values of Western civilization, and that it was "the white man's burden" to impose these values on

Africa. The policies followed by the colonial powers, however, differed widely.

The Belgian Congo was held by a private corporation headed by King Leopold II of Belgium from 1885 until 1908. Then world-wide indignation at the shocking treatment of the Congolese prompted the Belgian government to take over control. It has been said that from that day on Belgian policy was to give the Congo an administration as different as possible from that of Leopold II. Emphasis was on economic development, but no one, not even Belgian residents in the Congo, had any say in political matters. Under this paternalistic system, the average living standards of the Congolese were higher than those elsewhere in tropical Africa. The adult literacy rate was the highest, reaching perhaps 40 per cent. Independence, however, was regarded as far off in the future. The declared goal of Belgian policy was to raise the standards of the people as a whole and not to train an elite. Consequently, when independence came far sooner than had been planned, the Congo had only a handful of university graduates and semi-trained civil servants.

French colonial policy was influenced, at least in theory, by the "Liberty, Equality, Fraternity" of the French Revolution. The French did not regard independence for the Africans as the ultimate objective, but rather their assimilation as French citizens. All the French colonies sent representatives to the parliament in Paris. Emphasis was placed on educating an elite, and outstanding students were given the opportunity to continue their education either at such outposts of French culture as Dakar, in Senegal, or in France itself.

In 1958 General de Gaulle correctly foresaw the irresistible tide of nationalism and proposed a French Community in which all the members would have autonomy in local affairs but would look for guidance to Paris in the fields of defense, foreign affairs, finance, trade, and cultural affairs. If any member wished to follow a completely independent course, then it could do so, but without further help from France. All the French colonies in Africa, with the exception of Guinea, accepted membership in the Community in 1958. France immediately withdrew both its civil servants and financial support from Guinea.

The concept of the French Community, however, came too late to supersede the force of nationalism. The French African states began to opt for complete independence, and by the end of 1960 all were sovereign nations and all were members of the U.N. except Mauretania, which was admitted in 1961. Even though these states chose independence, France has continued technical, economic, and financial support.

British colonies in Africa were scattered all over the continent. The general policy was to prepare them for self-government. Land policies, perhaps because of climate, have varied. In Ghana, Nigeria, and Uganda white persons were not allowed to own land; in Nyasaland they were permitted but not encouraged to do so. In the Rhodesias and Kenya white settlement was actively encouraged. Great Britain realized, perhaps before the other colonial powers, that independence was inevitable and tried to prepare the Africans for it by providing higher education for many with ability and by working toward the Africanization of the civil service. The Gold Coast, taking the name of Ghana, became independent in 1957, the first colony in tropical Africa to do so.

The problem area in Africa for the United Kingdom today is the colony with the largest number of white settlers —Southern Rhodesia. The stumbling block to independence has been race relations. In Southern Rhodesia the white minority in control has been unwilling to accept a government based on the consent of the majority. Although the United Kingdom undoubtedly would like to be free of this responsibility, pulling out now would mean either leaving a white supremacist government trying to maintain power through increasing use of "apartheid" methods or abandoning British subjects to a black rule they fear.

Portugal regards its colonies as overseas provinces and has been unwilling even to consider independence for Angola and Mozambique. Although the Portuguese have de-emphasized color and race in their African territories, Europeans, nevertheless, retain power and authority firmly in their hands. They regard their mission as the Christianizing and uplifting of the Africans through assimilation. According to law, any inhabitant of the territories is to be treated the equal of the European if he can demonstrate through language, religion, and economic independence that he has cut his tribal ties and thinks and acts as a Portuguese. Africans who have achieved this recognition and mulattos constitute only 1 per cent of the population of the colonies. The other 99 per cent, formerly designated "indigenas," have scant opportunity for either higher or technical education.

In 1961 a bloody revolt broke out in Angola, resulting in casualties of over one thousand Portuguese and many thousands of Africans. More than 150,000 have fled Angola to find sanctuary in the Congo. The United Nations General Assembly adopted a resolution that year calling on Portugal to acknowledge the principle of self-determination for Angola. By supporting the resolution, the United States incurred Portugal's strong displeasure and this action made much more difficult the negotiations for renewal of the air base rights in the Azores, obtained in 1951.

The Portuguese position is being challenged in its other colonies. In 1962 a united Mozambique nationalist front, formed by exiles in Tanganyika, threatened to use violence if Portugal did not grant self-determination to the people of Mozambique. Several nationalist groups are also active in Portuguese Guinea.

AFRICAN PROBLEMS AND ATTITUDES

The colonial system broke down the old order. The introduction of a money economy attracted men away from the villages to work in plantations, mines, and factories. The chiefs began to lose their authority as cities gained thousands of new inhabitants who felt themselves less and less bound by tribal ties. Those who were able to make their way in this new economy and to acquire some education became the new elite. Their roots were no longer in the past, and they could not accept a future in which they would be permanently secondary to Europeans.

There appeared to be two avenues toward equality—assimilation, in which individual worth and not race would count, or independence. Assimilation would have meant giving Africans in the French African colonies the same rights as the Frenchmen in France. For a time many of the elite of the French colonies regarded assimilation as the ultimate objective. Assimilation implied, however, the granting of equal rights to Africans only if they passed certain tests administered by Europeans. Assimilation, viewed in this context, appeared realizable so far in the future that the elite instead concentrated its energies on seeking independence.

Once the elite made independence its objective, a colonial administration's days were numbered. A foreign rule imposed by outside force could never hope for an indefinite existence, because it would never really be accepted by the inhabitants of the colony as the legitimate government. Once the majority of the people gave support to the nationalist movement, the colonial government could enlist cooperation only insofar as it demonstrated that its aim was also independence.

World War II greatly hastened the move toward independence. A number of Africans served in European armies and acquired liberal ideas. The vulnerability of some of the colonial powers was demonstrated when they were defeated and occupied by the enemy. As the inhabitants of the colonies began to withdraw their passive allegiance from the colonial administration and give their support to the nationalist movements, the only logical course for the colonial power was to come to terms with the new elite. Great Britain, which had long assumed that its colonies would ultimately be independent, and France, which came to the same conclusion some years later, worked actively to make the transition as smooth as possible. In areas where there was no white settler problem, the move to independence was reasonably smooth. The longer the period of transition, the better was the opportunity to build up a party structure which would enable the government of the newly independent country to control the administrative machinery.

Once they had come to power, the new African leaders faced the difficult problem of the attitude of their own people toward government. Accustomed to opposing the colonial government, many of them did not feel any restraint in pushing their demands. Opposition groups trying to depose the government in power ran perilously close to destroying the state in the process.

Although African states have adopted some aspects of Western democracy, their political systems show significant differences from our own in theory and in practice. A democratic system heavily emphasizes the responsibilities as well as the rights of the individual—a concept not acquired in a few short years. African practices of democracy are influenced by the environment—the indigenous institutions; the shortage of trained people; the heavy demands which, falling abruptly on the new nations, have given their leaders the feeling of operating in a state of emergency. Because of these conditions, some African leaders believe that diversion of human talents to parties in opposition to the government is a luxury that their young countries cannot yet afford and that, once a party is elected to office, continued opposition is no longer justifiable and should be submerged.

We should, therefore, not be surprised at the drift in Africa towards one-party rule and the continuation in power of the revolutionary leader. By calling on the people's loyalty to him, the leader endeavors to obtain obedience to the laws of the state.

In a recent magazine article [1] President Sékou Touré of the Republic of Guinea listed African objectives. Among them were several identical to those backed so strongly by the nations of Latin America—the equality of all nations, respect for the character and institutions of each state, and no interference in the internal affairs of one state by another. President Touré continued:

> Our greatest victory, then will not be the one we are winning over colonialism by securing independence but the victory over ourselves by freeing ourselves from the complexes of colonialism, proudly expressing Africa's authentic values and thoroughly identifying ourselves with them. Thus the African peoples will become fully conscious of their equality with other peoples.

The "complexes of colonialism," bound to linger on even after independence was won, had many of their roots in the racial discrimination which prevailed even in areas which prided themselves on policies of assimilation. The educated elite quite naturally was the most aware of discrimination —the barrier against joining the white man's club or the difficulty of the trained engineer in securing a job in which he would be in a position to give orders to Europeans. The inevitable reaction to discrimination has taken such forms as emphasis on the past glories of African states before European colonization; the edification of "negritude," the unique qualities and attributes of the Negro; and the "chip on the shoulder" attitude sometimes shown toward Europeans and Americans, who in African eyes are associated with the colonial system.

It is not surprising, therefore, that African states have placed such importance on human dignity, on the equality of nations, and on their independence of decision—even to the extent of avoiding the appearance of being influenced by outsiders and particularly those with white skins. They have no desire or intention of being involved in the cold war.

[1] Sékou Touré, "Africa's Future and the World," *Foreign Affairs,* October 1962.

They insist upon the right to make their own decisions based on their own concepts of what is best for them.

Membership in the United Nations has assumed tremendous importance for the African states. The vote of the African delegate is just as important as that of the European delegate. Indeed, as of 1963, the African states, with 32 votes (excluding that of South Africa) out of the 111 in the General Assembly, could exert considerable influence when they worked together. Their strength has been particularly important in voting on questions involving colonialism. The United Nations has played an important role in the independence movement in Africa and particularly in the birth as nations of seven former U.N. Trust Territories—Burundi, Cameroon, Libya, Ruanda, Somalia, Tanganyika, and Togo.

REGIONAL GROUPS AND PAN AFRICANISM

Disputes between states over such issues as territorial claims and alleged interference in internal affairs are not unknown in Africa. Yet stronger than divisive issues has been a feeling of shared interests which has caused various states to join together in groups to promote their mutual interests.

All of the states belong to the Economic Commission for Africa, one of the four regional organizations of the United Nations Economic and Social Council. The Economic Commission for Africa has helped survey the needs of many of its members and is working to train statisticians, teach statistical techniques, and complete a statistical survey of Africa. It is sponsoring conferences for regional cooperation in power production and the creation of an iron and steel industry, and it has been instrumental in bringing together African finance ministers to confer on the creation of an African development bank.

Kenya, Uganda, and Tanganyika have formed the East Africa Common Services Organization, which may well form the basis for a political federation of these territories and perhaps of others.

In January 1961 leaders of Ghana, Guinea, Mali, Morocco, the United Arab Republic, and the Algerian provisional government met in Casablanca, Morocco. Among the interests that drew them together were dissatisfaction with the dismissal of Patrice Lumumba as prime minister of the Congo and the reluctance of the U.N. to use force to compel the reintegration of the province of Katanga. The charter signed at Casablanca urged the immediate "liberation" of all remaining African colonial territories and expressed the intention of the parties to establish an African consultative assembly and a common military command. Out of the deliberations at Casablanca and subsequent meetings, they framed positions on Algeria, the Congo, colonialism, and the Common Market that were generally in line with those of the Communist bloc. These statements and the fact that the Casablanca countries were all receiving assistance from Communist countries aroused a good deal of uneasiness in the West. By the middle of 1963, however, most of the Casablanca states, apparently realizing the danger of too close ties with the Soviet Union, were showing much friendlier attitudes toward the West.

Eighteen of the independent states of Africa had been either French colonies or under French administration as U.N. trust territories; most of them have retained close ties with France. Three (Morocco, Algeria, and Tunisia) are on the Mediterranean; one (the Malagasy Republic) is an island in the Indian Ocean off the east coast of Africa; and the other fourteen are in west and equatorial Africa. Eleven of these fourteen (with the exceptions of Guinea and Mali, which had joined the Casablanca group, and Togo) and the Malagasy Republic felt the need to coordinate their policies. They all belonged to the French franc zone, wished to continue close economic ties with France, and were associate members of the European Economic Community. In December 1960, these twelve states met at Brazzaville and expressed their respect for each other's sovereignty and integrity and their intention to establish common policies in economic, cultural, and foreign affairs. A second meeting at Yaoundé, Cameroon, in March 1961 resulted in the formation of the African and Malagasy Union. Ruanda joined the Union in 1962, and Togo, in 1963. The Union now has a joint airline, Air Afrique, which connects Paris to most of the capitals of the participating West African states.

At further meetings held at Monrovia in May 1961 and at Lagos in January 1962 the original twelve were joined by seven other African states. Agreement was reached to create, by easy stages, a series of regional customs unions, to coordinate campaigns against major human and animal diseases, to provide for pooling of medical and hospital facilities, and to lower the language barriers by encouraging the teaching of English in French-speaking states and the teaching of French in English-speaking states. Their aim, as set forth in the charter signed at Lagos, was the creation of a union of African states, but the approach was to be by gradual, non-political stages.

The Casablanca countries had been invited to the meetings in Monrovia and Lagos but did not attend. Although both groups shared the aim of African unity, their views and approaches were different. The two groups finally did get together, however, at a meeting of heads of state or government held at Addis Ababa, Ethiopia, in May 1963. Of the thirty-three independent states of Africa, all were represented except South Africa (not invited because of its racial policy), Togo (not invited because of the questionable legitimacy of the new government following the assassination of President Sylvanus Olympio), and Morocco (whose king boycotted the meeting because Mauritania, whose territory Morocco claims, was to be present).

The purpose of the meeting was to create an organization that would unite the African states. There were, however, wide differences of opinion as to what form the organization should take. President Kwame Nkrumah, of Ghana, urged a close union with a parliament based on the Congress of the United States. Many of the leaders, however, considered such close union premature. They were able to find common ground on the less far-reaching Ethiopian proposal for a loose federation, and signed a charter establishing an Organization of African Unity similar in concept to the Organization of American States. An assembly of heads of states and governments will meet once a year and will be the supreme organ of the organization. The permanent secretariat will for the time being have its seat in Addis Ababa. Specialized commissions may be established for economic, social, educational, military, and other affairs.

In addition to setting up an organization, the Addis Ababa conference adopted a number of resolutions involving cooperative effort.

1. The resolution on decolonization made clear that the independent African states would actively "support dependent peoples in Africa in their struggle for freedom and independence" by breaking off relations with Portugal and South Africa, refusing to trade with them, raising a special fund by voluntary contributions of member states to be administered by a Coordinating Committee of nine states to

aid national liberation movements, receiving "nationalists from liberation movements" on their territories in order to give them training, and establishing a body of volunteers "with a view to providing the various African national liberation movements with the assistance they need in the various sectors." A key passage of the resolution "informs the allies of colonial powers that they must choose between their friendship for the African peoples and their support of powers that oppress African peoples."

2. The resolution condemning apartheid and racial discrimination states that the conference

> Expresses the deep concern aroused in all African peoples and governments by the measures of racial discrimination taken against communities of African origin living outside the continent and particularly in the United States of America; Expresses appreciation for the efforts of the Federal Government of the United States of America to put an end to these intolerable mal-practices which are likely seriously to deteriorate relations between the African peoples and governments on the one hand and the people and government of the United States of America on the other.

3. The resolution on general disarmament affirmed the principle of declaring Africa a denuclearized zone, opposed all nuclear tests, undertook to bring about through negotiation the elimination from the African continent of military bases and nuclear tests, and appealed to the great powers to end the arms race.

4. Other resolutions provided for cooperation in economic, social, educational and health matters. They included a recognition of the need of the African states to pool their resources, the exploration of the establishment of an African free trade area, and the urging of international action to guarantee markets and stabilize prices for basic African exports.

UNITED STATES INTERESTS IN AFRICA

Our involvement with Africa goes back to the early years of our independent existence. In 1778 the Sultan of Morocco, Sidi Mohamet, recognized the United States and declared that all ships under its flag might freely enter Moroccan ports. In 1786, at Marrakech, the two countries signed a fifty-year Treaty of Peace and Friendship. Relations were not nearly so good with the other states of the north African coast. Like other maritime nations, the United States during the Washington and Adams administrations paid protection money to the Barbary pirates to safeguard its flourishing Mediterranean commerce. Thomas Jefferson, fed up with the humiliation of having to ransom Americans, sent warships to the Mediterranean. In 1805, through a show of force, he obtained a favorable treaty from Tripoli. Similar tactics in 1816 resulted in the signing of a satisfactory treaty with Algiers.

In the 1820's a number of Americans, distressed by the slave traffic, advocated freeing the slaves and sending them back to Africa. As a result of this activity, Negro Americans established colonies in what is now Liberia. A nation since 1847, Liberia is the second-oldest independent state in Africa. Many of its leading families are descendents of the freed slaves.

Today our interests in Africa are sizable. That continent takes 4 per cent of our exports and supplies 4 per cent of our imports. Direct private American investment is well over $1 billion.

American missionaries have been strongly attracted to Africa; some 6,500 are now there.

Military facilities have been confined to Morocco (where we are in the process of closing down our bases), Libya, and Ethiopia.

We maintain manned-space-flight tracking stations in Nigeria and Zanzibar and a deep-space probe station in South Africa.

UNITED STATES POLICY TOWARD AFRICA

The emerging nations of Africa have followed their own individual patterns. Several of them, in an emphatic reaction to the colonial ties they had just shed, turned to the Communist bloc for military and economic support. Once the initial reaction to colonialism began to wear off, African national individuality discovered that the Communist world of conformity was less congenial than the Western world of free choice.

The United States believes that its own interests, as well as those of Africa, would be best served by assisting Africans in developing free and independent nations. In the fiscal year 1963 our economic assistance to the whole of Africa except the United Arab Republic came to $500 million, including

$110 million under Food for Peace (PL 480). The Peace Corps has about 1,500 volunteers in Africa, at the request of the host countries. Increasing numbers of African students are coming to the United States. They now number about five thousand out of the total foreign student population of sixty-four thousand.

European countries, however, are giving far more assistance to Africa than we are. In 1962 France put in $600 million (including Algeria); the United Kingdom, $150 million; the Federal Republic of Germany, $155 million; and the Common Market has earmarked $800 million for a development program for the period 1963–68. The assistance given by the United States is designed to supplement—not supplant—that provided by the European countries.

The United States owes its own existence to its belief in the right of peoples to determine their own destinies. We accordingly have strongly supported the peaceful transition from colonialism to independence. The rapid drive toward nationhood in Africa at times, however, found us torn between our desire to see a quick end to colonialism and our obligations to those of our NATO allies who still have territories in Africa.

We believe (and this belief is reinforced by the experience of the former Belgian Congo) that independence requires preparation. When people are without experience in the operation of the administrative apparatus and yet attain independence, chaos may be the result. Chaos is an open invitation to intrusion by the Communist bloc. In order to keep the cold war out of Africa, the United States has given full support to the United Nations in the strife-torn Congo. The vast majority of African nations have expressed their appreciation for this support.

Avoiding a choice between the colonial power and the independence movements within its colonies is becoming almost impossible, as was pointed out in one resolution of the May 1963 conference, at Addis Ababa. The independent nations of Africa are determined to secure self-determination for the Portuguese territories and for the nonwhite population of South Africa. They will judge other countries by their actions on this question.

In the U.N. the United States has continuously supported measures calling for Portuguese recognition of the principle of self-determination and has privately urged Portugal to accept this principle and give it practical effect in its territories. In January 1962 we voted for a U.N. resolution reaffirming the "inalienable right of the Angolan people to self-determination and independence" and urging Portugal "to set up freely elected and representative political institutions with a view to transfer of power to the people of Angola." In July 1963 we abstained from voting on a U.N. resolution which called the situation in the Portuguese territories "seriously disturbing" to "peace and security in Africa" and which urged "the granting of independence immediately" to Portuguese territories. Although we supported the general aims of this resolution, we did not believe that its wording would encourage the discussions between Portugal and nationalist leaders that were necessary if any way were to be found out of the impasse between them. We believe that the United Nations' task is not to inflame a situation but to discover and support the most practical method of bringing about peaceful change.

Race relations in the United States have had repercussions far beyond our borders and particularly in Africa. The 1952 Supreme Court decision seeking to end segregation in schools improved our image, but events in Little Rock, Birmingham, and elsewhere have disappointed those who expect us to practice the democracy we advocate. African leaders are aware, however, that it is the avowed policy of the federal government to end discrimination.

On the contrary, the policy of the government of the Union of South Africa in fact denies equal rights and treatment to the nonwhites and by rigid segregation separates the races. The United States is unalterably opposed to this policy of "apartheid" and believes that its continuance can lead only to human tragedy for all races in Africa. Despite numerous U.N. resolutions on the subject of "apartheid," the government of South Africa has only intensified its repressive measures. In August 1963 the United States supported a U.N. resolution banning new shipment of arms to the government of South Africa and announced that it would suspend all arms shipments by the end of the year.

On the effectiveness of further measures there is disagreement. The African states have tried to expel South Africa, as well as Portugal, from U.N. bodies and have advocated economic sanctions. The United States believes that diplomatic isolation of South Africa and punitive measures against it would only harden the existing situation and would make impossible any communication that could possibly result in a change. Although many observers believe that conflict in South Africa is inevitable, the United States hopes that this impasse, like that on nuclear weapons testing, can be broken. Adlai Stevenson, our Representative to the United Nations, put it this way: [2]

> So I should like to suggest very emphatically that we approach the problem of "apartheid" in South Africa as a similar challenge to ingenuity, to the instinct for survival of humankind. As President Kennedy said with reference to the atomic treaty, we must not be afraid to test our hopes.

[2] Statement to the U. N. Security Council, 2 August 1963. From *The Department of State Bulletin* (Washington D. C.: U. S. Government Printing Office, 26 August 1963).

XI. THE CONGO

Upon gaining independence, the new nations of Africa, with one exception, have been able to maintain a reasonable degree of law and order. The Congo was the exception. When violence broke out five days after the proclamation of independence on June 30, 1960, the United Nations had to send forces. Their mission was to maintain order without using force unless absolutely necessary for their own protection.

Peace in the heart of Africa depended upon the success of the U.N. operation. Soon the bitter controversy over the scope of the U.N.'s mission threatened the organization's prestige and its solvency. To understand why the United Nations became involved in the first place and why the United States has been unflagging in its support requires a close examination of an exceedingly complicated situation.

BACKGROUND

Look at the map of Africa on page 237. The Republic of the Congo, one-third the size of the United States, occupies the heart of the continent. All of its neighbors to the north and east—the Congo Republic (Brazzaville), Central African Republic, Sudan, Uganda, Ruanda, Burundi, and Tanganyika—have recently acquired independence. In these countries, where white settlers were few, racial antagonism has not become a serious problem. This is not the case, however, of the lands to the south which, with the exception of the Union of South Africa, are not independent. In these lands the white settlers dominate political and economic life, and racial tension is increasing. The Congo's two immediate neighbors to the south are the Portuguese territory of Angola, with 190,000 whites (or 4 per cent) out of a total population of 4.5 million, and the British protectorate of Northern Rhodesia, with 72,000 whites (or 3 per cent) out of 2.3 million. Further to the south lie Southern Rhodesia, whose white population is 7 per cent of the total; the Portuguese overseas province of Mozambique, with 1 per cent; and South Africa, with 21 per cent.

The Congo had been under Belgian control since 1885. Its population of 14 million has some one hundred major tribal groups, several hundred dialects, and a feeling of nationhood which is only now beginning to grow beyond a small elite. The non-African population, mainly Belgian, was estimated in 1958 at 118,000. Almost one-third lived in the province of Katanga, which has a total estimated population of 1.7 million. Katanga was one of the six provinces into which, for administrative purposes, the Belgians had divided the Congo. It is the southernmost province and borders Angola, Northern Rhodesia, and Tanganyika.

The Congo is rich in tropical agricultural products and even more so in minerals. Copper, diamonds, cobalt, tin, gold, manganese, zinc, and other minerals accounted for more than half of the over $400 million in exports in 1958. Belgium, logically enough, tried to obtain the maximum economic return. Large private companies, usually with the Belgian Congo government as one of the principal shareholders, dominated the economy. The richest mines and 75 per cent of the country's hydroelectric power are located in the southern part of the province of Katanga.

The largest of the mining companies is the Union Minière du Haut Katanga, of which the Belgian Congo government owned 18.4 per cent of the shares and Tanganyika Concessions (British and South African interests) owned 14.67 per cent. Upon the independence of the Congo, ownership of the colonial government's shares was to pass to the Government of the Congo at Leopoldville. The Union Minière, with its subsidiaries, is in actuality the economy of the Katanga.

The Belgian administration and the private companies made a very good showing in providing the Africans with health and social services and education at the primary and trade school level. But not until 1956 did the first Congolese graduate from a university. In 1959 in the entire country there was not a single Congolese doctor, lawyer, or engineer. The army of 25,000, the Force Publique, was officered entirely by Belgians, as no Congolese held a rank above that of noncommissioned officer. The country was without Africans of administrative and executive experience vital to the running of a modern government.

The Belgians were preparing the Congolese for independence at a date many years in the future and were concentrating on the economic improvement of the masses rather than on the creation of an elite. The rising tide of nationalism in Africa was, however, not that patient. Unexpected riots in Leopoldville in 1959 led to a round table conference in Brussels in 1960, attended by the then current leaders of the Congo, including Moise Tshombe, who later became the president of the province of Katanga. The round table passed the resolutions which formed the base for the "fundamental law" establishing a centralized, rather than federal, structure of the government of the Congo. Although Tshombe would have preferred a federal form of government, he bowed to the wishes of the majority and afterwards praised the round table's decisions.

The Belgians precipitantly consented to grant independence effective June 30, 1960, assuming that some nine thousand Belgian administrators would remain in the country and would, together with about one thousand Belgian officers in the army, insure the continuance of government services and security. Joseph Kasavubu became the nation's first president and Patrice Lumumba its first prime minister.

THE FIRST SIX MONTHS

The road to nationhood is usually a long and arduous one. In the case of the Congo it came quickly, undoubtedly too quickly, for the Congo was not prepared for it. In the best of circumstances it would have had a difficult time making the transition, even with the help of foreign advisers, teachers, engineers, and businessmen, whose skills the Congolese could not as yet supply themselves. It was thought that the Force Publique under its Belgian officers would be a stabilizing force, but on July 5 and 6, 1960, it mutinied. In succeeding days various units went on rampages, not only in Leopoldville but in other cities of the Congo. Europeans started streaming for the frontiers; about ten were killed, others injured or raped. Outside force was obviously needed if order were to be restored. Under the terms of the independence agreement, Belgium retained in the Congo three military bases garrisoned by Belgian troops. Lumumba was unwilling to call them in, but Tshombe, in Katanga, was willing. Events then followed in rapid succession:

July 9–10: Belgium announced she was sending in troops to protect the lives of her citizens.

July 10: Force Publique troops in Elizabethville (the capital of Katanga) machine-gunned the Italian vice consul and five other whites; Belgian troops restored order; Tshombe appointed a Belgian to reorganize the army in Katanga; and Force Publique members who were not from Katanga were disarmed and sent home.

July 11: Tshombe declared Katanga to be independent.

July 12: The Congolese Government requested U.S. troops. The United States replied that the request should be addressed to the U.N.

July 12: The Congolese Government requested U.N. forces to get the Belgians out.

July 13–14: The U.N. Security Council, in an emergency, all-night meeting, adopted a resolution calling upon Belgium to withdraw her troops and authorizing the Secretary General to provide military forces. The vote was 8 for (including the U.S. and the U.S.S.R.), 0 against, and 3 abstentions (China, France, and the U.K.). The first soldiers reached the Congo on July 15. About 3,500 soldiers from African states, Ireland, and Sweden had been flown in, most of them by the U.S. Air Force.

July 22: The Security Council adopted a second resolution, this time unanimously, asking Belgium to speed the withdrawal, calling upon "all States to refrain from any action which might tend to impede restoration of law and order and the exercise by the Government of Congo of its authority and also to refrain from any action which might undermine the territorial integrity and the political independence of the Republic of the Congo," and inviting the U.N. specialized agencies to render assistance.

July 23: The Belgians completed the withdrawal of their troops from Leopoldville. Tshombe wanted them to remain in Katanga and bitterly opposed receiving any U.N. troops, although he later agreed to do so.

August 9: The Security Council adopted a third resolution, asking Belgium to withdraw its troops from Katanga, stating that the entry of U.N. troops was necessary, and affirming that the U.N. forces "will not be a party to or in any way intervene in or be used to influence the outcome of any internal conflict, constitutional or otherwise." The voting was 9 for, 0 against, and 2 abstentions (France and Italy).

Meanwhile, U.N. troops, which eventually were to number nearly twenty thousand (contributed at various times by thirty-four nations), were stationed in various parts of the country. They managed slowly to restore order, but they could not prevent savage tribal fighting in all areas, including northern Katanga. Southern Katanga, where the important mines were, remained relatively quiet and was policed by the Belgian-led Katanga gendarmerie.

The U.N., unfortunately, was not the only one sending men into the Congo. Russian Ilyushin planes landed with political agents. When Albert Kalonji, the leader of the Baluba tribe, in the province of Kasai, announced the secession of South Kasai from the Congo and the formation of the "Mining State" of South Kasai, Lumumba sent Congolese troops to Bakwanga, capital of the "Mining State." They took it and massacred a number of civilians in the process. The planes and trucks which made this movement of troops possible were supplied by the Russians. To limit the spread of fighting, the U.N. then closed the major airfields in the Congo to all but U.N. traffic. Prime Minister Lumumba called Secretary General Hammarskjold a Belgian puppet, demanded the removal of all white U.N. troops, and announced measures to abrogate freedom of speech, assembly, and association. He made clear that he thought the mission of the U.N. was to end Katangese secession by force. Congolese troops then started attacking U.N. troops.

The Congo was rapidly going to pieces when President Kasavubu on September 5 dismissed Lumumba as Prime Minister and appointed in his place Joseph Ileo, the President of the Senate. Lumumba refused to be dismissed, and the stalemate was only broken by a military coup led by Joseph Mobutu, the thirty-one-year-old Chief of Staff of the Congolese Army. He, cooperating with Kasavubu, dismissed both Lumumba and Ileo, put Lumumba under house arrest, ordered the Czech and Soviet embassies to close and their staffs to leave, and established a government of university graduates. Antoine Gizenga, Lumumba's Deputy Prime Minister, fled Leopoldville and in November established a rump government in Stanleyville, the capital of Orientale province.

Back in New York, the Soviets insisted that the U.N. bring the secession of Katanga to an end even if force were required. The Soviets proposed removal of all troops from the Congo, got nowhere with this, and then found themselves in the embarrassing position of vetoing a resolution sponsored by Ceylon and Tunisia (and the Soviets had always taken great pains to cultivate favor with the Afro-Asians) urging the Secretary General to carry out vigorously the earlier resolutions (which the Soviet Union had supported). The deadlock in the Security Council caused the General Assembly to take up the issue under the "Uniting for Peace" resolution of 1950. On September 20, 1960, the General Assembly adopted a resolution which:

> expressed full support of the three Security Council resolutions;
>
> requested the Secretary General to take vigorous action in accordance with them and to assist the Central Government in restoration of law and order and to safeguard its unity, territorial integrity, and political independence;
>
> appealed to all Congolese to seek "speedy solution by peaceful means of all their internal conflicts for the unity and integrity of the Congo, with the assistance, as appropriate, of Asian and African representatives appointed by the Advisory Committee on the Congo";
>
> appealed to all Member Governments for urgent voluntary contributions to a U.N. Fund for the Congo;
>
> requested "all States to refrain from the direct and indirect provision of arms or other material of war and military personnel and other assistance for military purposes in the Congo."

The vote was 70 in favor, 0 against, and 11 abstentions (including the Soviet bloc, France, and South Africa).

On September 23 Mr. Khrushchev, in the General Assembly, attacked Mr. Hammarskjold for his conduct of the Congo operation and made his "troika" proposal calling for replacement of the position of Secretary General by a three-man directorate. Since unanimous agreement would be required for any decision, the Soviets could thus block any action which they did not approve.

THE HEART OF THE MATTER

The Congo operation soon became much more complex than it first appeared. The United Nations had sent forces to the Congo to help the government of the Congo restore law and order and to make possible the withdrawal of the Belgian troops. This was a difficult, but not impossible, mission. Then a variety of other problems forced the United Nations, if it were to carry out its original assignment, to enter into fields it had not originally contemplated. These were the principal problems:

1. Lack of a stable government. How could the U.N. help the government restore law and order when the government itself was torn by internal dissension and lacked effective control of its own army?
2. Tribal fighting and the establishment in the provinces of South Kasai and Orientale of separatist governments.
3. The breakdown of the economy of the Congo.
4. The secession of Katanga.

The United Nations thus found itself engaged in far more than a peacekeeping mission such as it was performing in the Middle East. It was placed in the position of trying to help create a stable government, discipline an army, keep essential services in operation, and hold the country together. These tasks went far beyond the original mandate to the Secretary General and forced him not only to keep coming back to the Security Council and the General Assembly for further authority but also to exercise a great deal of latitude in interpreting his responsibilities.

Even if members of the U.N. had been in agreement as to what should be done, the Secretary General's task was excruciatingly difficult. But U.N. members were tugging in different directions—some openly, some covertly. The Soviet Union was looking for a way to build up its influence in Africa; continued disorder in the Congo was to its advantage. A number of countries with economic interests in Africa did not appear at times to be interested in taking the steps necessary to end the secession of Katanga.

Two attacks were aimed at crippling the U.N.'s ability to carry out its Congo operation. The first attack was the Soviet Union's attempt to curb the power of the Secretary General by proposing his replacement by a three-man directorate. The second attack was financial. The U.N.'s expenses in the Congo were running at the rate of $10 million a month. Belgium, France, Portugal, South Africa, and the Soviet bloc refused to pay their assessed shares of the Congo operation, and a number of other members failed to do so. Only loans, advance payments, and voluntary contributions, principally from the United States, prevented the operation from collapsing for lack of funds.

The United States was steadfast in its support of the United Nations, because it saw no better solution to the Congo problem. In July 1960, following the mutiny of Congolese armed forces and after Belgian troops were sent in, the Congolese government asked the United States and the United Nations for direct military assistance. Prime Minister Lumumba intimated that if help were not forthcoming from these sources he would have to turn elsewhere, meaning the Soviet Union. The United States had the choice of sending in its own troops, doing nothing and thus affording the Soviets an opportunity to establish their influence in the center of Africa, or supporting the recruitment by the U.N. of an international police force. The third choice was the least objectionable. The presence of a U.N. force could serve to keep other foreign troops out of the Congo and thus avoid the possibility of American and Soviet forces confronting each other.

The United Nations could then, hopefully, direct its attention to the Congo's internal problems. From the start of operations in July 1960, the U.N., directly and through the specialized agencies operating under an umbrella organization known as the U.N. Operations in the Congo (UNOC), had been trying to meet the country's urgent and massive needs for all types of trained personnel. Largely through its efforts, the essential services continued to function—public health, airport and meteorological operations, postal and telecommunications, health, and education. The number of personnel brought in for these purposes was eventually to exceed one thousand.

It was obvious, though, that stability in the Congo would be impossible unless some way could be found to bring about the reintegration of the province of Katanga. This was the foremost problem the U.N. faced in the Congo in 1961 and 1962.

KATANGA

Katanga was far from unified in support of Tshombe. The Baluba tribe, centered in the north, and related subgroups constituted half the province's population of 1.7 million. In the elections of May 1960 to the provincial assembly, Tshombe's Conakat party and its allies, with a bare majority of the popular vote, won twenty-seven out of the total of sixty seats. The Baluba party won twenty-five seats but because of harassment soon withdrew, leaving a rump parliament effectively under Conakat control.

In northern Katanga fighting broke out principally between the Balubas and the Katangese gendarmerie recruited from tribes who supported Tshombe. Harassment of Balubas in Elizabethville in 1961 was sufficient to cause about fifty thousand of them to seek U.N. protection and to live for months in a refugee camp.

Although Tshombe and his ministers were African, many in the army and the government apparatus were not. After Belgium removed her officers from Katanga in accordance with the various U.N. resolutions on the subject, Tshombe's government recruited foreigners—civilian Belgians, French officers who had fought in Algeria, Rhodesians, and soldiers of fortune of various nationalities. It is estimated that the foreign mercenaries totaled five hundred.

What made possible the payment of these mercenaries and the purchases of arms and equipment from abroad was the revenue the Tshombe government received from the Union Minière du Haut Katanga. Although the central government at Leopoldville was the rightful recipient, the company paid taxes and royalties to Tshombe on the grounds that it was forced to do so. (Before independence, taxes and royalties came to about $40 million a year.) The white interests in Katanga saw the Tshombe government as an effective shield against the chaos and disorder in the rest of the Congo. The secession of Katanga, however, made impossible the restoration of order or economic health to the rest of the Congo. The Congolese looked upon Katangan secession as a direct threat to their viability as a nation, and no central government had a chance of surviving unless it could take effective action to bring back Katanga. The mining revenues from Katanga were essential to the financial solvency of the whole of the Congo.

The Secretary General felt that if the foreign political advisers and mercenaries could be removed from Katanga, there was a chance of its coming peacefully back to the fold. Matters were not made easier when the news leaked out on February 13, 1961, that Lumumba had been murdered, with apparent Katangan complicity. Lumumba had been confined since his overthrow in September 1961, had escaped, been recaptured and then sent, for still unexplained reasons, to Katanga for safekeeping.

On February 21, 1961, the Security Council was again seized with the Congo question and adopted a two-part resolution. Part A asked the United Nations to "take immediately all appropriate measures to prevent the occurrence of civil war in the Congo, including arrangements for ceasefires, the halting of all military operations, the prevention of clashes and the use of force, if necessary, in the last resort"; urged that measures be taken "for the immediate withdrawal and evacuation from the Congo of all Belgian and other foreign military and paramilitary personnel and political advisers not under United Nations command, and mercenaries"; and called for an investigation into the death of Lumumba. Part B suggested to the Congolese that they convene the parliament and that they bring the Congolese army units under control.

On November 24, 1961, the Security Council authorized the Secretary General to use force if necessary to apprehend and deport foreign military personnel and political advisers.

The U.N.'s political work in the Congo then concentrated on three fronts—to try to get the Congolese to establish a more representative government, to persuade Tshombe and the Central Government to reach an agreement, and to remove the foreign advisers and soldiers from Katanga.

On the first front there was some success. On February 9, 1961, President Kasavubu terminated the military regime and installed Joseph Ileo as premier. In late July the national parliament met (under U.N. protection) at Lovanium University, near Leopoldville, although without delegates from Katanga, and on August 2 approved a government headed by Cyrille Adoula, a moderate labor leader. Antoine Gizenga, who had set up a rump government in Stanleyville and had the support of the Soviets and some of the African states, was named vice premier. He came to Leopoldville but did not remain. In January 1962 he lost the support of the Congolese soldiers who had made possible the Stanleyville regime and was arrested and imprisoned by the Central Government. This ended secession in Orientale province.

On the second front there was less success. Several times in 1961 and 1962 Tshombe met with Central Government leaders. Each time he appeared to agree to come to terms. Back in Katanga again he would repudiate them.

On the third front, removal from Katanga of the foreign

political advisers and mercenaries, the U.N. learned from direct experience that getting Tshombe to carry out an agreement was like trying to catch a fish with bare hands. In September 1961 the attempt of the U.N. to remove foreign personnel resulted in fighting between U.N. troops and Tshombe's forces. In December violence flared again after Katangese soldiers erected roadblocks and attacked U.N. personnel. On both occasions the U.N. troops replied by occupying key posts, such as the post office and radio station, in Elizabethville. Once the U.N. forces gained effective control of the city, Tshombe, who flitted back and forth across the border into Northern Rhodesia when things got hot, agreed to meet the U.N.'s requests. Once the U.N. forces withdrew to their bases, the advisers and mercenaries filtered back into Katanga and things went on as before. The disturbances were compounded by a tragedy in September: Dag Hammarskjold, the U.N. Secretary General, met his death when his plane crashed en route to a meeting with Tshombe in Northern Rhodesia.

His successor, U Thant, faced a dilemma. The Security Council and the General Assembly had instructed the Secretary General to use force, if necessary, to remove mercenaries but had not authorized the use of force to compel the reintegration of Katanga into the Congo. It was obvious that Tshombe believed that if he could stall long enough, the U.N. operation would collapse because it lacked funds and because the press and public opinion in many countries were strongly opposed to the use of force by a peacekeeping organization. Public sentiment was skillfully exploited by a Katangan information service which included an effective office in New York.

In August 1962 Acting Secretary General U Thant proposed a plan for Congo reconciliation: a federal constitution with greater autonomy for the provinces; a sharing on a 50-50 basis between the Central Government and a province of foreign exchange earnings derived from that province; integration of provincial forces into the national army; and a general amnesty. He made clear that Katanga's failure to agree to the plan could mean economic sanctions. Although Adoula and Tshombe agreed to the plan in principle, Tshombe dragged his feet on beginning discussions regarding the division of mining revenues.

Meanwhile, the Soviet Embassy in Leopoldville, which had increased its staff from 10 to perhaps 50 within a year, was intimating that if the U.N. could not solve the Katanga problem, the Soviets would be glad to supply the necessary military aid. At the U.N.'s request, the United States then sent a small military mission to see what equipment the U.N. forces needed. In late December 1962 Katangese forces fired on U.N. troops in Elizabethville. When Tshombe failed to stop their fire after nearly twenty-four hours of intermittent shooting, the U.N. troops then proceeded to reestablish freedom of movement. Effective resistance collapsed. After removing the roadblocks in Elizabethville, U.N. troops went on to occupy the major towns in Katanga. As U Thant said: [1]

> The time has passed for long delays, protracted discussions and talk of negotiations which in the past have served only Mr. Tshombe's interests, in any case. Only acts now can count.

In spite of the repeated assertions of Tshombe and his ministers that they would fight to the last man rather than give in, Tshombe capitulated, arranged the entry of U.N. forces into Kolwezi, and paid off his mercenaries. In spite of considerable damage to bridges and plants, U.N. troops by January 21, 1963, were able to complete the occupation of the important mining and power installations at Kolwezi, Tshombe's last redoubt.

IN RETROSPECT

Although the Belgian decision to grant the Congo independence was widely applauded at the time, in retrospect it was premature. The violence that flared in the Congo immediately after independence presented the Soviets with a long-sought opportunity to gain a foothold in the center of Africa. The only way to prevent the Congo from becoming a focal point in the cold war was to bring in a neutral presence and keep all others out. That was why the Belgian troops were asked to leave and why the U.N. sent troops in.

The U.N. gave itself a difficult mandate in Katanga—to bring about that province's reincorporation into the Congo without the use of force. That the U.N. after trying every other way to accomplish its task eventually was involved in fighting is lamentable, and yet it was the lesser of two evils.

[1] Statement made 31 December 1962, quoted in *The Washington Post*, 1 January 1963.

Failure to take decisive action would have led to the breaking up of the Congo. If the U.N. is to be an effective weapon for peace, the world must believe that it will shoot if necessary.

Was the U.N. guilty of depriving the people of the province of Katanga of the right of self-determination, one of the principles set forth in Article I of the U.N. Charter? To answer this we should look closely at the nature of the state of Katanga. For one thing, Tshombe's government represented a bare majority of the voters of the province. Then, too, Tshombe had participated in the meetings in Brussels where basic resolutions were passed establishing the structure of the government of the Congo. Although he was opposed to a centralized state, he nevertheless had accepted the principles of the "fundamental law" for the Congo as a whole and had stood for election under this law. Yet eleven days after Congolese independence he proclaimed the independence of his province. Not until the U.N. finally took effective action, did Tshombe's regime hastily came to terms with the Central Government.

XII. THE FAR EAST AND SOUTH ASIA

Excluding the Soviet Union, over 1.5 billion people inhabit Asia, from Pakistan in the west to Japan in the northeast and Indonesia in the southeast. Before World War II there were only four independent states in this vast area—Afghanistan, China, Japan, and Thailand. Today there are two Chinas, two Koreas, two Vietnams, and sixteen other states. Excluding the remote Pacific islands, the only remaining colonial possessions are British-held Hong Kong and Portuguese-held Macao and Timor. Over 700 million people live in Communist China, North Korea, and North Vietnam; 870 million live in the adjacent land areas and islands of what we might call free Asia. The countries of free Asia have a land area slightly smaller than our fifty states; their combined gross national products amount to only one-fifth of ours.

World War II brought about the decolonization of Asia. Surprisingly quick Japanese victories, which resulted in their occupation of much of Asia, showed the vulnerability of the colonial powers. In the last months of the war the Japanese transferred real power to indigenous governments in many of the occupied countries. Independence, even after an Allied victory, was inevitable. The only question was how and what form it would take.

The transition to independence was reasonably smooth when the colonial powers had made advance preparations and then proceeded without delay to grant independence. This was the case with the United States and the Philippines, and to a considerable extent with the United Kingdom and India, Pakistan, Ceylon, Burma, and Malaya. The nationalist leaders who came to power without a bitter struggle were reasonably well disposed toward their former sovereigns, and Communist elements were not able to assume charge of the independence movement. A different story occurred when the colonial powers were unwilling, as were the Dutch in Indonesia and the French in Indochina, to let go quickly and gracefully. This gave the Communist elements the opportunity to identify themselves with the struggle against colonialism and, in Vietnam, to take over the movement.

The problems of the new countries of Asia are indeed the problems of less-developed countries all over the world—poverty and disease, the development of stable government, reliance on exports of a few basic commodities, and an exploding population. These problems, however, have been particularly acute for the countries of Asia, because they have been the direct targets of Communist attempts to take them over. The struggle has been a bitter one and is still going on.

The Communists have worked on many levels and have used a number of methods. Among them are:

1. infiltration of labor and student organizations;
2. organized demonstrations and mob actions, such as those in Japan in 1960 to block signing of the United States-Japanese Treaty of Mutual Cooperation and Security;
3. direct use of military force in countries bordering on Communist China, as in Korea and India (as pointed out in the chapter on communism, the Chinese Communist aggression against India did not have the support of the Soviet Union);
4. internal subversion and guerrilla warfare, as in Burma, Malaya, the Philippines, Laos, and Vietnam;
5. massive economic aid from the Soviet Union, as in Afghanistan and India; coupled with military aid, as in Indonesia, with encouragement to use it to seize West New Guinea from the Netherlands.

Local quarrels, while they upset the peace of the area and are a drag on full economic development, would not be a threat to international peace if they could be kept out of the cold war. Unfortunately, they can't. For that reason, the United States has been trying to bring about settlements of local quarrels. Maintaining good relations with both parties becomes exceedingly difficult. No matter how neutral a great power tries to be in disputes among its friends, both parties sooner or later accuse it of favoritism. The following are among the more important disputes in the area in recent years:

1. Between India and Pakistan over the Indus waters. In

1960 the two countries and the International Bank signed an agreement providing for division of the waters and a development program.

2. Between India and Pakistan over possession of Kashmir.

3. Between Afghanistan and Pakistan over Afghanistan's desire to create a separate state of Pushtunistan for the Pathan tribes in the north of Pakistan. This resulted in the severance of commercial relations between the two countries and the need to ship U.S. aid intended for Afghanistan through Iran rather than the much more direct route through Pakistan.

4. Between Cambodia and Thailand over a disputed border area. The International Court of Justice in 1962 decided this case in favor of Cambodia.

5. Between Cambodia and Vietnam over alleged incursion of Vietnamese troops into Cambodian territory.

6. Between India and Portugal over the Portuguese holdings on the west coast of India. In 1961 India took them by force.

7. Between Indonesia and the Netherlands over possession of West New Guinea. In 1962, under U.N. auspices, an agreement was reaching providing for transfer of sovereignty to Indonesia and ultimately for a plebiscite.

8. Between Japan and Korea over fishing rights, Korean war claims, and other issues. The two countries still do not maintain normal diplomatic relations.

United States objectives in Asia are to contain further Communist encroachment, to help settle local disputes so as to prevent them from weakening the countries involved and giving the Communists a chance to intervene, and to strengthen the governments and improve their economies so that the countries concerned may have a better chance of maintaining their independence. In pursuing these objectives, the United States has used the usual tools of diplomacy—maintenance of military strength in the Far East, alliances, economic and military aid, and informational and cultural exchange programs. In many countries we are dealing with people who have had little experience in democracy and whose governments are fragile.

Asia is a large continent, and this is a small book. There will be no attempt, therefore, to explore our relations in depth with each country. Instead, this chapter will concentrate on those events and problems of broad significance.

COMMUNIST CHINA

In 1949 the Communists completed their conquest of mainland China. The government of the Republic of China, under President Chiang Kai-shek, with an armed force of 650,000 men and 1.5 million civilians from the mainland, took refuge on the island of Taiwan. Since then the main objectives of Red Chinese policy have been to take over Taiwan and the off-shore islands of Quemoy and Matsu, to destroy the government of South Korea and incorporate it with Communist North Korea, and to subvert the governments on its borders friendly to the free world and replace them with satellites. The obstacle in their path has been the strong United States presence in the Far East and the network of treaties committing the United States to the defense of South Korea, Japan, the Republic of China, the Philippines, Thailand, and Pakistan.

Communist China and the United States have already directly confronted each other in Korea and indirectly in the shelling of Quemoy and Matsu. Red China's lack of internal strength has perhaps deterred it from bolder ventures.

In 1958 Communist China introduced the commune system as the vehicle for achieving "the great leap forward." The leaders of Red China thought that regimentation of manpower in state-directed enterprises would be the fastest road to a great increase in agricultural and industrial output. The result was just the opposite. Poor planning, wasteful haste, and lack of incentive to the farmers and workers resulted in widespread apathy and discontent, chaos in production and distribution, shortages in raw materials and spare parts, the closing of many factories, and, coupled with flood and drought, in severe food shortages. Widespread famine was avoided only by the purchase of grain from abroad. By the end of 1961 at least $350 million had been so spent for grain. Like other countries which cling to socialist forms of economic organization, Communist China failed to solve the basic problem of providing an adequate supply of food for its people. With the economy about at the level it was in 1957, Peiping has changed its approach. First priority in investment is now given to agriculture rather than heavy industry, which now ranks last, after light industry.

Leaders talk of industrialization in 50 to 100 years rather than in 15.

Although Great Britain, France, and the Scandinavian countries have recognized Peiping as the legitimate government of China, the United States and most of the other countries of the free world have not. There are three questions a country normally asks itself before extending recognition to a new government:

1. Does the government have control over its territory?
2. Is it willing to live up to its international obligations?
3. Is recognition in the national interest?

Although Communist China qualifies on the first point, it has not lived up to the only agreement that it has made with the United States. Through talks at Geneva with the Chinese Communists, we reached an agreement in September 1955 under which all Americans in mainland China who wished to return to the United States would be allowed expeditiously to exercise this right. Nevertheless, the Chinese Communists have refused to release four Americans. They still remain in prison.

In chapter VII we explored the question of Chinese representation in the United Nations from the point of view of the U.N. Charter. Whether the United States should recognize Communist China is another question, one that must be decided purely from the point of view of our national interest. Communist China has made clear that it does not wish us well; its goals run counter to our interests. If increasing Chinese Communist influence should mean progressively limiting the independence of its neighboring states, then the power balance in the Far East and South Asia would shift against the United States. Our logical course of action then is to do all possible to minimize the power and prestige of Communist China, to help the free nations of Asia to maintain and strengthen their independence and integrity, and to give them confidence that a counterbalance to Communist China's power is available.

For these reasons the United States does not recognize Communist China. We have consistently supported the Republic of China on Taiwan as the legitimate government of China. The Republic of China has been a forceful example, particularly to the people in mainland China, that free Chinese can build a prosperous society while the Communist Chinese bring only totalitarian controls and economic chaos.

With its 650,000 men under arms, the best-trained and largest force in free Asia, the Republic of China is a powerful deterrent to Chinese Communist expansion. So is the Mutual Defense Treaty which we have with the Republic of China. The Communist Chinese demand that we abandon our support of the Republic of China and get out of the western Pacific. Under these circumstances, U.S. recognition of Red China would not be possible unless the U.S. were willing to meet these demands. To do so would mean abandoning the people and government of free China; it would be an indication to the other nations of Asia that the United States was no longer able or willing to exercise power in that area. Until the Chinese Communists show some sign of abandoning their hostility to the free world, there is little chance for improvement in relations with the United States.

There are some 12 million Chinese living in the countries of Southeast Asia. Through hard work and a keen business sense they have influenced commerce and business to a far greater extent than their number suggests. Both Communist China and the Republic of China have been wooing the overseas Chinese and encouraging them to send their children to school in mainland China or in Taiwan. Control of the overseas Chinese would give the Chinese Communists a powerful fifth column in Southeast Asia. Some of the overseas Chinese, although disliking communism, have been impressed by the fact that their homeland is a power which can make its influence felt. On the other hand, many of them are aware of the privations of life under the Communists and are concerned at the aggressive nature of the Peiping regime. The Republic of China on Taiwan provides the overseas Chinese with a focal point other than Peiping. This focal point is particularly effective in countries, such as the Philippines, Thailand, and Vietnam, which do not recognize Peiping.

JAPAN

Most economic experts in Japan during the Allied occupation saw scant hope for a prosperous future for that country. In 1945 Japan was as near prostrate as any modern industrial nation could be. Its cities were in ruins, its empire was gone, and with scant natural resources it was doubtful that its 75 million people would be able to support themselves. Yet, in less than twenty years Japan has achieved what has been termed an economic miracle.

The total area of Japan is somewhat less than that of California, and only 17 per cent of it is suitable for cultivation. Before the war almost half the people lived on the land and yet were not able to produce enough food to feed the population. Today slightly more than one-third lives on the land and yet is able to supply Japan's now 95 million people with all their rice and 85 per cent of their other food requirements.

In 1950 the Japanese iron and steel industry, heavily dependent upon imports of raw materials, produced 4.8 million tons of crude steel. In 1960 this figure was 22.3 million tons and in 1961 over 28 million tons, making Japan the fourth greatest steel producer in the world, exceeded only by the United States, the Soviet Union, and the Federal Republic of Germany. Japan now leads the world in fishing, shipbuilding, and exports of textiles and is fourth in electric energy production.

This productive outburst has been reflected in the consumer goods available to the Japanese. Their households are, next to those in the United States, the best equipped with electrical appliances. Nearly 80 per cent of urban households and nearly 50 per cent of rural households now have television sets.

In the decade of the fifties, Japan's gross national product increased at the rate of about 9 per cent a year and has somewhat exceeded that rate so far in the sixties. This is the highest rate of growth of any country in the world. The United States has a growth rate of under 3 per cent. Japan's gross national product now totals about $48 billion, about two-thirds that of the United Kingdom and West Germany. The per capita national income is about one-seventh that of the United States, one-fourth that of the United Kingdom, and one-third that of West Germany.

Perhaps even more revealing than economic statistics are these facts:

1. Higher education, once only for the privileged few, is now open to the many. Only the United States and Israel have a higher percentage of their youth in college.

2. Promoted in part by government encouragement of birth control, the birth rate is now half what it was in 1920 and actually a little lower than that of industrial countries of the West.

3. Life expectancy for men is now 65 and for women 70, ten years longer than in 1950.

A number of factors have made possible this transformation:

1. The occupation in Japan, unlike that in Germany, was in the main an American effort unhampered by controversies with the Soviets or the need to reconcile conflicting points of view with our allies. The occupation made sweeping changes in Japanese life but with the full cooperation of the Japanese. Perhaps the most significant was the land reform program, which made it possible for most of the farmers to own their own land. They were also able to profit from American agricultural methods such as new insecticides, improved seeds, and irrigation and reclamation techniques.

2. Japan has had stable governments. Since the Peace Treaty went into effect in 1952, Japan has been governed by a conservative party whose policy has been to maintain a close relationship with the West. Politically, a dominant conservative party or coalition of parties has commanded the support of about two-thirds of the electorate; an opposition party or coalition subscribes to socialist ideas. The Japanese Socialist Party specifically adheres to the concepts of class warfare and proletarian dictatorship. It is pledged to terminate the alliance with the United States; eliminate U.S. military installations in Japan; demand immediate reversion of Okinawa to Japan; establish diplomatic relations with Communist China; to sign a peace treaty with the Soviet Union, even at the expense of large territorial concessions; and to nationalize specified large industries in Japan.

3. Japan spends only about 2 per cent of its national income on defense, in comparison to 10 per cent spent for this purpose by the United States. In 1947 the Japanese people adopted a new constitution. Article nine provides that "land, sea, and air forces, as well as other war potential, will never be maintained." Since then this position has been modified, and confirmed by a unanimous decision of the Japanese Supreme Court, to permit Japan the forces needed for its self-defense. The United States has made a large contribution to Japan's defense power, both under the mutual security program and under the 1952 Security Treaty and its replacement, the 1960 Treaty of Mutual Cooperation and Security. Under these treaties American troops have been stationed in Japan. Over the years their number has steadily decreased as their functions have been taken over by the

Japanese Self-Defense Forces. There remains, however, in the minds of the Japanese people a strong revulsion toward all things military and particularly toward military use of nuclear energy.

4. Japan is a nation of savers. The rate of savings (about 30 per cent of gross national product) is perhaps the highest in the world, and a large proportion of savings has gone into the financing of industrial capacity and production. The labor force is skilled, literate, and hard-working. Business leadership has been adventurous and imaginative. However, with rising wages and living standards in Japan, Japan can now be undersold in some export fields (such as cheap textiles) by countries with lower labor costs. Business leaders, therefore, have turned attention to those more sophisticated industries which depend less on cheap labor—such as shipbuilding, electronics, and manufacture of machinery, trucks, and automobiles.

5. The government has pursued fiscal policies which encourage the more efficient industries.

6. U.S. economic aid to Japan has totaled about $2 billion, of which $600 million is being directly repaid. In addition, the outbreak of the Korean War created a heavy demand for the output of Japanese factories just at the time the economy needed a shot in the arm.

7. Japan has been able to export. Its imports of goods have, however, consistently exceeded exports. Japan, although running an unfavorable balance of trade, has been able to show a favorable balance of payments—chiefly because of the expenditures in Japan of the U.S. Government and military personnel, foreign long-term investment, and foreign short-term credits.

Far and away, Japan's largest trading partner is the United States, which supplies over 35 per cent of Japan's imports and purchases almost 25 per cent of Japan's exports. Japan consistently buys more from the U.S. than the U.S. does from Japan.

Japan has a special commercial interest in the political stability and economic advancement of the less developed countries. In 1961 they received more than half of Japan's exports and supplied more than 40 per cent of its imports. Japan has recognized the importance of these countries to its own future and has extended economic assistance. The countries of Asia have been the principal recipients, chiefly in the form of war reparations. Agreements with these countries have provided for payment of reparations in the form of Japanese goods and services with deliveries timed to fit in smoothly with Japan's own economic program.

So far, trade with the Sino-Soviet bloc has been a small factor in the total Japanese trade picture. The Soviets and the Chinese Communists have tantalizingly held out the prospect of tremendous orders that might come to Japanese industry for the development of mainland China and Siberia if only Japan would change its political orientation.

Japan's expansion of trade has not had entirely smooth sailing. Many European countries, perhaps unduly fearful of Japan's lower wages even though its other costs of production may be higher than theirs, have declined to extend to Japan the tariff concessions granted to other signers of the General Agreement on Tariffs and Trade (GATT). Payment of higher duties in these markets puts Japanese exports at a disadvantage. Japan has also voluntarily limited exports of certain items (such as textiles, hardwood, plywood, and tuna fish) to the United States so as to avoid injury to U.S. industries which might justify restrictive measures against Japanese imports. The coin has two faces, however. Japan restricts imports by high tariffs and exchange controls, although the government has begun to take measures to liberalize trade.

Rapid changes have not been without their effect on the Japanese people. Juvenile delinquency, almost unknown twenty years ago, is becoming a problem. University students have been particularly susceptible to Communist influence and restive with their government's policies, as during the violent student demonstrations in 1960 against the United States-Japan Treaty of Mutual Cooperation and Security. In short, as the old values have been breaking down, new values have not replaced them. Many people are disenchanted with today's politics and parties and are groping for national goals. As yet no political party has presented a program charting Japan's future in terms such as to give the electorate a feeling of national purpose.

We have examined very briefly some of the changes that have taken place in Japan and some of the reasons for them. Let us now look at the significance of these changes, particularly in the light of Japan's relationship to the United States.

The great increases in agricultural and industrial production have made possible Japan's breakthrough into a consumer-oriented economy which promises a decent standard of living for all its people. Japan is the first nation in Asia to reach this goal. Japan's success then is of particular importance, because it demonstrates that a non-Western nation can make this breakthrough by using methods which permit freedom as well as economic growth. The less developed nations, therefore, are closely watching Japan's relationship with the West. If the restrictions placed on Japan's trade continue, the less developed nations may well conclude that similar restrictions will apply to them if they try to develop within the free enterprise system.

A high rate of economic growth, sufficient to absorb the growing labor force and at the same time provide continued improvement in standards of living, is essential to the political stability of Japan. This high rate of growth depends upon trade. Its success in trade has given Japan a truly global outlook. As long as Japan is able to trade throughout the world without insurmountable obstacles, it will not have to turn its eyes to mainland China, as it did in the decades before World War II. Japan, however, has little control over the external forces which influence this trade. Since the United States is Japan's largest trading partner, it is, therefore, the key to Japan's economic stability and, in turn, to its political stability.

The United States, in turn, believes that a strong, democratically-oriented Japan is essential to the maintenance of the free world's position in the Far East. The United States, therefore, has been trying to bring Japan into full membership in the free world community in terms of both benefits and responsibilities, for economic discrimination decreases the efficiency of the free world economy and also strains free world political solidarity. Liberalizing international trade, through such measures as negotiations made possible by the Trade Expansion Act of 1962, will promote Japan's economic and political stability. But full partnership has its responsibilities as well as its benefits; Japan will have to assume a much greater share of the free world's defense and assistance to the less developed countries, if it is to become the third pillar of the free world.

VIETNAM

During World War II the Japanese occupied the French colony of Indochina. French forces returned late in 1945 and proceeded to reoccupy the country, not without some fighting with nationalist forces under the command of Ho Chi Minh, a dedicated Communist. Negotiations to find a satisfactory road to full independence broke down, and for nearly nine years the French fought an appallingly expensive and frustrating war against guerrilla bands that were everywhere and yet nowhere. One never knew whether the peaceful-looking peasant working during the day in the rice paddy was or was not a guerrilla fighter at night.

Under the circumstances, the French decided to seek a negotiated end to "the dirty war." In 1954 a conference of interested powers was held in Geneva for that purpose. Agreement was reached that the three major components of Indochina—Cambodia, Laos, and Vietnam—would receive full independence and would be neutral. Vietnam was partitioned at the 17th parallel, but elections were to be held in two years in both the north and the south to determine a government for the whole country. The elections were never held, because of the unwillingness of the northern regime to guarantee truly free voting processes. An International Commission for Supervision and Control (ICC), composed of India as chairman, Canada, and Poland, was created to carry out the Geneva accords. It could not, however, make any recommendations or take any action without a unanimous vote.

Ho Chi Minh, the leader of the Communist movement, became the chief of state of North Vietnam; Ngo Dinh Diem was elected president of South Vietnam. Nearly a million refugees fled from the north to the south. Few observers would have predicted more than a year of independent existence for South Vietnam. Ngo Dinh Diem's energetic actions, however, revived the spirit of the people, and the United States contributed heavily to refugee relief and economic development. The state not only survived but made economic headway. By 1960 the gross national product of its 12 million people was greater than that of the 14 million in North Vietnam, and its rice production had recovered sufficiently to feed its people and leave a surplus for export. This economic recovery was undoubtedly one of the reasons why North Vietnam in 1960 began in South Vietnam a campaign of accelerated terrorism, subversion, and guerrilla warfare, aided and abetted by Communist China and the Soviet Union. The purpose was to disrupt the economy, undermine the government, and absorb the country into Communist North Vietnam.

Only a small minority in South Vietnam, the Viet Cong, as the Communist forces there are called, were engaged in guerrilla fighting and subversion directed from North Vietnam. The Viet Cong's hard core is estimated at between 20,000 and 25,000. To enter South Vietnam, Communists from the north either land at night along the long coastline, slip across the frontier at the 17th parallel, or walk through Laos and infiltrate through the mountains and forests of the border region.

Before going into an account of what is being done in South Vietnam, we should look first into the nature of terrorist warfare. A relatively small body of men supported from an external base can wreak havoc in a developing country. The objective of terrorist warfare is not territory but the minds of men. A band of terrorists can swoop by night into an undefended village and extract from the villagers food and information on the location of government forces. The villagers know that failure to oblige can mean death, and that reporting to the government on the terrorists will bring retaliation a few nights later.

A determined government, however, can cope with guerrilla-terrorist warfare and ultimately be successful if it can do these things:

1. Demonstrate to the people through provision of health services, schools, and roads, that the government is of benefit to them. They will thus have a stake in the outcome of the war.
2. Provide protection to the people so that they are not at the mercy of terrorist raids.
3. Cut off the terrorists' lines of communication and supply with their external base.
4. Cut off their food supplies within the country.
5. Keep the terrorists on the defensive by attacking their local bases of operation. This means training the armed forces in anti-guerrilla tactics and providing mobility, such as helicopters to carry out a quick strike.
6. Maintain an efficient communications system so that the presence of terrorists in a particular area can be reported immediately.

These methods have been successfully used in Malaya and the Philippines.

By 1961 the United States realized that the struggle was going against the Diem government in South Vietnam. Either that government would have to seek a compromise with North Vietnam, an unsatisfactory arrangement at best, or would require a much greater commitment of American military and economic assistance. President Kennedy sent General Maxwell Taylor to make an on-the-spot appraisal. The result is the presence today in South Vietnam of some 16,500 American military advisers and technicians, and a stepping-up of economic aid, some of it in the form of medical and social services going directly to the communities. The American military personnel are there to train, advise, and support the Vietnamese army. Although they are not in Vietnam in combat status, maintaining an observer role in the middle of a battle is not always possible. American personnel can and do fire back when fired upon by the enemy.

Protecting the people in the countryside is essential. The "strategic hamlet" program was designed to do so by giving the villagers arms to protect themselves and radio transmitters to call for help when needed, and by fortifying the villages with watchtowers, barbed wire barricades, ditches filled with bamboo spikes, and booby traps. Identity cards are required for everyone over twelve years of age, in order to prevent infiltration by the Viet Cong. Only in exceptional cases are villages relocated. An estimated 60 per cent of South Vietnam's rural population is now living in the strategic hamlets.

Even with American military and economic assistance, now running about $500 million a year, the government of South Vietnam will not be able to win the war unless it has popular support behind it. By the spring of 1963, it was apparent that the actions of the government of President Ngo Dinh Diem were alienating influential segments of the population. Army officers complained privately that commands were being given on the basis of political loyalty rather than merit and that the palace was not supporting the aggressive tactics needed to subdue the Viet Cong. Buddhist protests against restrictions on their activities evolved into widespread demonstrations which the government attempted to break up by force. The regime resorted to increasingly repressive measures and in August 1963 raided Buddhist temples and arrested many priests and students. Generally held responsible for these harsh tactics were the

President's brother, close adviser, and head of the secret police, Ngo Dinh Nhu, and his wife, Mme. Nhu.

These events put the United States on the spot. We believed that a Communist take-over in South Vietnam would encourage similar efforts elsewhere by demonstrating that American assistance was ineffectual in coping with guerrilla tactics. Our objective was to help the Vietnamese win the war against the Viet Cong and then get out. In the eyes of the Vietnamese people, however, the United States was becoming increasingly associated with the repressive actions of the Diem government. Our problem was to find a means—whether by persuasion or pressure—of convincing President Ngo Dinh Diem to change his policies. Attempts to persuade had not been successful. We could exert pressure by threatening to withdraw our aid, but the carrying out of this threat would insure a Viet Cong victory.

In a television interview of September 2, 1963, President Kennedy frankly stated that the war could not be won unless the people supported the effort, that the Diem government had gotten out of touch with the people, and that perhaps it could regain popular support by changes in personnel and policy.[1] To demonstrate its seriousness, the United States suspended certain types of economic assistance.

The Vietnamese, however, took matters into their own hands. On November 1 and 2, President Ngo Dinh Diem was killed in a coup led by Major General Duong Van Minh and supported by most of the top officers of the armed forces. Former Vice President Nguyen Ngoc Tho was named premier of a provisional government, to which the United States extended recognition on November 7.

During November and December 1963, the Viet Cong took advantage of the temporary loss of momentum occasioned by the change of government in Saigon to step up its attacks on Government forces and fortified hamlets, especially in the Mekong delta region where the Communists have always been strongest. The regime in Saigon and its forces in the provinces met these attacks as effectively as they could, but their task was not easy while an almost complete reorganization in government personnel was in progress, and the Communists made substantial gains during this period.

[1] Television interview with Walter Cronkite, 2 September 1963. From *The Washington Post,* 3 September 1963.

On January 30, 1964, Major General Nguyen Khanh seized power in a bloodless change of government. The majority of the other senior Vietnamese officers rallied to him, and General Duong Van Minh (Chairman of the Military Revolutionary Council in the previous government) agreed to serve as chief of state. A new government was named on February 8, with General Khanh as premier heading a mixed military and civilian cabinet. General Khanh also retained the post of chairman of the Military Revolutionary Council, which he had assumed on January 31. Since the change of government General Khanh has restated the Vietnamese Government's dedication to free-world principles and his intention to prosecute the war against the Viet Cong more energetically and efficiently than had been done previously.

LAOS

Laos is a country of 2 million people inhabiting a landlocked area slightly larger than the state of Idaho. Most of the people live in isolated villages without any feeling of belonging to a nation. In 1954 the United States began an aid program for the purpose of developing the country's primitive economy through improved agricultural methods, education, financing essential imports, and a small military program designed to train the Laotians to cope with internal security problems. Some progress was made despite corruption in the Lao government and some looseness in the administration of the aid program. Progress was further hampered by the development of a three-cornered struggle between conservatives, with General Phoumi Nosavan as the principal figure; the neutralists, under Prince Souvanna Phouma; and the pro-Communist Pathet Lao, under his half-brother, Prince Souphanouvong.

In 1960 this struggle broke out into civil war. The United States provided assistance to the legitimate government, whereas the Soviets assisted the anti-government forces. It became obvious that the Pathet Lao were in a position to take over the whole country. A serious threat of a big power confrontation in Laos existed.

The United States had three possible courses of action:

1. Do nothing and accept the resulting Communist control of Laos, which would make much more difficult the

struggle in South Vietnam and would be a distinct danger to the rest of Southeast Asia.

2. Send in American troops for protracted jungle fighting with a strong possibility that the Chinese Communists would do likewise.

3. Try to reach an agreement for the withdrawal from Laos of all foreign military personnel and the neutralization of that country.

Given the circumstances, the third course of action seemed the least undesirable. The major powers agreed to attend, at Geneva in 1961, a fourteen-nation conference to settle the Laotian question. First it was necessary to bring about a cease-fire, and the International Control Commission, which had been dormant since 1958, again came into action. The next step was to bring the three contending factions in Laos together to agree upon a government in which each was represented. After long, drawn-out discussions, agreement was reached in July, 1962, providing for a neutral Laos and evacuation of foreign military personnel.

The situation in Laos has remained unsettled, however, and national reconciliation and unity have not been achieved, despite Prince Souvanna Phouma's efforts as Prime Minister of the tri-partite government. In May, the relative stability of the military situation was shattered when Pathet Lao forces, supported by those of North Vietnam, drove Kong Le's neutralist forces from the strategic Plaine des Jarres and precipitated a virtual military crisis in the country. The United States has withdrawn its military personnel, but North Vietnam has violated the agreements by keeping troops in Laos and using Laotian territory to support the Viet Cong in South Vietnam. We cannot be sure how much influence the Soviet Union has over North Vietnam, the source of supply and leadership for the Pathet Lao. At best, this is a precarious agreement held together by Communist realization that the alternative could be a direct confrontation between the Communist and free worlds.

Why was the United States only willing to participate in negotiations to end the fighting in Laos, whereas in Vietnam it aided the government in its fight to prevent the Communists from taking over the country? The answer lies in the circumstances peculiar to each country. In Laos much of the general populace was apathetic; competing factions were struggling for power. Also, because Laos is landlocked, it is extremely difficult and precarious to supply outside military assistance. In South Vietnam the government was determined to fight to preserve its independence and requested American assistance against the North Vietnamese aggression. The country's location on the sea made it feasible to supply this assistance.

Nevertheless, the United States has given its full support to the Geneva settlement on Laos and continues to assist the Royal Laotian government, headed by Prince Souvanna Phouma, in its efforts to preserve Laotian independence.

INDONESIA

Indonesia, with almost 100 million people living on over 3,000 islands, extends from Sumatra on the east through Java and on to West Irian (formerly West New Guinea), 3,000 miles to the west. Potentially it is wealthy, but internal rebellion, mismanagement of the economy, and the building up of large armed forces have contributed to serious inflation and a steadily deteriorating economic situation.

When the Netherlands conceded independence to Indonesia in 1949, the two parties were unable to agree on the status of West New Guinea, a territory administered as part of the Netherlands East Indies. Its status, accordingly, was left undetermined, to be settled by further negotiations within a year. In the interim, the Dutch were to retain control of the territory. These and subsequent negotiations failed to resolve the issue, both sides continuing to claim sovereignty over the territory. Attempts by Indonesia to promote a settlement through the U.N. General Assembly were also fruitless. During this period the issue became, to an ever increasing extent, the dominant factor in Indonesia's foreign relations. In the late 1950's Indonesia turned to a policy of direct political, economic, and, eventually, military pressure on the Dutch in an effort to force the issue. Determined to modernize and expand their armed forces, the Indonesians attempted to obtain arms from the United States and other Western countries. While the United States responded with a small military aid program, the Western nations as a whole were reluctant to provide arms on the scale desired by the Indonesians, in large part because of the distinct possibility that they would eventually be used against the Dutch in New Guinea.

The Indonesians then turned to the Soviets, and what started as a local quarrel became a cold war issue. Chairman Khrushchev visited Indonesia in February 1960. Since then, Indonesia has become a major target for Soviet aid and influence. Credits from the Soviet bloc now exceed $1.5 billion, and about half has been drawn upon. Of this amount, approximately $600 million was for economic aid, slightly less than the amount of aid extended by the United States. The balance was for military aid, and Indonesia today, equipped with Soviet jet fighters, ships, submarines, and a military force of about 300,000, has far and away the largest indigenous military force in Southeast Asia. It is deeply indebted to the Soviet Union, whose aid has been extended entirely on a loan basis, repayable in hard currency, rather than in the form of grants. Having supplied the equipment, the Soviets encouraged the Indonesians to use it to take over West New Guinea.

This explains, in part, the interest of the United States in doing everything possible to bring about a peaceful settlement of the New Guinea question. As the dispute continued, the Dutch progressively lost interest in holding this undeveloped and primitive territory but were unwilling to relinquish it to Indonesia. By early 1962 the dispute had reached a stage in which limited hostilities had broken out between Indonesian infiltrators and Dutch units. Indonesian forces had begun to mobilize for a major assault on the territory. At this point the Acting Secretary General of the United Nations was able to bring the two parties together for a final attempt at a negotiated settlement with Mr. Ellsworth Bunker, a former American ambassador acting in a private capacity as mediator. Agreement was reached in August 1962 for interim control of West New Guinea by the United Nations and its transfer to Indonesian administration in May 1963. The agreement also provided for an expression of self-determination by the inhabitants before the end of 1969 to choose whether they wished continued association with Indonesia.

Where Indonesia goes from here remains to be seen. President Sukarno, leader of the independence movement, is a hero to the masses of his people. He governs with the aid of the army and the tacit support of the Communist party, which, with perhaps two million members, is the largest in the free world. Sukarno, however, is a neutralist, not a

Communist, and has so far managed to avoid naming any Communists to his cabinet. There is no other leader to challenge his position.

INDIA

India's basic problem is revealed in a statistic. Upon independence in 1947 its population was 347 million; in 1963 its population was nearly 460 million and growing by over 8 million a year. All these people live in an area of 1.25 million square miles, a little over one-third the size of the United States. The late Prime Minister Nehru and his government were determined to provide a better existence for India's millions and to accomplish the necessary agricultural and industrial revolution through peaceful methods. The government's Planning Commission set up targets to be reached in five years, and the government then directed its resources to that end. Over the period of the first two plans (1951–1961) national income increased by about 42 per cent and per capita income by about 20 per cent (from $59.64 a year to $69.30).

The third five-year plan called for a total outlay of $25 billion, of which about one-fourth is supplied through foreign aid. The United States is a member of a 10-nation AID Consortium sponsored by the World Bank to coordinate free world assistance to India. For 1965, AID assistance to India will be continued principally on a loan basis; the U. S. pledge will probably be comparable to the $385 million pledge for each of the past two years. A number of private U. S. organizations have also been assisting. Chief among them are the Ford and Rockefeller foundations, which have expended over $50 million toward projects mainly for community development.

India has followed a policy of nonalignment in international affairs and has accepted aid from whatever source offered, as long as no political strings were attached. India has been the recipient of nearly $1 billion in Communist bloc aid up to June 30, 1962.

Why have the United States and other Western powers made heavy commitments of aid to India? Because it is in the interests of the free world for the Indian effort to succeed. Communism has long claimed that its system of forced saving and collectivization is the only way possible for an underdeveloped country to push ahead. The Indian plans, although combining state socialism with free enterprise, were approved by the elected representatives of the Indian people, and are being carried out in the democratic tradition. The underdeveloped areas of the world are watching with keen interest this contest between the methods being used by India and Communist China. If India is not able to make a go of it, then other countries can only assume that democracy cannot supply the answers to their problems.

Economic development has already placed a severe strain on India's economy, and yet progress may still not be fast enough to cope with the ever-mounting population increase. The government is carrying on a campaign of birth control but finds that success in this venture depends to a great degree on improving education and economic standards. The problems are inseparable. Diversion of a sizeable proportion of India's limited resources to military expenditures could defeat the development effort. For that reason, relations with Pakistan and Communist China assume a double importance.

Until the fall of 1962, India's modest military establishment concentrated on what was regarded as the potential danger from Pakistan. At the time of independence in 1947, the subcontinent, because of religious antagonisms between Hindus and Moslems, was divided into two parts. Besides causing the mass migration of over 11 million people, partition brought forth two major problems—the allocation of the waters of the Indus and other rivers, and the future of the princely states of Kashmir and Jammu. Through the good offices of the International Bank, agreement was reached in 1960 for a division of the Indus waters and the financing of the proposed dams, canals, and irrigation systems.

No solution has yet been found to the problem of Kashmir. The population of the state was 77 per cent Moslem, but the Maharajah of Kashmir was a Hindu. He vacillated between whether to join India or Pakistan. After Pakistani tribesmen invaded the state in October 1947, he opted for India. Both India and Pakistan then sent troops to Kashmir, and the ensuing bitter fighting did not come to an end until negotiation of a cease-fire under U.N. supervision took effect on January 1, 1949. India was left in possession of two-thirds of the state including the fertile Vale of Kashmir. Although several U.N. resolutions have urged a plebescite, New Delhi has been unwilling to agree. The Kashmir dispute has embittered relations between the two countries and has caused both to make larger defense expenditures than would otherwise have been considered necessary. The Chinese Communist invasion of India in October 1962 prompted the United States to renew its efforts to bring the two countries to an agreement. Several conversations between them have not shown much promise.

The world's highest mountains, the Himalayas, lie along the frontier between India and China. The Chinese Communists have claimed two frontier areas: on the west, part of Ladakh in Kashmir and, on the east, part of the Northeast Frontier Agency. In 1914 British and Chinese negotiators agreed on the so-called McMahon Line as the border on the east between Assam and Tibet. The Chinese government, however, did not ratify the treaty, and neither Peiping nor Taipei today accepts the line as the border. India's right to possession of this desolate area in the high Himalayas was not, however, challenged by China in 1954 when the two nations signed a general treaty on Tibet, undertaking to respect each other's territorial integrity and to refrain from aggression against each other.

Beginning in 1959, the Chinese Communists made a number of forays into Ladakh. When India sent troops into the area, the Chinese Communists in October 1962 undertook a full-scale invasion of both Ladakh and the Northeast Frontier Agency. India was no match for the Chinese forces and, after heavy fighting, had to retreat. In December the Chinese inexplicably halted their advance, announced they were drawing back to their previous positions, and suggested that the two countries negotiate. Meanwhile, India's request to the United Kingdom and to the United States for military assistance was promptly met.

We do not know the Chinese motives for the invasion and for its abrupt halt. Was it a means of diverting public attention from deteriorating economic conditions at home? Was it to assure the security of a road the Chinese had built across Ladakh, connecting Tibet and Sinkiang? Was it to demonstrate to the Soviet Union the futility of the Soviet policy of peaceful coexistence with the West and aid to the neutrals and that, as far as Asia was concerned, Peiping rather than Moscow had the power? Was it to demonstrate, in the ideological conflict within the Communist bloc, the Chinese conviction that force was the only road to ultimate victory for communism and that there was no room for nonalignment? Did China, fearing the probable success of India's economic development, wish to sabotage it by compelling a diversion of resources to defense?

The Chinese action has caused a good deal of reflection among those neutrals in Asia and Africa who thought the cold war had nothing to do with them. Mr. Nehru, in commenting on the invasion, made this frank admission: [2]

> We were getting out of touch with reality in the modern world and we were living in an artificial atmosphere of our own creation. We have been shocked out of it, all of us, whether it is the government or the people; some might have felt it less and some more.

This external threat may, however, serve one desirable end. It has brought to India a unity of feeling and has submerged regional differences. It may supply the stimulus needed for the success of India's economic development and its welding together as a nation.

[2] Prime Minister Nehru's speech to conference of state information officers. Quoted in *Indiagram,* No. 202 (Washington, D. C.: The Indian Embassy, 25 October 1962).

XIII. THE MIDDLE EAST

The term "Middle East" is not an exact one. Centuries ago Europeans considered as "the East" all lands lying beyond the eastern portals of their then known world. The area bordering the eastern shore of the Mediterranean came to be known as "the Near East" and the area bordering the distant Pacific as "the Far East." The vast expanse of land lying in between was often referred to as "the Middle East." Today the terms "Near East" and "Middle East" have come to be used interchangeably. The Middle East is now generally considered to include the independent countries of Turkey, Iran, Cyprus, Syrian Arab Republic (Syria), Iraq, Lebanon, Israel, Jordan, the United Arab Republic (U.A.R., Egypt), Saudi Arabia, Yemen, and Kuwait; the British crown colony of Aden; and the small states under British protection lying along the coast of the Arabian peninsula.

This is an area of intense international rivalry and of bitter local conflict. To give an idea of the scope of the problems the area presents for American foreign policy, I have placed the emphasis in this chapter on three countries —Iran, Israel, and the United Arab Republic.

CHARACTERISTICS OF THE AREA

GEOGRAPHY. Fertile coastal plains, arid plateaus, mountains, deserts, and river valleys are the predominant features of the Middle Eastern landscape, and water is the all important factor. Less than 8 per cent of the land can at present be used for agriculture. Where water is plentiful, as in the valleys of the Nile and the Tigris-Euphrates rivers, intensive cultivation makes possible the feeding of millions of people.

From the beginning of history, the Middle East has been a crossroads, and this strategic position has made it the object of great power rivalry. The Turkish Straits provide the only way for ships to reach the Russian ports on the Black

Sea. The Suez Canal, opened in 1869, transports roughly half the commerce between Europe and the Far East. Jet planes today fly over the routes used for centuries by camel caravans.

PEOPLE. The some 90 million people of the Middle East are a mixture of many races, and trying to sort them out ethnically would be a fruitless task. There are three main language groups—Semitic, Persian or Iranian, and Turkish. The two major Semitic languages are Hebrew, the official language of Israel with over two million people, and Arabic, the principal language of some 40 million people in the Arabian peninsula, Egypt, Jordan, Iraq, Lebanon, and Syria. Although written Arabic is the same everywhere, spoken Arabic differs widely in various parts of the Arab world.

A persistent cause of tension has been the existence of minority groups—such as the Armenians, who live in Lebanon, Syria, Turkey, and also the Soviet Union; the Kurds, who live in Turkey, Syria, Iraq (where they form about one-quarter of the population), Iran, and also the Soviet Union; and nomadic tribes such as the Bakhtiari, in Iran.

RELIGIONS. The Middle East is the cradle of three of the world's major religions—Christianity, Judaism, and Islam.

Islam, the world's youngest major faith, has nearly 700 million adherents, who live mainly in the lands extending from Morocco to Indonesia. Founded by Mohammed, who was born in Mecca, Arabia, about 570 A.D., Islam means the peace of God gained through submission to His will. A Moslem is one who makes this submission. Mohammed's followers spread from the Arabian peninsula to conquer most of the Middle East, North Africa, and Spain; their expansion into Europe was halted only by their defeat at the Battle of Tours, in France, in 732.

Twenty-three years after Mohammed's death, civil war broke out over the succession to the Moslem leadership, the caliphate, and split Islam into two denominations—Sunni and Shia. Today, most Iranians and perhaps half the Iraqis are Shiites. In other Moslem countries of the Middle East the Sunnis predominate.

OIL. In 1908 in Iran the British opened the first oil well in the Middle East. Not until the end of World War II, however, did Middle Eastern oil assume its present great importance to the economy of Europe. With over 190 billion barrels in proven reserves, the Middle East has two-thirds of the world's known oil reserves. In 1962 it produced an average of 6.2 million barrels a day and shipped nearly one-half of it to Europe. If this oil were to be cut off, as it was during the Suez crisis, Europe would be hard pressed to meet from other sources its daily requirements of 5.2 million barrels.

The revenues from oil received by the principal oil-producing states are very large. In 1962 Kuwait received $400 million; Saudi Arabia, $310 million; Iran, $250 million; and Iraq, $235 million.

Kuwait's huge income, in comparison to its population of less than 350,000, and the farsightedness of its ruler have made possible a paternalistic program of free medical service and hospitalization, education, and extensive construction of roads, public buildings, and low-cost housing. Over the years Kuwait's expenditures have been less than its revenues. The surplus, now estimated at $750 million, has been invested in London.

In the oil-producing countries other than Kuwait, revenues from oil are only beginning to affect the living standards of the masses of the people. In Iran and Iraq oil revenue is being channeled into development programs such as flood control and irrigation which over a period of time will raise living standards. In the past, Saudi Arabian oil revenue has gone largely to supporting the numerous members of the royal family in luxury far removed from the subsistence level of the ordinary citizen.

Although not oil-producing countries, Lebanon, Jordan, Syria, and Egypt have to some extent profited through charges on oil transit by pipelines crossing their territories, or by tankers passing through the Suez Canal.

The uneven distribution of oil revenues has been a disruptive influence. The Arab states without large oil revenues have long cast a covetous eye at the riches discovered beneath the barren sands of their neighbors. In 1961 the government of Kuwait wisely decided to establish a fund for the economic development of less fortunate Arab lands.

IRAN

The determination of the people of the Middle East to better their way of life has led to intense unrest and in a number of countries to the overthrow of the government. In Iran, the politically astute Shah, realizing that change was inevitable, has assumed its leadership. By undertaking a series of reforms, the most important of which is the breaking up of the large landholdings, the Shah hopes to gain allegiance from the 15 million peasants, by far the largest segment of Iran's 21 million population. Without their support there can be no firm foundation for the continuation of the Pahlavi dynasty.

Three classes form Iran's social structure. At the top is a small upper class whose wealth came from ownership of land and whose political power rested on its ability to dominate the elections for the Majlis, the lower house of parliament. Although many of the wealthy have been educated abroad and are intelligent and sophisticated, they have not as a class demonstrated any strong sense of social consciousness or national purpose.

Peasants, illiterate and apathetic, form the bulk of the population. Most of them are either small tenants, bound to the land by almost feudal forms of land tenure, or are day laborers. They live in some fifty thousand villages, most of which are owned by less than one thousand wealthy families. In recent years there has been a mass migration from the farms to the cities. In less than thirty years, Tehran, the capital, grew from 400 thousand to 2 million.

The middle class is small but growing—government civil servants, oil company employees, small merchants, professional men, university professors and students. They are concentrated in the cities, particularly in Tehran.

Three forces cut across class lines:

1. The army, about 200,000 strong, takes a large percentage of the budget, has been equipped through U.S. military assistance, and comes under the direct command of the Shah. The security forces of the country, which have been well treated, have been the mainstay of the Shah in putting through reforms which have been unpopular with influential elements in the country.

2. The Shia religious establishment, unlike the Sunni Moslems, has a priesthood. In Iran the "mullahs" have engaged actively in politics.

3. The nomadic tribes constitute about 3 million people. When the central government was weak, the tribal leaders exercised authority in their areas. Their influence is now waning.

Since the beginning of the nineteenth century, Iran attracted the interest of European powers and became the object of the contending ambitions of Great Britain and Russia. Although in the Anglo-Russian agreement of 1906 the two powers stipulated that Great Britain's sphere of influence would be in the south and Russia's in the north, their underlying conflicts of interest, which the Iranians became adept at using, helped make possible Iran's continued existence as an independent state. In World War I both countries moved troops into Iran. In the anarchy that followed their withdrawal a military commander by the name of Reza Khan was able to gain control of the government. In 1925 he deposed the dynasty and made himself Shah.

Reza Shah, like his contemporary in Turkey, Kemal Ataturk, was undisputed master of his country and tried to drive it into the twentieth century. He created a national army, restored the authority of the central government throughout the country, built a railroad from the Persian Gulf to the Caspian Sea, stood up to attempted interference by foreign powers, began industrialization, and made a start on the educational and administrative reforms necessary to create a modern state. His methods were authoritarian.

After the outbreak of World War II the British and the Russians again moved troops into Iran. Reza Shah, suspected of pro-Axis sympathies, abdicated in favor of his son, the present Shah, Mohammed Reza Pahlavi. The United States took charge of shipping lend-lease supplies on this vital route from the Persian Gulf to the Soviet Union.

After the end of the war the Soviet Union refused to withdraw its troops from the northern provinces and backed revolts which set up pro-Soviet governments in the provinces of Azerbaijan and Kurdistan. Action by the United Nations, strongly supported by the United States, finally forced the Soviets out in 1946. With the entry of Iranian troops into the area, the puppet regimes collapsed.

A strong wave of nationalism resulted in the nationalization in March 1951 of the Anglo-Iranian Oil Company's holdings, of which the British government owned the controlling interest, and the coming into power of an ultranationalist, anti-foreign government under Dr. Mohammed Mosadeq. His National Front regime increasingly relied upon police-state methods to maintain itself in power but faced serious financial difficulties because oil revenues diminished when they could not sell Iranian oil abroad. In 1953 the

Shah, persuaded that Dr. Mosadeq's intention was to form a republic, dismissed the prime minister. The Shah almost lost his throne when he left the country but was saved by the army, which thwarted Mosadeq's attempt to remain in power. Nine days after his departure the Shah returned to Tehran and was greeted by popular acclaim.

Since then the Shah has no longer been content merely to reign. He rules the country but has been able to do so more or less within the constitutional framework. By control of appointments, he has made sure that only men loyal to him reach or stay in positions of authority.

These are the major policies he has followed:

1. Close association with the West, particularly the United States. Following the downfall of the Mosadeq government, American economic aid kept the government afloat until oil revenues began to flow in; U.S. economic aid through June 30, 1962, totaled $731.5 million, and military aid totaled $653 million. In 1955 Iran joined the Bagdad Pact, later known as the Central Treaty Organization. Relations with the Soviet Union have at times been tense, but Iran has stood up to Soviet pressures.

2. Settlement of the oil question. In 1954 Iran reached an agreement with an international consortium of oil companies providing for exploitation of Iran's oil on the basis of a 50–50 split of the profits between Iran and the consortium. Members of the consortium are the British Petroleum Company, formerly Anglo-Iranian Oil Company (40 per cent), 14 American oil companies (40 per cent), Royal Dutch Shell (14 per cent), and the French National Oil Company (6 per cent). This arrangement greatly increased Iran's oil revenues, which are expected to be more than $400 million in 1964–65.

3. An economic development program, financed by a major share of the oil revenues and by foreign grants and loans. Perhaps the most spectacular project is the construction of dams and development of irrigation and power facilities in the southwestern province of Khuzistan.

4. A series of reforms designed to give the people a stake in the regime. In 1951 the Shah began selling the crown lands, containing perhaps 2,000 villages, to the peasants who worked them. Terms were moderate and payments spread over a number of years. Few landowners followed the Shah's example.

In January 1962, land redistribution was made compulsory. A decree provided that all landholdings in excess of one village would have to be surrendered to the government against compensation payable over a ten-year period. The value of the land was calculated at the amount the owner used for tax purposes. The government in turn is to sell the land to the peasants, who pay over a fifteen-year period. As of October 1963, lands connected with 6,000 villages had been distributed to 230,000 families.[1]

As expected, the efforts of the Shah to modernize his country have aroused opposition from a number of groups, including landlords, religious leaders (who are particularly opposed to greater freedom for women), and intellectuals and students (who have resented the government's authoritarian methods). Six reform decrees (land distribution, nationalization of forest areas, sale of government-owned factories to help pay for the cost of the land distribution program, a workers' profit-sharing program, the creation of a Literacy Corps of 50,000 to teach illiterates to read and write, and electoral reform) were submitted to the voters in a referendum held in January 1963. They were overwhelmingly approved. In March 1963 the cabinet approved a decree granting suffrage to women. Nevertheless, in June 1963 the opposition groups were able to stage in Tehran a number of nasty riots against the reform program. The elections of September 1963, although carried out with some controls, selected for the Majlis a majority of representatives in favor of the reform program, including a number of persons not allied to the wealthy upper class.

In a few years the Shah and his government are attempting to carry out changes which elsewhere have taken centuries. Forcing Iran to move ahead in spite of its people's cynicism and apathy is a hazardous task for the Shah but necessary for Iran if it ever is to emerge as a modern state.

ISRAEL

Although Palestine was their biblical homeland, very few Jews lived in this neglected province of Turkey until events in Europe forced their migration. A series of pogroms (organized massacres of Jews) began in Russia in 1881. Within twenty years some six hundred thousand Jews from Eastern Europe fled to America. During the same period,

[1] Jay Walz, "Iran's Shah Leads a White Revolution," *The New York Times Magazine*, 27 October 1963.

about 25,000 went to Palestine. Among these were the first Zionists. They believed that they never could hope to identify themselves completely with the non-Jewish people among whom they had lived and that the only permanent solution was to create a national homeland for Jews, preferably in Palestine. This movement was known as "Zionism," after the hill in Jerusalem on which had been built the palace of David and the temple of Solomon.

The first of a series of Zionist Congresses was held in 1897 in Basle, Switzerland, under the leadership of Theodore Herzl. The Congress established the World Zionist Organization and declared as its objective "the securing for the Jewish people a home in Palestine guaranteed by public law." Two financial institutions—the Jewish Colonial Trust and the Jewish National Fund—were established to purchase land in Palestine. Although settlement of Jews in Palestine quietly progressed, the Zionist movement lost much of its vitality with the death of Herzl in 1904.

World War I gave the movement new impetus. Turkey entered the war on the side of Germany and Austria-Hungary. In 1917 Arthur James Balfour, the British Foreign Secretary, issued a statement on Palestine. Perhaps he was influenced by the hope of swinging full Jewish support, particularly in the United States, behind the Allied cause, and by the nationalist movements of the time. Among those he consulted was Dr. Chaim Weizmann, a distinguished British chemist of Russian origin and a leading Zionist who was later to be the first president of Israel. The Balfour Declaration, which was to have a far-reaching effect on the Zionist movement and on the history of the Middle East, stated:

> His Majesty's Government view with favour the establishment in Palestine of a National Home for the Jewish people, and will use their best endeavors to facilitate the achievement of this object, it being clearly understood that nothing shall be done which may prejudice the civil and religious rights of the existing non-Jewish communities in Palestine or the rights and political status enjoyed by Jews in any other country.

With the defeat of Turkey, the League of Nations awarded Great Britain the mandate for Palestine. Jewish immigrants arrived in a steady trickle, constructed towns, and through reclamation of swamplands and irrigation made progress in developing agricultural settlements. The Nazi persecution of Jews in Europe caused a fresh flow of immigration to Palestine. The Jewish population of Palestine, which at the time of the Balfour Declaration was about 60,000, approached 500,000 by the end of 1939. Palestine's total population was about 1.5 million.

Although the Arabs in Palestine benefited from Jewish purchases of land and from the improvement in the mandate's economic life, they resented the intrusion of an alien people. Arab outbreaks and rioting against the Jews increased in intensity and became particularly violent in 1936.

In 1939 the British Government, in an official document known as a White Paper, announced a change of policy which it hoped would placate the Arabs and restore peace to the Holy Land. Henceforth, Jewish immigration into Palestine was to be limited to 75,000, to be spread out over a period of five years. The White Paper intimated that by 1949 the British would withdraw from Palestine, leaving the way clear for an independent country with a permanent Jewish minority. In spite of tight immigration restrictions, an estimated 120,000 Jews managed to enter the country between 1940 and 1947, although half of them did so illegally.

After World War II, relations between the Arabs and Jews and between the British and the Jews reached the breaking point. The British, realizing that governing a million Arabs and 650,000 Jews was not only a thankless but an impossible task, announced their intention to give up the mandate as of May 15, 1948.

In November 1947 the United Nations adopted a plan for the partition of Palestine into two states—one Arab, one Jewish—politically separate but economically united. Jerusalem was to be a free city administered by the United Nations. The Arabs at that time were unwilling to accept the partition plan, and no state was willing to commit to the U.N. the forces that would have been needed to enforce partition. On May 14, 1948, the Jews announced their acceptance of the partition plan and the birth of the state of Israel. Over seven hundred thousand Arabs fled Palestine, although about two hundred thousand remained. Armies of the neighboring Arab states attacked Israel but were no match for the numerically smaller but far better organized and equipped Jewish forces.

The United Nations was able to bring about a truce in the fighting and in 1949 to bring together Israel and Egypt,

Jordan, Lebanon, and Syria for the signing of armistice agreements. The U.N. resolution on Jerusalem was not carried out. Israeli forces occupied the modern city, and Jordanian forces took over the old, walled city. The United Nations Truce Supervision Organization (UNTSO) was set up in Jerusalem to see that the armistice agreements were carried out. Its officers serve as the neutral chairmen of the four mixed armistice commissions on which Israel and one of its Arab neighbors are equally represented. The UNTSO investigates border incidents and attempts to determine responsibility for them in the hope that the spotlight of publicity may discourage repetitions. In flagrant cases the aggrieved party has appealed to the U.N. Security Council.

In spite of the presence of the UNTSO, Arab forays across Israel's borders and Israeli retaliation have been the pattern. In 1956, just prior to the Anglo-French attack on the Suez Canal, Israeli forces invaded the Sinai Peninsula of Egypt and succeeded in capturing large quantities of military equipment. Withdrawal of the Israeli forces took place in March, 1957, under U.N. auspices. A U.N. Emergency Force, hastily recruited to supervise the removal of foreign troops from Egyptian soil, today patrols the Egyptian-Israeli frontier and has been able to keep this sector free of dangerous incidents.

Israel, which now has a population of 2.3 million, has managed to make steady economic progress in spite of the large sums it has felt compelled to spend on defense and on the care and settlement of the nearly one million Jews who have come to Israel since the founding of the state. This progress has been possible because of an intelligent, industrious population with a strong sense of purpose and because of heavy infusions of foreign capital. Funds have come from restitution and reparation payments from West Germany, from economic assistance supplied by the United States Government, and from loans and contributions of Jews abroad, principally in the United States. The standard of living today in Israel is far higher than in other countries of the Middle East and is approaching that of the industrialized countries of Europe.

Israel would like nothing better than to achieve a definite peace settlement with its Arab neighbors but has no intention of giving up any of the territory it gained by force of arms in excess of that contemplated by the U.N. partition plan. It would like a defensive alliance with the United

States which would put the stamp of legitimacy on the present armistice lines. This the United States is unwilling to do. However, Israel is prepared to fight and has a modern, efficient fighting force to protect itself. Israel regards Nasser as the greatest threat to its security and would strongly oppose any attempt by the U.A.R. to take over Jordan, perhaps to the extent of moving in troops to that part of Jordan lying west of the Jordan River, formerly part of the Palestine mandate.

ARAB ATTITUDES

For four centuries, beginning with the occupation of Egypt in 1517, the greater part of the Arab world was under Turkish domination. After the outbreak of World War I, some Arabs, notably Hussein, the head of the Hashemite family of Mecca, and his two sons Faisal and Abdullah, were persuaded to join the Allied cause in the belief that an Allied victory would mean freedom and self-rule for those Arab lands under Turkish rule. Although Arab expectations were encouraged, they were not met. The French obtained Lebanon and Syria as mandates and removed Faisal from the throne he had assumed in Damascus. The British received as mandates Palestine, Iraq, and Transjordan and discharged their debt to the Hashemite family by making Faisal king of Iraq and Abdullah emir of Transjordan. Egypt, which had been occupied by the British since 1882, was granted nominal independence but with the British maintaining control of foreign affairs and defense. The only truly independent Arab states were Yemen, so backward that it has been characterized as rushing headlong into the thirteenth century, and Saudi Arabia. In 1924–25 a leading sheikh by the name of Ibn Saud drove the Hashemites out of Mecca and proceeded to bring most of the Arabian peninsula under his control. Not until after World War II were all the major Arab states to obtain full independence.

The long period under foreign domination had a strong effect on the character of the Arabs. They have felt compelled to prove to the rest of the world, and to themselves, that they are as capable as the West. These are the principal attitudes which have shaped their actions:

1. Emotional reaction against the political, military, and economic domination of the former colonial powers, with which the United States is identified.

2. The conviction that Israel is a form of Western imperialism and must be eliminated.

3. The willingness to use either the free world or the Communist bloc in pursuance of objectives. This does not mean that the Arab states are pro-Communist, merely that they do not regard the Soviet Union as a serious threat to them.

4. Awareness of the pressing need to build modern states and economies.

5. The feeling that the Arabs, with a common religion, language, and culture, should work together and, if united, could play a more significant role in the world. But they cannot agree on the question of leadership.

All these attitudes form a catalyst known as Arab nationalism. It includes a deep dissatisfaction with the ways of the past and a determination to achieve self-respect. Perhaps the state of mind can be understood better by a closer look at recent developments in the United Arab Republic.

THE UNITED ARAB REPUBLIC

The United Arab Republic, known as Egypt until its union with Syria in 1958, has 26 million people, far more than any other Arab state. During World War II, Egypt was the center for Allied forces in the Middle East. On important matters British wishes prevailed. In 1942, for example, British tanks drawn up in front of the royal palace convinced King Farouk that he should follow the British suggestion as to his choice of prime minister. Although this action accomplished an immediate objective, it may have been to Great Britain's long-run disadvantage, for it incurred Egyptian resentment.

Arab weakness was driven home even more painfully in 1948 by Israel's defeat of the Arab armies sent to put the newly-created state out of existence. The humiliating revelation of their weakness had a traumatic effect on the Arabs. Many blamed Zionist success on British and American support, but a number of young Egyptian officers more realistically placed the responsibility for the defeat of their army on their own government. Prominent officials, including the King, were implicated in scandals which involved supplying the army with defective equipment and shoddy supplies. In July, 1952, these young officers easily and almost bloodlessly overthrew the old regime and sent King Farouk into exile. The ostensible leader was General Naguib, but in 1954 he was forced out by Colonel Gamal Abdel Nasser.

Nasser views Cairo as the center of three concentric and overlapping circles. The first embraces the world of Islam; the second, the Arab world; and the third, Africa. He believes that Egypt and he have leading roles to play in all three circles. At the same time, he faces an extremely serious economic problem at home. Egypt's population is increasing as fast as the national income.

Nasser's objectives and the methods he has used to achieve them can be briefly summarized as follows:

1. To remove the last vestiges of Western imperialism from Egypt. In 1954 Egypt obtained the U.K.'s agreement to remove its troops within twenty months and to close down its large base at Suez. In July 1956, following the announced decision of the United States not to proceed with its proposed financing of part of the costs of the Aswan High Dam, Nasser nationalized the Suez Canal. Following the Anglo-French attack on Suez that October, Nasser proceeded to take over British and French business firms in Egypt. Contrary to many predictions, Egypt has run the canal efficiently.

2. Unremitting hostility toward Israel. Egyptian forays into Israel provoked the Israel raid on Gaza in 1955. Despite U.N. resolutions, the U.A.R. refuses to permit Israeli ships or cargo to transit the Suez Canal.

3. A determination to make Egypt strong militarily for the dual purpose of (a) defeating Israel and (b) assuring unquestioned leadership of the Arab world. In 1951, before Nasser came to power, the Egyptian Government refused to take part in a Western plan for regional defense known as the Middle Eastern Defense Command. The British base at Suez would have been its nerve center. The United States had hoped that once British troops left Egyptian soil in compliance with the 1954 agreement, Egypt might then be inclined to consider a regional defense arrangement. The United States was willing to supply Egypt arms and training under the supervision of a U.S. military advisory group. Although Nasser wanted arms, he was unwilling to accept any conditions as to their use. He continued to oppose the adherence of Egypt or any Arab state to a Western military alliance. In February 1955 Iraq signed the Bagdad Pact, and the Israelis made a lagre raid on Egyptian-held Gaza. In September, Nasser entered into a deal with the Soviet bloc for arms in exchange for cotton.

4. To speed economic development in order to raise the miserably low standard of living of the majority of Egypt's people. To gain this objective, Nasser has followed a threefold approach:

First he planned to even out the great inequalities in wealth with a land reform program breaking up the large estates and followed some time later by nationalization of the larger industrial and business enterprises.

Secondly, he planned to increase the amount of land that could be irrigated by building a high dam at Aswan. This project, estimated to cost over $1 billion, should make possible a one-third increase in the amount of land that can be farmed. In 1955 the United States had offered to finance part of the cost. Nasser dragged his feet in accepting the offer. In 1956 the United States withdrew its offer on the grounds that Egypt could scarcely devote its resources to the project since it had mortgaged its cotton crop for years to come in order to pay for Communist arms. In 1958 the Soviet Union undertook to finance the first stage of the dam.

The third approach was rapid industrialization. Since private capital showed little inclination to invest in Egypt, the government itself stepped into the field and took over the operation of most of the country's business enterprises.

5. To bring about some form of unity in the Arab world under his leadership with the revenues of the oil-rich states supplying the financial support. In 1945 the League of Arab States was established, with headquarters in Cairo, to bring about a close coordination of the policies of the Arab states. Egypt and Nasser have played the dominate role. By nationalizing the Suez Canal, Nasser overnight became a hero to the Arabs. He had been able to defy the West and to get away with it. After the withdrawal of the Israeli, British, and French forces following the attack on Sinai and the Suez Canal, his prestige rose even higher. In Arab eyes it was Nasser who had won the victory, even though withdrawal had come about as a result of pressure brought by the United States, the Soviet Union, and world-wide opinion working through the United Nations.

Nasser has devoted a great deal of attention to fostering his image as an Arab leader. He has sent Egyptian school teachers by the thousands to teach in neighboring lands, even though Egypt itself needed their services. For many hours each day, Radio Cairo beams entertainment and propaganda to the Middle East and Africa. Although many of the people of the Arab lands have been enthusiastic supporters of Nasser, their governments have good reason to fear his influence. His agents have actively worked for the downfall of the governments in nearly all the other Arab states.

In 1958 Syrian leaders, in an effort to forestall what they feared would be a take-over of the government by internal Communist forces, asked for and obtained the union of Syria with Egypt. The union, known as the United Arab Republic, initially sparked strong feelings of Arab nationalism. It was to last, however, only three years. Syrians resented the number of Egyptian officials and attempts to impose the socialist Egyptian pattern on the free-enterprise Syrian economy. In 1961 an army coup overturned the government in Syria and dissolved the union with Egypt. Nasser decided not to try to hold the union together by force.

The only serious rival to Nasser for leadership of Arab nationalism is the Baath Socialist Party. The word "Baath" means "reawakening." The party is a nationalist, socialist group with aims similar to those of Nasser but opposed to his domination. In early 1963 the party, with the support of military elements, was able to overthrow the governments of Iraq and Syria and seize power. On April 17, 1963, the Baathist governments of these two countries and the U.A.R. signed an agreement for union of the three nations. Baathist distrust of Nasser's intentions, however, has resulted in mutual recriminations and the suspension of any further steps toward unity.

THE UNITED STATES IN THE MIDDLE EAST

How the United States Came on the Scene. The major role the United States plays in the Middle East is a recent development. Until World War I our interests were largely missionary and educational, such as the American University in Beirut, which since its founding in 1866 has educated many of the area's leaders. Between the wars American oil companies gained participating rights with European companies in the development of oil concessions in Iraq and Kuwait and obtained exclusive rights in Saudi Arabia.

Up through World War II the British had assumed responsibility for maintenance of peace and stability in the Middle East so as to assure that their shipping lanes to India and to the Persian Gulf oil ports would remain open. Great Britain kept in the area the forces needed to accomplish its objectives. There were British bases at Suez in Egypt, Cyprus, Iraq, Jordan, and Aden; the British-trained and officered Arab Legion in Jordan; and close political relationships with the small coastal sheikhdoms of the Arabian peninsula. The strains of World War II, the unwillingness of the Labour Government to play an imperialist role, and the rising forces of nationalism in the Middle East contributed to Britain's decision that it could no longer maintain its former position of strength in the area. Soviet pressures on Greece, Turkey, and Iran convinced the United States that the Soviets would try to fill any vacuum left by Great Britain's withdrawal. In his message to Congress in March, 1947, President Truman asked for the authority and funds to provide economic and military assistance to Greece and Turkey. The enabling legislation passed by Congress made us active participants in the defense of the area. The following year Great Britain's decision to give up its Palestine mandate and to deposit the Palestine problem in the lap of the United Nations propelled the United States into an active role in the internal problems of the Middle East.

OBJECTIVES. The key objectives of the United States in relation to the Middle East can be simply stated:

1. To prevent the Soviet Union from dominating the area.
2. To prevent conflicts and rivalries within the area from touching off a war that would involve both the Soviet Union and the United States.
3. To achieve sufficient stability to make possible orderly political and economic development and insure the continued flow of Persian Gulf oil to Europe.

DEFENSE OF THE MIDDLE EAST. In attempting to protect the Middle East against direct Communist aggression, the United States has used these methods:

1. Direct military and economic assistance, such as that extended to Greece and Turkey in 1947 under the Truman Doctrine.
2. Military alliances. The Bagdad Pact of 1955 brought together in a defensive alliance Turkey, Iraq, Iran, Pakistan, and the United Kingdom. In 1958 Iraq withdrew, and the name was changed to the Central Treaty Organization (CENTO). Although the prime mover of the pact, the United States believed it wisest not to become a full member. The United States is, however, a member of CENTO's working

committees and has bilateral security agreements with Turkey, Iran, and Pakistan.

3. The Eisenhower Doctrine, embodied in a resolution passed by Congress in 1957, states that the United States is prepared to use its armed forces to assist, on request, any Middle Eastern state subjected to overt attack by a state controlled by international communism. In 1958 civil war broke out in Lebanon, and the President of Lebanon asked the United States for help on the basis of the Eisenhower Doctrine. U.S. forces landed in Lebanon on July 15, 1958, and remained until October 25 when order had been restored.

A Middle Eastern nation desiring U.S. protection through one of these methods is forced to stand up and be counted on the side of the West. Few governments have the internal strength to be able to do so. Turkey and Iran, independent for centuries, do not have the fear of Western imperialism held by the Arab states and accordingly have been able to enter into and maintain defensive alliances with the West. Other governments have found that too close identification with the West can cause their downfall. Many Iraqis bitterly opposed their country's adherence to the Bagdad Pact, and one of the causes of the revolution in 1958 was Iraq's close identification with the West. The new revolutionary government promptly announced Iraq's withdrawal from that alliance. In 1956 King Hussein of Jordan almost lost his throne as riots raged in the capital city of Amman in protest against the apparent intention of the government to join the Bagdad Pact.

The strong stand of the United States against direct aggression prompted the Soviet Union to use more subtle methods to gain a position in the Middle East. Supplying arms to Egypt in 1955 provided a foothold. The Soviets realized that the minimum return on their investment would be an arms race with Israel and the strengthening of Egypt's potential to use force in asserting its claim to Arab leadership. The Soviets' obvious next steps were either to lead Nasser willingly into the Communist camp or to increase their strength sufficiently within Egypt so as to make possible a Communist take-over. As the Soviet Union was to discover, however, Nasser was perfectly willing to use Soviet assistance as a lever against the West, but had no intention of becoming a Soviet tool. He cracked down on Communists within his own country and in 1958 agreed to the union of Egypt and Syria in order to forestall a Communist coup in that country. Relations between Egypt and the Soviet Union cooled and became cooler yet when the Soviet Union in 1958 gave strong support to the revolutionary government of General Qasim in Iraq. Nasser did not relish the build-up of a potential rival for Arab leadership. General Qasim soon showed that he also had no intention of becoming a Soviet tool; as soon as he had sufficient strength, he took steps to curb the growing power of the Communists in Iraq.

ARAB-ISRAEL RELATIONS. In its dealings with the Arab countries the United States has two strikes against it—its close relationship with France and Great Britain and its close identification with the birth and support of the state of Israel. We have attempted to maintain good relations with both the Arab states and Israel and at the same time to exert our influence to bring about a settlement of the disputes between the two parties. We have perhaps overestimated our influence. The Arab states refuse to recognize the existence of Israel and, had they possessed the military strength, would have crushed it at birth. Failing in that attempt, they have tried economic strangulation by boycotting Israeli products, blacklisting firms that have factories and branches in Israel and foreign ships that call at Israeli ports, and denying the use of the Suez Canal to ships flying the Israeli flag or even carrying cargoes to or from Israel.

American efforts at improving relations between the Arab states and Israel have followed these lines:

1. Supporting the efforts of the United Nations to prevent border incidents from developing into conflict. Incidents have ranged from the shooting of Israeli farmers by small groups of Arab infiltrators to large-scale reprisal raids carried out on Arab villages by Israeli army commandos.

2. Attempting to get Israel and Lebanon, Syria and Jordan to cooperate in a plan for harnessing the waters of the Jordan River. All wish to use its water for irrigation and power. The Arab states, however, would rather suffer economically than enter into discussions with Israel on this matter. The United States hoped that, by serving as a broker between the parties and offering to pick up the check, it might not only get them to work together but might also settle some of the Palestinian refugees on the newly irrigated land. In the early 1950's Mr. Eric Johnston, as the President's special representative, made several trips to the area. Although he

was finally able to obtain general agreement on technical questions concerning division of water, the Arab states could not bring themselves to make the political decision to go ahead with the project. Since then both Israel and Jordan have been carrying out independent projects for diversion of the Jordan waters. These have given rise to considerable friction.

3. Trying to work out a plan for resettlement of the Arabs who fled Palestine in 1948. The refugees now number over one million; most of them live in camps in Jordan and the Gaza Strip. Few have found permanent homes. They are fed and housed by the United Nations Relief and Works Agency for Palestine Refugees (UNRWA), for which the United States contributes the largest part of the funds. No settlement has been reached because of the opposing views held by the Arab states and Israel. The Arab states have insisted that Israel agree to compensate the refugees for their property and to permit them to return to their former homes. Israel, while willing to consider some compensation and perhaps repatriation of a token number, maintains that it neither has the room nor can take the security risk of agreeing to repatriation of all the refugees. The United States has on a number of occasions expressed its willingness to help finance the resettlement of the refugees in underpopulated Arab lands such as Syria and Iraq. These proposals have not been welcomed. The refugees appear convinced that any acceptance of resettlement would rule out forever any return to Palestine, and the Arab states view resettlement as recognition of the permanence of Israel.

4. Keeping a balance of arms. With the aim of trying to make effective the 1949 armistice agreements, France, the United Kingdom, and the United States in 1950 issued what became known as the Tripartite Declaration. The three powers served notice that they would not permit any armed aggression across the existing armistice lines and would strive to maintain a balance in the supply of arms to Israel and the Arab states in order to prevent the creation of any imbalance that might endanger the peace. As long as the West was the sole supplier of arms to the area, this limitation on arms was reasonably effective. The West lost control when Egypt in 1955 was able to conclude an arms deal with the Soviet bloc. Israel and the Arab states are now spending far more on arms than they can afford. The West has on occasion sold Israel

arms and aircraft to prevent the power balance from shifting to Egypt's side. The situation is becoming increasingly dangerous since both Israel and the U.A.R., with the help of German scientists, have been experimenting with rockets.

General Policy. In a relatively few years the United States has learned a great deal about the Middle East. Perhaps the most important fact is that problems of long-standing are not going to be solved overnight and that the people of the area are the only ones who can solve them. The United States cannot force them to; the most effective role it can play is one of helpful support.

With this realization, the United States since 1958 has adopted a much less tense attitude in its relations with the Middle East. In the early summer of 1958 it appeared that the area was deliberately and joyfully jumping aboard the Communist train. Egypt had accepted the Soviet offer to finance the Aswan High Dam. Although a Communist take-over in Syria had been thwarted for the moment by Syria's union with Egypt, the U.A.R. appeared dangerously dependent upon Soviet bloc economic and military aid. The new military government in Iraq was receiving strong Communist support. Yet these passengers on the Communist train elected not to ride through to the final destination. As they became more and more aware of the dangers of too close involvement with the Soviet Union, they themselves have sought to strengthen their ties with the West.

Although the United States can perhaps prevent external aggression and in emergencies can land troops, as it demonstrated in the case of Lebanon, there is little we can effectively do about inter-Arab power struggles. We have therefore tried to stay out of them. An exception was the civil war in Yemen, where the U.A.R. and Saudi Arabia, in their support of opposing sides in the civil war, seemed embarked on a collision course. In this case we gave strong support to the efforts of the United Nations to bring about a disengagement.

By becoming less involved in the internal rivalries of the Middle East, the United States has been able to profit from Soviet mistakes. By providing economic aid to those governments which show sincere interest in coping with their extremely difficult economic problems, we have sought to direct their energies to internal development and away from rivalries with their neighbors. We believe that the development of healthy national economies that can make visible headway in meeting the aspirations of their people will give them a greater stake in peace and stability and reduce the pressures toward conflict with their neighbors.

XIV. LATIN AMERICA

Latin America is a convenient term for the lands south of the border. In this continent-and-a-half stretching some seven thousand miles from the Rio Grande to Cape Horn live some 220 million people. With the inclusion of the islands of the Caribbean, there are twenty-two independent republics and several areas still associated with European nations and with the United States. Of the independent states, eighteen were once ruled by Spain; one (Brazil), by Portugal, one (Haiti), by France; and two (Jamaica and Trinidad-Tobago independent since 1962), by Great Britain. This chapter concerns itself with the twenty states which, with the United States, founded the regional body known as the Organization of American States (OAS).

Mutual interests and objectives have been drawing the members of the OAS into ever closer interdependence. Inevitably, an event in one of the states reverberates in the other states. The hemisphere today faces two main tasks. The first is to bring about, within a democratic framework, essential economic development and social reforms so that millions of restless people may have a better way of life. The second is to protect and perfect democratic institutions against the attempts of "Castro-communism" to undermine and destroy them. These tasks are intertwined. Conditions of economic and social discontent provide the seedbed in which communism germinates.

The roots of Latin America's problems lie deep. Solutions are neither quick nor easy. Seeking to put into perspective our policy toward Latin America, this chapter first looks at conditions typical of much of Latin America. It then examines the history of relations between the United States and Latin America, the development of the inter-American system, and the efforts to bring about economic development and social progress through the Alliance for Progress. The next chapter, "Cuba," discusses the rise of the Castro regime, the missile crisis, the threat to the hemisphere of Communist penetration, and the need for some changes in attitudes towards the traditional concepts underlying the inter-American system.

The countries of Latin America vary in size from El Salvador, roughly the size of Massachusetts, with 2.6 million inhabitants, to Brazil, slightly larger than the continental United States, with a population of over 75 million. Although the countries of Latin America have certain common characteristics and common problems, in many respects they are so different that generalizations become meaningless. For example, one might say that 40 per cent of the population of Latin America is illiterate. This is true but misleading. Illiteracy ranges from a mere 8 per cent of the population of Argentina to a massive 90 per cent in Haiti. Guatemala has a very large Indian population; its neighbor, Costa Rica, has very few. Brazil is troubled by inflation; some of its neighbors have stable currencies. Countries such as the Dominican Republic have had long and bitter experiences with dictatorships; others, such as Costa Rica and Uruguay, have had long experience with elective governments.

UNITED STATES-LATIN AMERICAN RELATIONS

Three threads stand out in the fabric of our relations with Latin America. They are:

1. Protection of the hemisphere against foreign encroachment.

2. Tensions in the relationship between the United States and its sister republics to the south.

3. Cooperation among the American states for common purposes.

The concept that the United States has a special interest in the protection of the Western Hemisphere was clearly stated in 1823 by President Monroe, in his year-end message to the Congress on the State of the Union. There were indications that Russia had territorial ambitions in the Pacific Northwest and that the continental European powers might seek to reimpose Spanish sovereignty upon the New World colonies which had just won independence. President Monroe's words, which came to be known as the Monroe Doctrine, set forth the U.S. attitude: [1]

> . . . the occasion has been judged proper for asserting, as a principle in which the rights and interests of the United States are involved, that the American continents, by the free and independent condition which they have assumed and maintain, are henceforth not to be considered as subjects for future colonization by any European powers. . . .
>
> . . . We owe it, therefore, to candor and to the amicable relations existing between the United States and those powers to declare that we should consider any attempt on their part to extend their system to any portion of this hemisphere as dangerous to our peace and safety. . . .

Over a century passed before this unilateral declaration was transformed into a continental undertaking. The Second Meeting of Foreign Ministers, held in 1940 at Havana agreed that an act of foreign aggression against an American state would be considered an act of aggression against all American states. This concept, which provided the basis for wartime cooperation against the Axis powers, was broadened at Mexico City in 1945 to include aggression on the part of any nation, American or non-American. It is the basis of the Inter-American Treaty of Reciprocal Assistance, signed at Rio de Janeiro in 1947.

The second thread in the relations between the United States and its neighbors to the south is, regrettably, woven of tensions and misunderstandings. Although the Organization of American States (OAS) is composed of twenty-one sovereign states, one of them, the United States, has far more wealth and power than the other twenty put together. The United States has the capacity to act alone on the world scene; they do not. A number of events in the past have given Latin Americans cause to suspect the motives of their large neighbor to the north. They well remember the war between the United States and Mexico in 1846–1848 which resulted in the cession of a large part of Mexico to the United States. They remember that, although Cuba achieved independence following the Spanish American War of 1898, the United States reserved the right under the Platt Amend-

[1] Extracts from President Monroe's Seventh Annual Message to Congress, 2 December 1823. From *Documents of American History*, Vol. I, edited by Henry Steele Commager (New York: F. S. Crofts and Co., 1938), p. 236.

ment to intervene in Cuba to maintain order and on several occasions did so. Not until 1934 did the United States rescind the Platt Amendment. They remember President Theodore Roosevelt's words, "Speak softly and carry a big stick; and you will go far," and the Roosevelt corollary to the Monroe Doctrine which he expressed as follows: [2]

> If a nation shows that it knows how to act with reasonable efficiency and decency in social and political matters, if it keeps order and pays its obligations, it need fear no interference from the United States. Chronic wrongdoing, or an impotence which results in a general loosening of the ties of civilized society, may in America, as elsewhere, ultimately require intervention by some civilized nation, and in the Western Hemisphere the adherence of the United States to the Monroe Doctrine may force the United States, however reluctantly, in flagrant cases of such wrongdoing or impotence, to the exercise of an international police power. . . .

The Roosevelt corollary was used to justify sending U.S. troops to the Dominican Republic (1916), Haiti (1915), and Nicaragua (1912) for the maintenance of order. Many Latin Americans have apparently forgotten that, although the U.S. did intervene, it always withdrew. Even before President Franklin D. Roosevelt enunciated the Good Neighbor Policy in 1933, our attitude was changing from that of the policeman and mentor of the hemisphere to that of one of the team.

The Seventh International Conference of American States meeting at Montevideo in 1933 unanimously accepted the principle that "no state has the right to intervene in the internal or external affairs of another." By disavowing intervention, the United States, represented by Secretary of State Cordell Hull, opened the door to a new approach.

The concept of partnership is the third thread in the fabric of our relations with Latin America. Over the years the areas of cooperation have steadily enlarged. They now include commerce, health, agriculture, education, settlement of disputes between states, common political action, and economic assistance. The Alliance for Progress is by far the most ambitious of these cooperative efforts.

[2] Annual Message to Congress, 6 December 1904. From *Documents of American History,* Vol. II, edited by Henry Steele Commager (New York: F. S. Crofts and Co., 1938), p. 213.

THE INTER-AMERICAN SYSTEM

ORGANIZATIONAL DEVELOPMENT. The inter-American system had its beginning in 1826 when Simon Bolivar, one of the great leaders in the wars of independence against Spain, called a conference of the American republics in Panama. Although the United States decided to send two representatives, political bickering in Congress over their appointment so delayed their departure that they never reached the conference. Bolivar hoped that the new nations would unite in a permanent association for their collective defense, but his vision was ahead of his times.

A permanent organization did not come into existence until 1890, when the American states met in Washington at the invitation of James G. Blaine, Secretary of State. This meeting, known as the First International Conference of American States, created the International Union of American Republics together with its working secretariat, the Commercial Bureau of the American Republics. In 1910 the Bureau was renamed the Pan American Union, and permanent headquarters were built in Washington, D.C.

In 1948 at Bogota, Colombia, representatives of the twenty-one American states signed a Charter reorganizing the inter-American system and giving it the name of Organization of American States (OAS).

THE MACHINERY. The OAS has three major representative bodies:

1. The Inter-American Conference, the supreme body, decides general policy and action and has the authority to consider any matter relating to relations among the American states. Each state is represented by a number of official delegates but has only one vote. The chief delegate is usually the foreign minister. Regular meetings are supposed to be held at five year intervals. The last regular Inter-American Conference, the tenth, was held in Caracas in 1954. The Eleventh Inter-American Conference was scheduled to meet in Quito in 1959, but a number of circumstances, including internal troubles in Ecuador, resulted in an indefinite postponement. With the approval of two-thirds of the American governments, a special Inter-American Conference may be held.

2. The Meeting of Consultation of Ministers of Foreign

Affairs, which may be called at the request of any member state upon decision of the Council of the OAS, considers problems of an urgent nature. By the end of 1962 there had been a total of eight such meetings. The first three were held during World War II and dealt with the defense of the hemisphere. The other five have been held since 1951 and have been primarily concerned with the threat to the hemisphere of aggressive communism and with tension in the Caribbean arising out of the activities of the Trujillo regime in the Dominican Republic and of the Castro regime in Cuba.

The Meeting of Consultation also serves as the Organ of Consultation provided for under the Rio Treaty in case of an armed attack on, or threat to, the independence of any American state. By a two-thirds vote, the Meeting of Consultation can adopt measures binding on all members.

3. The Council, the permanent executive body, is composed of one representative from each member republic. It takes care of the day-to-day business and can act provisionally as the Organ of Consultation, in case of a threat to the peace, when it has invoked a Meeting of Consultation of Foreign Ministers. The Council's headquarters are in the Pan American Union building in Washington, D.C.

There are three separate bodies to advise the Council—the Inter-American Economic and Social Council (IA-ECOSOC), the Inter-American Council of Jurists, and the Inter-American Cultural Council.

The Pan American Union serves as the secretariat of the OAS.

There are six special organizations dealing with technical matters of common interest—health, children, women's rights, geography and history, Indians, and agriculture. There are also several special agencies and commissions which have independent status within the OAS. Noteworthy among them are the Inter-American Defense Board, which coordinates defense measures, and the Inter-American Development Bank.

From time to time specialized conferences—such as on economic development, housing, education, and agriculture—are held.

The regular annual budget of the OAS comes to about $15 million, of which, under the quota system based on population and income, the United States pays two-thirds.

In 1945, at the conference in San Francisco which drew up the U.N. Charter, the American states insisted that the U.N. recognize the existence of regional organizations and their primary responsibility for settlement of regional disputes. Article 52 of the U.N. Charter does so. Members of the OAS are to make every effort to achieve pacific settlement of disputes through the OAS before referring them to the Security Council of the United Nations. The Inter-American Peace Committee, established by a resolution adopted at Havana in 1940, is composed of representatives of five governments chosen by the Council of the OAS. It has been successful in bringing together conflicting parties and helping them to solve their disputes. One accomplishment was the resolution in 1961 of the long-standing border dispute between Honduras and Nicaragua.

PURPOSES, PRINCIPLES, and PROCEDURES. The Charter of the Organization of American States, signed at Bogota in 1948, pulled together in one document the purposes, principles, and procedures of the inter-American system which had been agreed to at successive conferences.

The purposes, set forth in Article 4, show how broad is the area of cooperation:

> a. To strengthen the peace and security of the continent;
> b. To prevent possible causes of difficulties and to ensure the pacific settlement of disputes that may arise among the Member States;
> c. To provide for common action on the part of those States in the event of aggression;
> d. To seek the solution of political, juridical and economic problems that may arise among them; and
> e. To promote, by cooperative action, their economic, social and cultural development.

Listed below are the main principles set forth in the charter that are of particular importance today.

1. No state or group of states has the right to intervene, directly or indirectly, in the affairs of any other state (non-intervention). (Article 15)

2. The territory of a state is inviolable; it may not be the object, even temporarily, of military occupation or of other measures of force taken by another state. (Article 17)

3. Measures adopted for the maintenance of peace and

security in accordance with existing treaties do not constitute a violation of the principles set forth in Articles 15 and 17. (Article 19)

4. Each state has the right to develop its cultural, political, and economic life freely and naturally (self-determination).

5. The solidarity of the American states and the high aims which are sought through it require the political organization of those states on the basis of the effective exercise of representative democracy.

6. An act of aggression against one American state is an act of aggression against all the other American states.

Under the Inter-American Treaty of Reciprocal Assistance, signed at Rio de Janeiro in 1947 and usually referred to as the Rio Treaty, each state undertakes to assist in meeting an armed attack against any other American state. The Organ of Consultation (the foreign ministers) is to meet without delay to decide on collective measures for the common defense. Measures may include breaking of diplomatic relations and use of armed force. Decisions in the Organ of Consultation are taken by a two-thirds majority.

7. Controversies between American states are to be settled by peaceful means.

A state involved in a controversy with a neighbor may (a) ask the Inter-American Peace Committee to attempt to settle the dispute; (b) may use one of the formal methods for resolving differences, including an appeal to the International Court of Justice, set forth in the American Treaty on Pacific Settlement (signed at Bogota at the same time as the charter of the OAS); or (c) appeal in extreme cases to the entire hemisphere to come to its defense under the Rio Treaty.

8. Economic cooperation is essential to the common welfare and prosperity of the peoples of the continent. The member states agree to cooperate with one another to achieve just and decent living conditions for their entire populations. Social justice and social security are bases of lasting peace.

The principal agent that carries out the principles in paragraph 8 is the Alliance for Progress.

Representatives of the American states have met on a number of occasions since drawing up the charter at Bogota in 1948 and have developed further principles and procedures. These are discussed later in relation to the events with which they are concerned—principally the Alliance for

Progress and the menace to the hemisphere of Communist subversion.

THE ALLIANCE FOR PROGRESS

The signing of the Inter-American Treaty of Reciprocal Assistance at Rio de Janeiro in 1947 marked the high point of our relations with Latin America. Cooperation against the common enemy during World War II had brought to the twenty-one states an identity of interest. From 1947 on, however, the slow erosion in this relationship became steadily more apparent. Perhaps one of the principal causes, which was only dimly perceived at the time, was that United States attention was directed to other parts of the world. In 1947 we put our energies into the Marshall Plan for European recovery, and in 1949 we concluded the NATO alliance. We interpreted these moves to our own citizens as the most effective way of safeguarding the security of the U.S. We did not make clear at the time that these moves also safeguarded the security of the Western Hemisphere. Whereas we had implicitly rejected isolationism, the other twenty states had not. The Latin America nations did not regard the cold war as a direct concern to them, but rather as a contest between two superpowers. They did not feel endangered by Sino-Soviet expansion and were unable to associate their interests with ours. This perhaps explains why Latin American nations so grudgingly subscribed to the Caracas resolution of 1954 labeling international communism a menace to the hemisphere and why many of them did not take seriously the threat of the Castro regime until Soviet offensive missiles were discovered in Cuba.

To the Latin Americans, their internal economic and social problems were far more important than the cold war struggle. They felt that the United States, which had been so liberal with its expenditures elsewhere in the world, was badly neglecting them. The boom in commodity prices caused by the Korean War had stimulated the Latin American economies, but by the late fifties prices had dropped whereas spending had not. A number of Latin American countries saw themselves in serious economic difficulties. If they were to get themselves on their feet, outside help was needed.

In May 1958 President Kubitschek of Brazil wrote to President Eisenhower concerning the need of undertaking economic measures to strengthen the inter-American system.

Giving his plan the name "Operation Pan America," he suggested increased private investment, control of inflation, increased loans from the U.S., establishment of a regional development bank, stabilization of export prices, eventual establishment of a Latin American common market, consideration of the impact of the European Common Market on Latin America, and increased technical assistance. At first, the U.S. was rather cool to these proposals but soon considered all of them. The foreign ministers, meeting informally in Washington in September 1958, established a special committee under the OAS, the Committee of 21, to work out measures that might be taken under Operation Pan America.

In 1959 all the representatives of the Latin America republics except Cuba agreed to the establishment of the Inter-American Development Bank (IDB) with a capital stock of $850 million and a Fund for Special Operations with a capital of $150 million. The Bank operates on the principle of any other bank, that is, of making loans for projects that show some promise of paying off. The Fund makes loans for projects that would ordinarily not be bankable, such as roads and educational facilities that are not going to be self-liquidating.

In September 1960 the Committee of 21 held its third period of sessions in Bogota. The resulting Act of Bogota (nineteen signed, Cuba dissented, the Dominican Republic was not present) agreed to "launch a program for social development in which emphasis should be given to those measures that met social needs, and also promote increases in Productivity and strengthen economic development." Congress meanwhile had responded to President Eisenhower's request to authorize $500 million for this program and another $100 million for rehabilitation in Chile, which had been badly hit by an earthquake.

President Kennedy carried his predecessor's initiative even further. On March 13, 1961, at a White House reception for members of Congress and Latin American diplomats, he suggested a ten-year plan for the Americas with a goal of transforming the 1960's into "an historic decade of democratic progress." This would not be just a United States aid program but a joint undertaking—an Alliance for Progress—in which the Latin American states would have heavy responsibilities.

Although President Kennedy's proposals were very well received throughout Latin America, public attention was soon focused on the abortive Cuban invasion attempt of April 17–19, 1961. The Alliance was a genuine attempt to meet the needs of the hemisphere and not an attempt to buy support for our Cuban stand; but the situation in Cuba had made us realize the urgency of the problems in the rest of the hemisphere.

In August, 1961, the Inter-American Economic and Social Council met in Punta del Este, Uruguay, to see what could be done toward putting the Alliance for Progress on the tracks. The meeting was at the ministerial level, and our delegate was Douglas Dillon, the Secretary of the Treasury. Agreement on a course of action was reached after eleven days of deliberation.

The Cuban delegate, Ernesto "Che" Guevara, at first tried to disrupt the meeting. When he saw that these tactics were winning Cuba no friends, he hinted at possible Cuban participation in the Alliance. This, of course, would have made the U.S. Congress and public less than enthusiastic about providing the necessary funds. In fact, the Foreign Assistance Act of 1961 specifically prohibited aid to Cuba. A declaration of intent was then drawn up stressing that "This Alliance is established on the basic principle that free men working through the institution of representative democracy can best satisfy man's aspirations . . ." Cuba could not bring itself to sign.

The Declaration to the Peoples of America and the Charter of Punta del Este set forth the determination of their signers to work toward the following goals:

To improve and strengthen democratic institutions.

To accelerate economic and social development.

To carry out urban and rural housing programs.

To encourage programs of agrarian reform.

To wipe out illiteracy.

To press forward with programs of health and sanitation.

To assure fair wages and satisfactory working conditions for all workers.

To reform tax laws.

To maintain monetary and fiscal policies which will protect the purchasing power of the many.

To stimulate private enterprise.

To find a solution to the grave problem created by excessive price fluctuations in the basic exports of Latin American countries.

To accelerate the economic integration of Latin America.

The countries of Latin America agreed to devote a steadily increasing share of their own resources to economic and social development, to make the reforms necessary to insure that all their citizens shared fully in the results, and to draw up comprehensive national development programs. To reach the goals, it was realized that the rate of economic growth in all countries of Latin America would have to be at least 2.5 per cent per capita per year and that over the ten-year period they would have to devote at least $80 billion of their own resources. For its part, the United States undertook to provide a major part of the external financing, estimated at $20 billion over the ten-year period, and specifically to make $1 billion available in the year ending March 1962.

The charter emphasized the need to speed up the broadening of markets through lowered tariff barriers among the Latin American countries. A start had already been made by the Montevideo Treaty of 1960, establishing a seven-nation Latin American Free Trade Association (LAFTA), and the Central America Treaty on Economic Integration, also signed in 1960.

The charter provided a mechanism for screening each country's plans. A government, if it wishes, presents its development plan to a committee composed of up to three of "nine wise men," attached to the Inter-American Economic and Social Council, and an equal number of experts proposed by the country. The committee studies the development program, exchanges opinions with the interested government, and reports its conclusions. Arrangements can then be made for financing, whether by the IDB, AID, the International Bank, other countries, or private banks. This service is available to a country only if it wishes it. Alternatively, it can go directly to possible sources of funds.

A first year progress report showed mixed results. Economic development plans submitted by Chile and Colombia had received favorable review, and the International Bank had formed a consortium to finance the Colombian plan. Several countries had drawn up land reform and tax reform measures and had tightened up their system of tax collection. A number had made good progress in construction of low-cost housing and schools. The main criticism was that progress had not been fast enough and that some of the countries needed to realize that this was not merely a program of U.S. economic assistance but required much more self-help on their part.

XV. CUBA

The Castro take-over of the Cuban government under President Batista demonstrates how a small group of very determined men can overthrow a government that is more interested in staying in power than in bringing about the social and economic reforms the country desperately needs. Without a basis of popular support, the government must depend upon the army. Once President Batista lost the allegiance of the army his days were numbered.

Cuba prior to Castro was better off economically than most of its sister republics. Sugar exports, the mainstay of the economy, were booming, and trade with the United States alone was in the neighborhood of $1 billion a year. There was, however, entirely too large a gap between the very rich in Havana and the very poor who made up the majority of the population. Castro's promises of a better life, added to the corruption and increasing brutality of the Batista regime, swung popular support to Castro. The developing middle class of doctors, lawyers, businessmen, and teachers, who realized the need for reform, responded to Castro's moving declarations concerning his plans for political freedom and social justice.

Much has been written, after the fact, that the United States government should have realized from the very beginning that Castro was a Communist and should have taken steps to prevent his ever coming to power. Many of his closest associates, even those who had fought with him in the Sierra Maestra, were equally mistaken in their evaluation of the man. Of the nineteen members of his first cabinet for the revolutionary government, over two-thirds are now dead, in prison, or in exile because of their opposition to Communist control of Cuba. When Castro fled to the mountains in December, 1956, to carry on the fight against the Batista government, he did not have the support of the Cuban Communist Party, which dismissed him as "bourgeois." Only when the party saw he had a chance of winning did it lend him support.

As early as 1957 the United States Government expressed its concern over political unrest in Cuba. In 1958 we suspended arms shipments to the Batista government. The purpose of sending arms to Cuba, as well as to other Latin American governments, was for hemispheric defense rather than the suppression of local revolutionary movements. President Batista fled Cuba on January 1, 1959, and Dr. Castro came to power. As did most of the countries of Latin America, we recognized his government almost immediately and welcomed his promises of a new deal for the Cuban people.

THE CASTRO REGIME

Few countries have changed so completely as did Cuba in the next three years. These were the main aspects of the change:

THE BETRAYAL OF THE PROMISES OF THE REVOLUTION AND THE CONVERSION OF CUBA TO A TOTALITARIAN STATE. Fidel Castro came to power with the near unanimous support of the Cuban people. Manuel Urrutia, a respected judge, was made President, and Jose Miró Cardona, a distinguished lawyer, was named Prime Minister. Dr. Miró Cardona lasted six weeks and Dr. Urrutia, slightly over six months. Dr. Urrutia, after charging in a television broadcast that communism was a danger to the Cuban revolution, was accused of treason by Castro. He resigned, was placed under house arrest, and subsequently was permitted to go to the United States. The head of the Cuban Air Force, a leader of the Cuban labor movement, and many other early enthusiastic supporters of Fidel Castro found that the consequences of protesting the Communist take-over of the revolution meant either exile or imprisonment. As the original Castro supporters were purged, Communists were placed in positions of authority and control over education, agriculture, industry, labor, communications—in short, over every aspect of Cuban life.

Any lingering doubts as to where Fidel Castro stood were put to rest on December 2, 1961, when he declared in a television speech: [1] "I am a Marxist-Leninist and will be a

[1] *The New York Times,* 3 December 1961.

Marxist-Leninist until the last day of my life." He admitted that he had hid his true political ideology during his revolutionary struggle because he felt that ". . . if we, when we began to have strength, had been known as people of very radical ideas, unquestionably all the social classes that are making war on us would have been doing so from that time on . . . ."

THE IDENTIFICATION OF CUBA WITH THE SINO-SOVIET BLOC. The Cuban agreement on December 31, 1959, to sell 50,000 tons of sugar to Communist China was followed by an agreement on February 13, 1960, with the Soviet Union for the sale of one million tons of Cuban sugar in each of the next five years and the extension by the Soviet Union of a credit of $100 million for the purchase of Soviet equipment. Within a year Cuba had established diplomatic relations with all the bloc countries except East Germany and had entered into economic agreements with many of them, including East Germany. This series of trade and financial agreements integrated the Cuban economy with that of the Communist world.

Along with economic aid from the Communist countries came military assistance in large quantities and assurances of Soviet support. On July 9, 1960, Chairman Khrushchev stated that the U.S.S.R. is ". . . raising its voice and extending a helpful hand to the people of Cuba . . . Speaking figuratively, in case of necessity, Soviet artillerymen can support the Cuban people with rocket fire . . ." [2] With the help of bloc arms, Cuba under Castro built up a military establishment at least ten times as large as that under Batista.

During the sixteenth session of the U.N. General Assembly in 1961, Cuba voted with the Soviet bloc on thirty-three out of thirty-seven major issues and only five times with the majority of the American republics.

A CAMPAIGN OF HOSTILITY AGAINST THE UNITED STATES. For over a year after Dr. Castro's accession to power the United States expressed its sympathies for the purposes of the revolution, its desire to be helpful, and its hope for friendly relations. In response, Cuba accused the United States of having aided Batista, of sponsoring counterrevolutionary activities, and even of responsibility for the explosion

[2] *The New York Times,* 10 July 1960.

in Havana harbor of a French munitions ship. Three months after Castro came to power, the Cuban Government took over control of the Cuban Telephone Company, the first seizure of a U.S.-owned firm, and in succeeding months took over U.S.-owned ranches, sugar refineries, oil refineries, hotels, banks, and other properties, altogether valued at about one billion dollars. On January 2, 1961, Castro demanded that the staff of the U.S. embassy be reduced to eleven persons. In view of this demand, which would have placed crippling limitations on the ability of the United States to carry out normal diplomatic and consular functions, the United States broke relations with Cuba.

THE ASSAULT ON THE HEMISPHERE. During the first six months of 1959, in the flush of victory, Castro aided or supported armed invasions of Panama, Nicaragua, the Dominican Republic, and Haiti. These unsuccessful expeditions served only to arouse the suspicions of the other Latin American countries and to generate action by the OAS. Castro then shifted his tactics and resorted to the following actions:

1. Supported the formation of front organizations in other countries of the hemisphere in the form of friendship societies or committees for the defense of the Cuban revolution, such as The Fair Play for Cuba Committee in the United States.
2. Engaged in an intensive propaganda campaign by printed materials, press, and radio.
3. Furnished covert material support, largely financial, to subversive groups.
4. Sponsored the indoctrination and training of hundreds of Latin Americans in Cuba, including training in sabotage, terrorism, and guerrilla tactics.

ACTIONS BY THE UNITED STATES AND BY THE ORGANIZATION OF AMERICAN STATES (OAS)

After months of trying to find some means of getting along with the Castro regime and of great forbearance in the face of many provocations, the patience of the United States wore thin. By midsummer of 1960 it had become clear that the Castro regime had no desire for friendly relations with the United States, that it had firmly identified its interests with those of the Sino-Soviet bloc, and that its aim was to promote Communist revolutions in its sister republics in Latin America. Our policy was then directed toward nullifying Cuba's usefulness as a source of infection for international communism while at the same time rendering it more costly for the Sino-Soviet bloc to maintain for that purpose. In pursuit of this objective we took a number of steps, both unilaterally and in collaboration with our friends and allies.

The process of isolating Cuba economically first began in July 1960. Pursuant to congressional authorization, President Eisenhower ordered a cut of 700,000 tons in Cuba's 1960 sugar quota (the amount Cuba was permitted to sell to the United States at premium prices). The reason given for this cut was that Cuban commitments to pay for Soviet goods with Cuban sugar had raised serious doubts as to whether the United States could depend upon Cuba as a source of sugar. In October 1960 the United States prohibited the export of U.S. goods to Cuba except for nonsubsidized foodstuffs, medicines, and medical supplies. In December 1960 the President set the Cuban sugar quota at zero.

In January 1961 Castro's demand that we drastically reduce the number of officers in our embassy in Havana resulted in our terminating diplomatic relations. On April 17 19 occurred the ill-fated landing at the Bay of Pigs by Cuban exiles determined to free their country.

Prior to the missile crisis of October 1962, many of the Latin American countries failed to take seriously the menace to them of Castro-Communist subversion. Some regarded Cuba as primarily the concern of the United States and seemed to fear U.S. intervention more than Communist infiltration. In August 1960 the Sixth and Seventh Meetings of Consultation of the Ministers of Foreign Affairs of the American States were held in San Jose, Costa Rica. The sixth meeting was called to consider charges that the Trujillo regime in the Dominican Republic was implicated in an assassination attempt on President Betancourt of Venezuela. The seventh meeting, called to consider the question of Cuba, could agree on nothing stronger than a condemnation of outside intervention in the affairs of the hemisphere. The resolution did not specify Cuba by name, and some delegations said that it should not be interpreted as applying specifically to Cuba. Although the foreign ministers had no hesitation in taking action against the Trujillo dictatorship, they were not prepared to take concrete steps aimed at the Communist offensive in general and Cuba in particular.

In January 1962 the foreign ministers met in Punta del Este, Uruguay, for their Eighth Meeting of Consultation. In the seventeen months since the previous meeting in San Jose the nature of the Castro regime had become much more apparent to both the governments and peoples of Latin America. This time the foreign ministers were in agreement (unanimous except for Cuba) that

1. The Castro-Communist offensive in this hemisphere is a clear and present danger to the unity and freedom of the American republics.

2. ". . . the present government of Cuba, which has officially identified itself as a Marxist-Leninist government, is incompatible with the principles and objectives of the inter-American system."

3. The struggle against communism in this hemisphere is not merely a question of defense against subversion but of the positive measures of reform set forth in the Alliance for Progress.

The conference, being in agreement on principles, was then able to adopt specific courses of action, including:

1. The exclusion of Cuba from the Inter-American Defense Board.

2. The prohibition of traffic in arms between Cuba and the other American countries.

3. The exploration of further trade restrictions.

4. The establishment of special machinery within the OAS to recommend joint action to block Communist subversive activities.

5. The exclusion of the present government of Cuba from participation in the inter-American system.

On this last point, the conference agreed by only a two-thirds majority. Abstaining were the three largest countries—Argentina, Brazil, and Mexico—and Bolivia, Chile, and Ecuador. Some governments questioned the legality of exclusion of a member; others were troubled by domestic political considerations.

In the months following the meeting at Punta del Este, Cuba had become increasingly isolated, not only because credits and goods were cut off, but also by shipping restrictions imposed by the United States and its allies. We were becoming increasingly concerned, however, by the step-up, beginning in July 1962, in shipments of Soviet arms to Cuba.

These arms included surface-to-air missiles with a range of 25 miles, coastal defense missile installations effective to a range of 30-35 miles, modern jet interceptors, "Komar" class guided missile patrol boats, and tanks, self-propelled guns, and other ground force equipment. About 4,200 Soviet military specialists and technicians, we calculated, arrived in connection with the shipments. As far as we could ascertain at the time, however, these weapons were of a defensive character.

TWO WEEKS OF CRISIS

The Cuban crisis began late on Monday night, October 15, 1962, when the analysis of aerial photographs revealed the presence in Cuba of medium and intermediate range missiles capable of the nuclear bombing of a large part of the Western Hemisphere. The crisis ended on Sunday, October 28, 1962, when Chairman Khrushchev notified President Kennedy that he had ordered the dismantling of the sites and the shipment of the equipment back to the Soviet Union.

The President first saw the photographs early Tuesday morning, October 16, and summoned to the White House a number of the key men in his administration. During the next two weeks an informal group, which came to be known as the Executive Committee of the National Security Council, worked directly with the President. In this group were: Dean Rusk, the Secretary of State; Robert McNamara, Secretary of Defense; Douglas Dillon, Secretary of the Treasury; Robert Kennedy, the Attorney General; John McCone, Director of the C.I.A.; General Maxwell Taylor, Chairman of the Joint Chiefs of Staff; McGeorge Bundy, Special Assistant to the President; and Theodore Sorensen, Special Counsel to the President. Working closely with this nucleus and attending some of the meetings were other high officials and Dean Acheson, Secretary of State under President Truman.

The two weeks of the Cuban crisis brought into play every aspect of foreign policy and well illustrated the five main steps in the policy-making process:

1. Collection of reliable information.
2. Evaluation of the information.
3. Determining the objective.
4. Determining a course of action to accomplish the objective.
5. Carrying out the course of action.

Step one was the taking of the aerial photographs. *Step two,* their evaluation, showed the presence of Soviet missile sites. *Step three* was to determine our objective. Was it to be limited to getting the Soviet missiles out of Cuba or was it to include destroying the Castro regime? What was immediately possible? Pressure on Khrushchev could conceivably bring about the removal of the missiles but could not directly result in a change of government in Cuba. The missiles were the immediate menace to our security; the President decided to make their removal the primary objective.

The fourth step was to determine the best way of accomplishing the objective of securing the removal of the missiles. These were the possibilities:

1. Send a stiff note of protest to the Soviet Union and at the same time ask for a meeting of the U.N. Security Council.
2. Invade the island of Cuba.
3. Bomb the missile sites.
4. Institute a quarantine of Cuba to prevent further delivery of offensive military equipment.

Alternative one as the sole course of action was never seriously considered. The menace to the security of the United States was too grave to resort only to diplomatic protests. *Alternatives two* and *three* would inevitably result in loss of life and perhaps in Soviet countermeasures in Berlin or elsewhere. *Alternative four* seemed most likely to accomplish the withdrawal of the missiles and at the same time to present the fewest disadvantages.

The final step in the policy-making process is to carry out the decision. The fact that we were aware of the missile bases had been kept secret. The problem now was to preserve this secrecy until we had made all the necessary preparations, so as to avoid giving the Russians any opportunity to take evasive action. We could not wait too long, however, as our action could only be effective if taken before the missile sites became operational.

President Kennedy broke the news in a radio and television broadcast to the nation at 7 P.M., Monday, October 22. He announced the following:

1. A quarantine on all offensive military equipment under shipment to Cuba. This meant, if necessary, the searching and turning back of Russian ships.
2. Continued and increased surveillance of Cuba.
3. "It shall be the policy of this nation to regard any

nuclear missiles launched from Cuba against any nation in the Western Hemisphere as an attack by the Soviet Union on the United States, requiring a full retaliatory response upon the Soviet Union."

4. Reinforcement of our naval base at Guantanamo (established on the southeastern coast of Cuba under a 1903 lease agreement) and the evacuation of naval dependents from that base.

5. A call for an immediate meeting of the Organ of Consultation of the OAS to consider this threat to hemispheric security.

6. A call for an emergency meeting of the Security Council "to take action against this latest Soviet threat to world peace."

7. A call upon Chairman Khrushchev to halt this threat to the peace and to join in an effort to end the arms race.

The smooth execution of this program required careful advance planning and rapid follow-through. The following were among the actions taken on a broad range of fronts:

I. DIPLOMATIC

A. Notification of allies.

1. A personal letter from the President to the chief of state of each of the forty-two nations with which we have alliances and also to the Mayor of Berlin. Direct communication with Prime Minister Macmillan.

2. Mr. Acheson was sent to Paris in time to inform General de Gaulle on the afternoon of October 22. That evening Mr. Acheson informed the NATO Council and the following day conferred with President Adenauer in Bonn.

3. Ambassadors in Washington were briefed by the Department of State shortly before the President's address. Ambassadors to the OAS were given copies of the resolution we planned to introduce in the meetings of the Council of the OAS the following day.

B. Cables to our embassies informing them of the actions to be taken and alerting them to the possibility of Communist-inspired riots.

C. At the meeting of the Security Council on October 23, Ambassador Stevenson submitted a resolution calling for the immediate dismantling and withdrawal from Cuba of all missiles and other offensive weapons and requesting the Acting Secretary General to send observers to report on compliance with this resolution.

D. Meeting on October 23 in Washington of the Council of the OAS. Constituting itself provisionally as Organ of Consultation, it passed a resolution calling for dismantling and withdrawal from Cuba of all offensive weapons and recommending that the member states, in accordance with the Inter-American Treaty of Reciprocal Assistance, take all measures, including the use of armed force, to insure that the government of Cuba cannot continue to receive offensive weapons from the Sino-Soviet bloc. This action provided OAS authorization for the quarantine measure.

E. Letter from President Kennedy to Chairman Khrushchev, the first of several letters sent and received during the crisis.

II. MILITARY

A. Sending of naval forces to the Caribbean.
B. Build-up of troops and air power in Florida.
C. Alerting of U.S. military commands throughout the world.
D. Continued and intensified aerial surveillance of Cuba.
E. Reinforcement of Guantanamo and evacuation of dependents.

III. POLITICAL and LEGISLATIVE

A. Key Members of Congress were called to Washington and briefed by the President a few hours before his address to the nation. Congress had already expressed its feelings on the necessity for a firm position vis-a-vis Cuba in a joint resolution, approved on October 3.
B. Former Presidents were notified by President Kennedy of our proposed course of action.
C. The Foreign Aid and Related Agencies Appropriations Act, approved on October 23, stated that no assistance was to be furnished any country which sells or permits its ships to carry to Cuba items of economic assistance unless the President determines withholding of assistance would be contrary to the national interest.

IV. INFORMATIONAL

A. Briefing of newspaper correspondents.
B. Foreign language broadcasts on the Voice of America.
C. Spanish language broadcasts to the Cuban people.

V. LEGAL

Drafting of the quarantine proclamation.

These were only some of the many steps involved in carrying out the course of action. On October 24, U Thant, Acting Secretary General of the United Nations, in letters to Mr. Kennedy and Mr. Khrushchev, suggested suspension of arms shipments and suspension of the quarantine for several weeks while the two powers discussed the matter. Ambassador Stevenson was instructed to inform U Thant of our determination to get the missiles out of Cuba. On October 25, twelve of twenty-five Soviet ships headed for Cuba turned around. On October 28, Chairman Khrushchev informed the President that he had ordered the dismantling of the missiles and their return to the Soviet Union.

So ended the critical two weeks.

THE SOVIET POINT OF VIEW

Why did the Soviet Union construct missile bases in Cuba? All we can do is speculate. Mr. Khruschev has stated, and there is no reason to doubt him, that the Soviet Union has missiles in its own territory that are capable of reaching the United States. He also knew that the United States had long-range missiles in its own territory, intermediate-range missiles in Great Britain, Italy, and Turkey, and Polaris missiles in submarines, all capable of hitting selected targets in the Soviet Union. Soviet leaders recognized that the United States had the preponderance of strength. Putting medium- and intermediate-range ballistic missiles into Cuba would not only contribute toward equalizing military strength but would also be a devastating psychological blow. And in this peculiar type of cold war, the battle for men's minds and psychological attitudes is important. American reaction would also be a gauge as to how far the Soviet Union could probe in other directions. If the United States failed to respond, as perhaps Khrushchev thought it might, he could assume that the U.S. would likewise fail to respond if he took over West Berlin. Success in Cuba would also give him new strength vis-a-vis the Chinese Communists, who had been accusing the Soviets of becoming soft in their stand toward the West. If the worst happened from Khrushchev's point of view and he had to withdraw the missiles, as he did, he risked only a loss of face which perhaps could be made up by posing as the savior of world peace. But when the United States insisted upon removal of the missiles, Chairman Khrushchev must have realized that he was skirting very close to a nuclear war which the Soviet Union wanted no more than the United States.

THE AFTERMATH OF THE CRISIS

In his letter of October 27 to Chairman Khrushchev, President Kennedy wrote: [3]

> As I read your letter, the key elements of your proposals —which seem generally acceptable as I understand them— are as follows:
>
> 1. You would agree to remove these weapons systems from Cuba under appropriate United Nations observation and supervision; and undertake, with suitable safeguards, to halt the further introduction of such weapons systems into Cuba.
>
> 2. We, on our part, would agree—upon establishment of adequate arrangements through the United Nations to ensure the carrying out and continuation of these commitments—(a) to remove promptly the quarantine measures now in effect and (b) to give assurances against an invasion of Cuba. I am confident that other nations of the Western Hemisphere would be prepared to do likewise.

Castro's consent to United Nations observation was necessary, however, and this the Soviet Union could not deliver, despite the trip to Cuba of Anastas Mikoyan, the Soviet First Deputy Premier. We therefore had to depend upon continued aerial surveillance and on naval inspection of departing Soviet vessels to confirm their removal. The statements by some Members of Congress questioning whether the missiles had really been removed resulted in an unprecedented two-hour press briefing in February 1963 by the Secretary of Defense. He and an associate gave an amazingly frank account, illustrated by photographs, of the methods we had used to assure ourselves of the missiles' removal from Cuba. Nevertheless, Cuba continued to be a domestic political issue.

Although Cuba without nuclear missiles is not a direct menace to the United States, its subversive activities do threaten the stability of many countries in Latin America. The missile crisis, in exposing the Castro regime as a tool of Moscow, caused it to lose popular support in Latin America. While still abetting open revolt, the Castro regime changed the emphasis of its campaign in Latin America from

[3] *The Department of State Bulletin* (Washington, D. C.: U. S. Government Printing Office, 12 November 1962), p. 743.

one of popular front, mass-movement tactics to one that encouraged terror.

Venezuela is a principal target. Through a campaign of sabotage and terrorism, Communists have attempted to overthrow the popularly elected and popularly supported government of President Betancourt. Their activities have included hit-and-run raids, setting off homemade pipe bombs in the streets of Caracas, burning warehouses of foreign enterprises, blowing up oil company power installations, kidnapping, and attempted assassination. The Castro regime has supported these activities by supplying funds and weapons and by training Venezuelans in Cuba in the techniques of sabotage and guerrilla warfare.

The United States is directly attacking the problem of Communist subversion in the Western Hemisphere in two ways:

1. By isolating Cuba from contacts with the rest of the hemisphere and by discrediting the image of the Cuban revolution.

2. By supplyimg arms and training to selected personnel of the armies and police forces of countries which request this assistance in order to improve their capability to maintain internal law and order against Communist-inspired violence.

These actions are helpful, but it would be wishful thinking indeed to assume that they alone will make the Western Hemisphere safe for democracy. That day will come only when the conditions which encourage the growth of communism are no longer prevalent and when a government which does not rest upon the consent of its people, expressed through free elections, will no longer be able to remain in power. Peaceful evolution can take the place of violent revolution if the American states possess the will and ability to act and to coordinate their efforts with one another. Two courses of action are indicated:

The first is to provide a democratic alternative to Castro-Communism by a vigorous campaign to modernize Latin American society.

The second course of action depends upon whether the American states will be as concerned about the practice of democracy itself as they are about public education, health, and industrialization. Yet traditional attitudes toward the principles of self-determination and nonintervention have hindered collective action to promote the effective exercise of representative democracy.

As the President of Panama noted in a speech in 1962 before the Council of the OAS, in applying these principles the hemisphere runs the risk of "drifting toward a new formula of eyes shut and hands off" resulting in an "almost complete indifference to the fate of brother peoples who, within their national boundaries, are deprived by force of all chance of self-determination, and for whom the principle of nonintervention, carried to its most extreme interpretation, becomes a universal condemnation to live forever subject to the oppression that incurably affects them." Article 19 of the Charter of the OAS, however, specifies that measures adopted for the maintenance of peace and security in accordance with existing treaties do not constitute a violation of the principles of nonintervention and the inviolability of the territory of a state.

The principles of self-determination and nonintervention are being used as a cloak behind which Cuba and local Communist movements carry on activities threatening the peace and security of Latin American countries. Yet the Castro regime flagrantly violates both principles. It has not held the elections it promised before coming to power. It is actively intervening in the affairs of its neighbors.

The thinking of the United States Government was well set forth in a speech on April 16, 1963, by Edwin M. Martin, Assistant Secretary for Inter-American Affairs. He said: [4]

> We need to give the principle of self-determination its true and vital meaning: freedom for the people periodically to decide through elections who their leaders should be and the policies they should follow. It has been said that we should not concern ourselves with changing the present regime in Cuba, for that would violate the principle of self-determination. Until that regime is ready to seek the sanction of a free election, as Castro often promised to do in the early days, it has no claim for the protection of this great principle. And we should come to the realization that the active pursuit of ways for improving the quality of democracy in our respective countries does not constitute a violation of the principles of nonintervention.

[4] Address before the Pan American Society of the United States. Department of State Press Release No. 196, 16 April 1963.

MAPS

United States Collective Defense Arrangements

NORTH ATLANTIC TREATY—signed April 4, 1949:

1 United States
2 Canada
3 Iceland
4 Norway
5 United Kingdom
6 Netherlands
7 Denmark
8 Belgium
9 Luxembourg
10 Portugal
11 France
12 Italy
13 Greece
14 Turkey
15 Federal Republic of Germany

RIO TREATY—signed September 2, 1947:

1 United States
16 Mexico
17 Cuba
18 Haiti
19 Dominican Republic
20 Honduras
21 Guatemala
22 El Salvador
23 Nicaragua
24 Costa Rica
25 Panama
26 Colombia
27 Venezuela
28 Ecuador
29 Peru
30 Brazil
31 Bolivia
32 Paraguay
33 Chile
34 Argentina
35 Uruguay

ANZUS (AUSTRALIA-NEW ZEALAND-UNITED STATES) TREATY—signed September 1, 1951:

1 United States
36 New Zealand
37 Australia

PHILIPPINE TREATY—signed August 30, 1951:

1 United States
38 Philippines

JAPANESE TREATY—signed January 19, 1960:

1 United States
39 Japan

REPUBLIC OF KOREA (SOUTH KOREA) TREATY—signed October 1, 1953:

1 United States
40 Republic of Korea

SOUTHEAST ASIA TREATY—signed September 8, 1954:

1 United States
5 United Kingdom
11 France
36 New Zealand
37 Australia
38 Philippines
41 Thailand
42 Pakistan

REPUBLIC OF CHINA (FORMOSA) TREATY—signed December 2, 1954:

1 United States
43 Republic of China (Formosa)

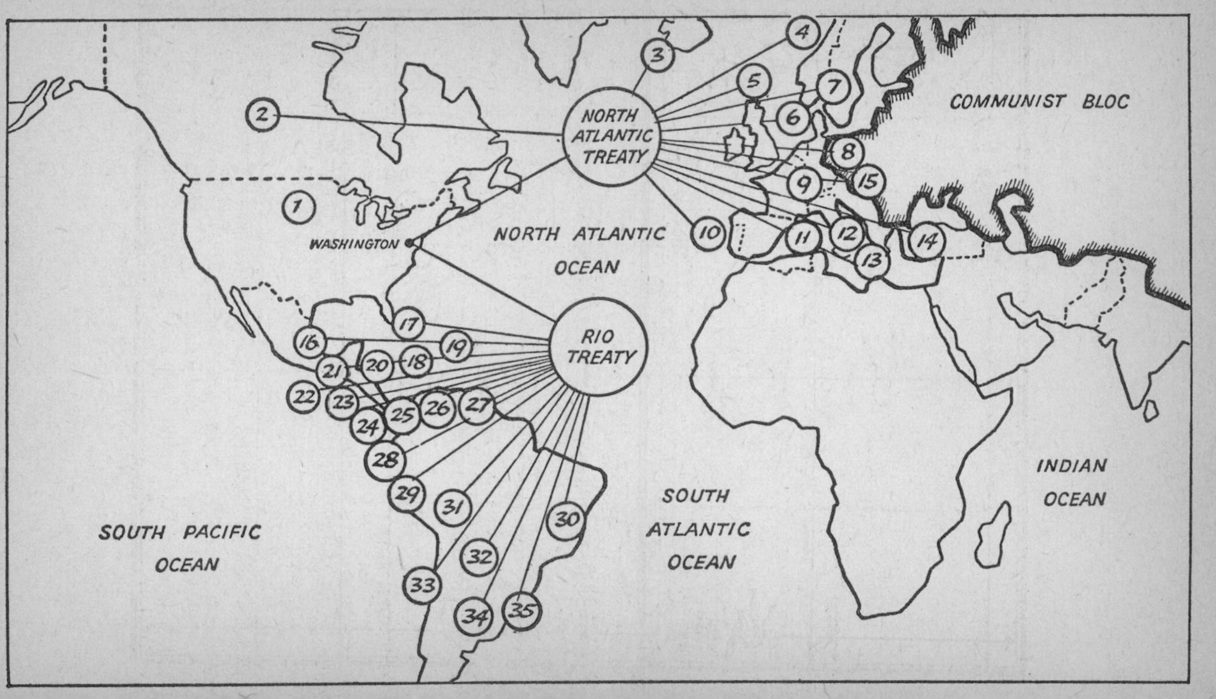
COMMUNIST BLOC
NORTH ATLANTIC TREATY
NORTH ATLANTIC OCEAN
WASHINGTON
RIO TREATY
SOUTH ATLANTIC OCEAN
SOUTH PACIFIC OCEAN
INDIAN OCEAN
1
2
3
4
5
6
7
8
9
10
11
12
13
14
15
16
17
18
19
20
21
22
23
24
25
26
27
28
29
30
31
32
33
34
35

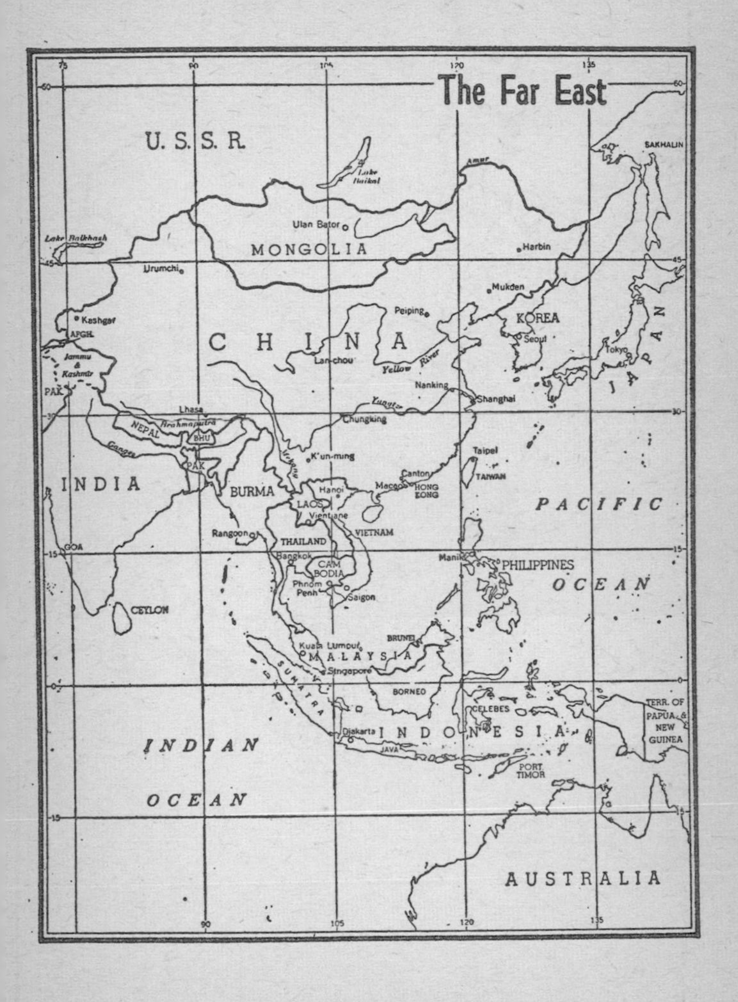
The Far East
U.S.S.R.
SAKHALIN
Amur
Lake Baikal
Ulan Bator
MONGOLIA
Harbin
Lake Balkhash
Urumchi
Mukden
Kashgar
AFGH.
Jammu & Kashmir
PAK.
Peiping
KOREA
C H I N A
Seoul
Tokyo
J A P A N
Lan-chou
Yellow River
Nanking
Shanghai
Lhasa
Brahmaputra
Yangtze
Chungking
NEPAL
BHU.
Ganges
PAK.
K'un-ming
Mekong
Taipei
TAIWAN
INDIA
BURMA
Hanoi
Canton
Macao
HONG KONG
LAOS
Vientiane
PACIFIC
Rangoon
THAILAND
VIETNAM
GOA
Bangkok
CAMBODIA
Phnom Penh
Saigon
Manila
PHILIPPINES
OCEAN
CEYLON
BRUNEI
Kuala Lumpur
MALAYSIA
Singapore
SUMATRA
BORNEO
CELEBES
TERR. OF PAPUA & NEW GUINEA
Djakarta
INDONESIA
JAVA
PORT. TIMOR
INDIAN
OCEAN
AUSTRALIA
75
90
105
120
135
60
45
30
15
0
15

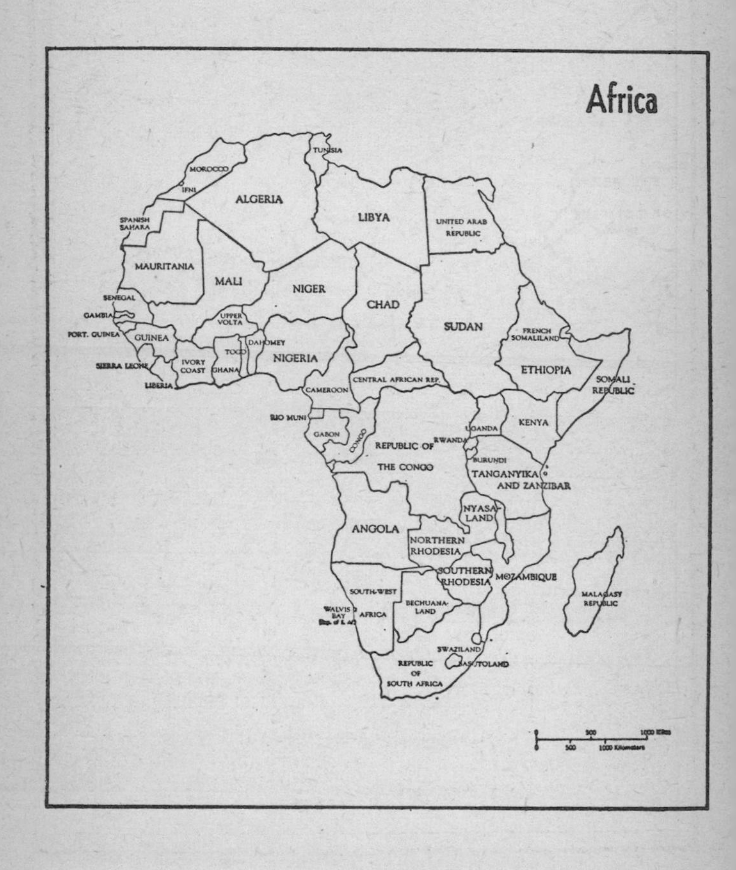
Africa
TUNISIA
MOROCCO
IFNI
ALGERIA
LIBYA
UNITED ARAB REPUBLIC
SPANISH SAHARA
MAURITANIA
MALI
NIGER
CHAD
SUDAN
SENEGAL
GAMBIA
PORT. GUINEA
GUINEA
UPPER VOLTA
DAHOMEY
TOGO
NIGERIA
SIERRA LEONE
IVORY COAST
GHANA
LIBERIA
FRENCH SOMALILAND
ETHIOPIA
SOMALI REPUBLIC
CENTRAL AFRICAN REP.
CAMEROON
RIO MUNI
GABON
CONGO
REPUBLIC OF THE CONGO
RWANDA
UGANDA
KENYA
BURUNDI
TANGANYIKA AND ZANZIBAR
NYASALAND
ANGOLA
NORTHERN RHODESIA
SOUTHERN RHODESIA
MOZAMBIQUE
MALAGASY REPUBLIC
SOUTH-WEST AFRICA
WALVIS BAY
BECHUANALAND
SWAZILAND
BASUTOLAND
REPUBLIC OF SOUTH AFRICA
0
500
1000 Miles
500
1000 Kilometers

The European Soviet Satellites

Latin America
MEXICO
México
Rio Grande
GULF OF MEXICO
Havana
CUBA
JAMAICA
Kingston
HAITI
Port-au-Prince
DOMINICAN REPUBLIC
Santo Domingo
Puerto Rico
CARIBBEAN SEA
BRITISH HONDURAS
GUATEMALA
Guatemala
San Salvador
EL SALVADOR
HONDURAS
Tegucigalpa
NICARAGUA
Managua
COSTA RICA
San José
Panamá
PANAMA
NORTH ATLANTIC OCEAN
Caracas
Port-of-Spain
TRINIDAD & TOBAGO
BRITISH GUIANA
SURINAM
FRENCH GUIANA
Georgetown
Paramaribo
Cayenne
VENEZUELA
Rio Orinoco
Bogotá
COLOMBIA
Quito
ECUADOR
GALÁPAGOS IS.
Manaus
Amazon
Belém
BRAZIL
Recife
Rio São Francisco
Salvador
PERU
Lima
La Paz
BOLIVIA
Brasília
PARAGUAY
Asunción
São Paulo
Rio de Janeiro
PACIFIC OCEAN
Antofagasta
Pôrto Alegre
Rio Paraná
ARGENTINA
Santiago
Rosario
URUGUAY
Buenos Aires
Montevideo
CHILE
SOUTH ATLANTIC OCEAN
FALKLAND IS.

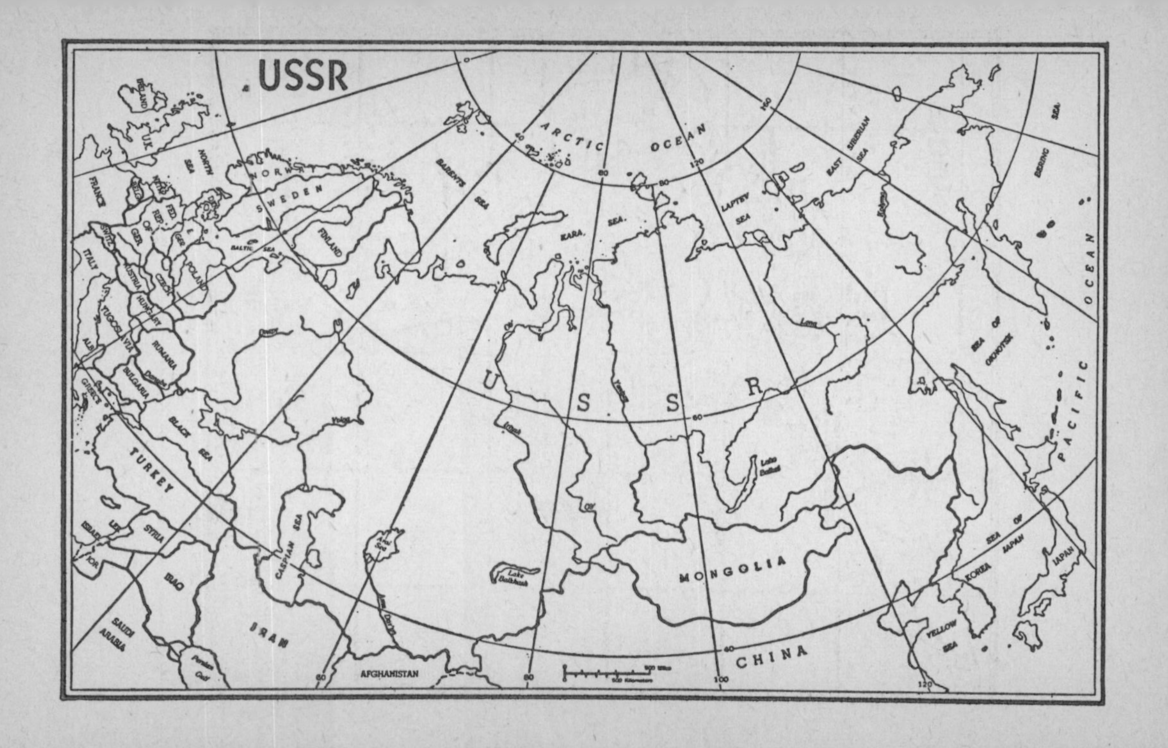
USSR
ARCTIC OCEAN
PACIFIC OCEAN
BERING SEA
EAST SIBERIAN SEA
LAPTEV SEA
KARA SEA
BARENTS SEA
SEA OF OKHOTSK
SEA OF JAPAN
YELLOW SEA
U S S R
MONGOLIA
CHINA
KOREA
JAPAN
Lena
Yenisei
Ob
Irtysh
Volga
Dnepr
Danube
Amu Darya
Lake Baikal
Lake Balkhash
Aral Sea
CASPIAN SEA
BLACK SEA
BALTIC SEA
NORTH SEA
Persian Gulf
IRAN
AFGHANISTAN
TURKEY
SYRIA
IRAQ
LEB
ISRAEL
JOR
SAUDI ARABIA
IRELAND
U.K.
FRANCE
BELG
NETH
DEN
NORW
SWEDEN
FINLAND
FED. REP. OF GER
E GER
POLAND
CZECH
SWITZ
AUSTRIA
HUNGARY
ITALY
YUGOSLAVIA
RUMANIA
BULGARIA
ALB
GREECE
0
40
80
120
160
60
100
500 Miles
500 Kilometers

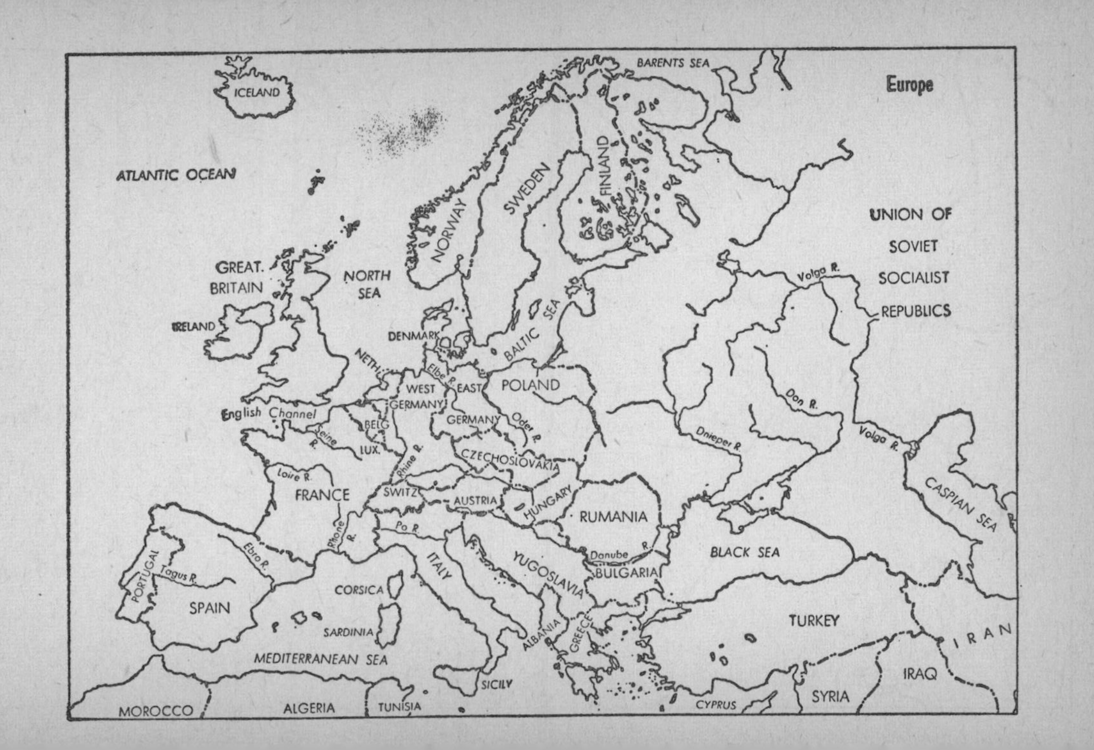
Europe
ICELAND
BARENTS SEA
ATLANTIC OCEAN
NORWAY
SWEDEN
FINLAND
UNION OF
SOVIET
SOCIALIST
REPUBLICS
GREAT.
BRITAIN
NORTH
SEA
IRELAND
DENMARK
BALTIC SEA
Volga R.
NETH.
Elbe R.
WEST
GERMANY
EAST
GERMANY
POLAND
English Channel
BELG.
Oder R.
Don R.
Seine R.
LUX.
Dnieper R.
Volga R.
Rhine R.
CZECHOSLOVAKIA
Loire R.
FRANCE
SWITZ.
AUSTRIA
HUNGARY
RUMANIA
CASPIAN SEA
Rhone R.
Po R.
Ebro R.
ITALY
Danube R.
BLACK SEA
PORTUGAL
Tagus R.
YUGOSLAVIA
BULGARIA
CORSICA
SPAIN
TURKEY
SARDINIA
ALBANIA
GREECE
IRAN
MEDITERRANEAN SEA
IRAQ
SICILY
SYRIA
MOROCCO
ALGERIA
TUNISIA
CYPRUS

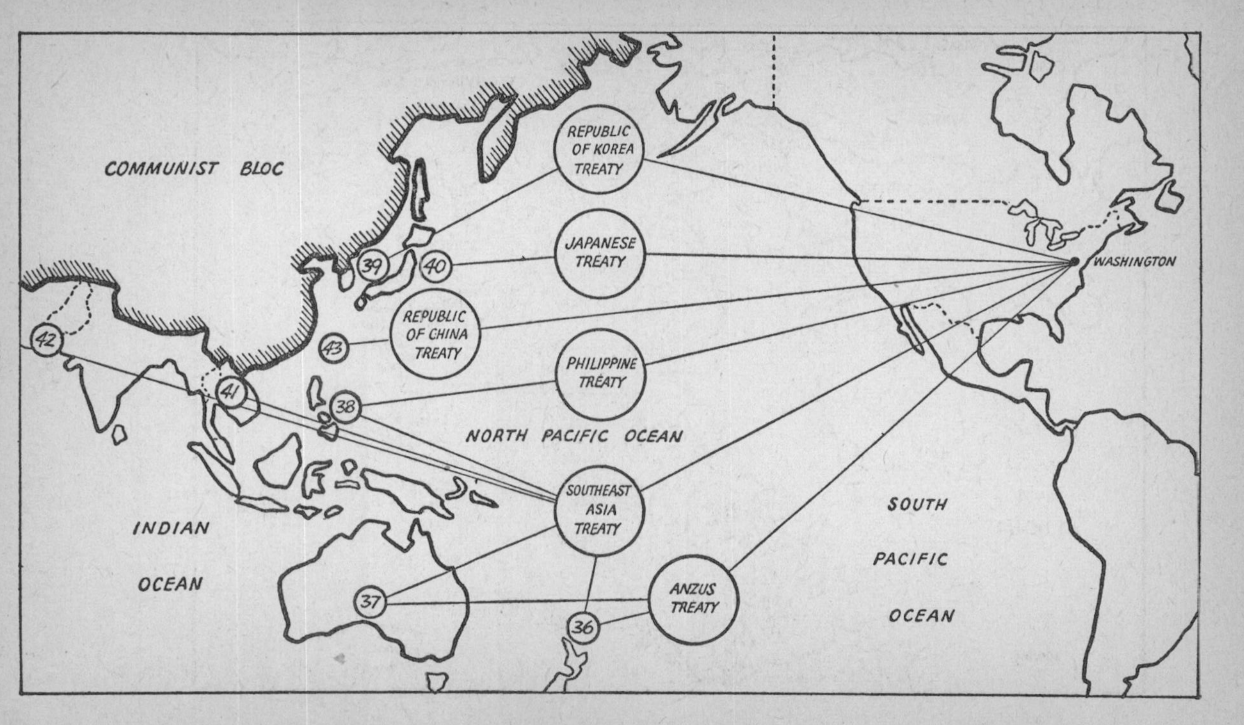
COMMUNIST BLOC
REPUBLIC OF KOREA TREATY
JAPANESE TREATY
REPUBLIC OF CHINA TREATY
PHILIPPINE TREATY
NORTH PACIFIC OCEAN
SOUTHEAST ASIA TREATY
ANZUS TREATY
WASHINGTON
INDIAN OCEAN
SOUTH PACIFIC OCEAN
39
40
42
43
41
38
37
36

INDEX